COMMENTARY ON THE BOOK OF

ISAIAH

AN IN-DEPTH LOOK AT THE
GOSPEL OF THE OLD TESTAMENT

COMMENTARY ON THE BOOK OF

ISAIAH

AN IN-DEPTH LOOK AT THE GOSPEL OF THE OLD TESTAMENT

FR. MITCH PACWA, S.J.

TAN Books
Gastonia, North Carolina

Cover design by Jordan Avery

Cover image: *Isaiah's Lips Annointed with Fire* by Benjamin West (1738–1820). The Picture Art Collection/Alamy Stock Photo.

Library of Congress Control Number: 2023947938

ISBN: 978-1-5051-2990-8
Kindle ISBN: 978-1-5051-3350-9
ePUB ISBN: 978-1-5051-3349-3

Published in the United States by
TAN Books
PO Box 269
Gastonia, NC 28053
www.TANBooks.com

Printed in India

Contents

Introduction

The scroll of Isaiah is the longest of all the prophets' works and is the second longest book of the Bible. (Psalms is more than twice the length.) Its importance for communities of faith was recognized very early, as evidenced by more copies of the Isaiah scroll being found among the Dead Sea Scrolls than any other book, and it is the second most cited Old Testament book in the New Testament (sixty-three citations; Psalms has sixty-seven). When Saint Jerome penned his famous line, "Ignorance of Scripture is ignorance of Christ," he wrote it in his introduction on Isaiah, which he saw as the Gospel in Old Testament form. Isaiah appears prominently throughout the lectionary, but especially during Advent and Holy Week. The book of Isaiah is also the main source for the Office of Readings during the Advent and Christmas seasons. Because Israel and the Christian Church treasure the book of Isaiah, as seen by its influence on her liturgical calendar, it should be studied well.

The reader of the Hebrew text does notice a variety of writing styles in various sections of the book. The historian of the ancient world recognizes that some sections of the book refer to events in the mid through late eighth century BC, while other parts contain historical references to the 540s BC, and still others assume a situation in the late sixth or early fifth century. Traditionally, the mention of late historical references was understood as Isaiah's ability to foresee the future, though that does not explain either the change in style, vocabulary, nor forms of speech that also appear in those sections. Scholars sought explanations for these anomalies.

Amazing advances in Old Testament studies took place in the nineteenth century AD as various Europeans took interest in the ruins of the ancient world that they discovered in their territorial or mercantile empires. The science of archaeology was born, and tremendous advances in its methods continued to be made through to the present. Among these advances was the work of ingenious pioneers in translating ancient languages. Jean-François Champollion was the first, learning to translate Egyptian hieroglyphs. Soon afterwards, others cracked the codes of ancient Persian and Akkadian (Assyrian and Babylonian) cuneiform, while still more scholars learned to read Ugaritic, Eblaite, and other languages. Tens of thousands of clay tablets, papyri, and wall inscriptions were discovered and translated, offering the world an understanding of languages that had been forgotten and unread for thousands of years. Ancient historical and religious documents became available to help modern people study the Bible with new insights. Scholars learned more about the meaning of Hebrew words by comparing them to cognate words in other Semitic languages used throughout the region. Ancient historical records gave new insights into the ancient Near Eastern situations with which Israel was dealing. Scholars noticed patterns in the forms of speech found in the ancient documents, helping them see the forms of speech that the Bible used in an international culture. Some theories proved to be unfounded after research advanced, but many remain critical for understanding the ancient history and biblical texts better—therefore helping our faith.

Among these theories, one sound theory accepted by scholars states that Isaiah was composed by six authors in at least five different periods. This theory is based on the differences of style and historical data. The six authors are as follows:

- Proto-Isaiah (First Isaiah) in the eighth century, generally including chapters 1 through 23, 28 through 33, with historical narratives from 2 Kings added in chapters 36 through 39.
- Isaiah 36–39 is historical material taken from 2 Kings, which was finished being written and edited by 560 BC, since the last event mentioned was the release of King Jehoiachin from a Babylonian prison, which occurred in 561 BC.
- Deutero-Isaiah (Second Isaiah), written in the late 540s BC in Babylon, includes chapters 40 through 55.
- Isaiah Apocalypse, including chapters 24 through 27, was probably written in the sixth century.

- Isaiah 34–35, could have been written in the sixth or even fifth century BC.
- Trito-Isaiah (Third Isaiah), including chapters 56 through 66, was written in the late sixth or even early fifth century BC.

Regarding this theory, why did different prophets from different periods add their prophetic words to the already existing Isaiah scroll? Why did they not simply use their own names for each of their writings? Two complementary explanations can be offered. One, the modern value of taking credit for your own work was not particularly high in ancient times. It was commonly considered more valuable to associate oneself with an already well-known person and share in his fame or add to it. An example is in 1 and 2 Samuel, which begins with material about that famous prophet but includes much more about Saul and David, and then includes other prophets within books named for Samuel. Samuel inspired the writing but the book was completed decades after his death.

A second explanation is more theoretical, though it is plausible. Isaiah had disciples who were taught by him: "Bind up the testimony, seal the teaching among my disciples" (8:16). In 8:18 he mentions his "children," which naturally refers to his son Maher-Shalal-Hash-Baz and any other children born to him and his wife. However, this may well have been extended to his disciples, since disciples of the prophets are elsewhere known as the "sons of the prophets" (see 1 Kgs 20:35; 2 Kgs 2:3, 5, 7, 15; 4:1, 38; 5:22; 6:1; 9:1) as well as "bands of prophets" (1 Sm 10:10–12; 19:20). These groups, who even addressed their prophetic leader as "father" (1 Kgs 2:12; 13:14), were the ones who wrote down the stories of their prophetic leader. Notice that in both cases of being addressed as "father," the prophet Elijah was about to ascend to heaven or Elisha was about to die, indicating that neither of them could have written that last episode of life.

Furthermore, these followers' similar writing styles indicate that they probably wrote all their stories about their leaders, most likely after their death. The existence of such schools that wrote about their founding prophet posthumously makes it possible that Isaiah's disciples continued his legacy, not only transcribing his prophecies while he lived, but also supporting subsequent prophets who arose from their midst in later periods of history to address the new situations of Israel's history with a word from the Lord. Catholics can understand the existence of an ongoing Isaiah school along the lines of the Benedictines, Dominicans, Franciscans, Jesuits, and other orders who are inspired by their founders to continue a community with a distinctive quality or charism that can be traced back to the founder. Isaiah's prophetic charism may well have inspired a group of disciples that continued on for centuries, parallel to movements like the Pharisees or various Catholic religious orders. In this way, we can understand the rise of Isaianic prophets even into the fifth century with Trito-Isaiah.

This theory of different levels and periods of composition is useful in guiding the reader to interpret Isaiah's text within its historical context. The oracles make more sense within the dynamics of each historical period, and their meaning and its application illuminates the texts for the modern reader.

This last point is extremely important in understanding how to make such ancient texts relevant for today. The first step in interpreting Scripture is to understand the text in its own proper context—linguistically, historically, and culturally. From understanding the situation of the ancient writers and audiences, modern people can see into the cultural and historical differences and recognize the common humanity we share. Seeing that the texts come from a variety of ancient human struggles with sin, social disorder, and historical and natural forces, the modern reader can see the similarities to modern problems and situations. Just as Isaiah and other writers approached life with faith in God, so also can the modern reader come to understand the sensitive application of the principles of faith to present-day problems.

Such an approach avoids the path of both atheists and literalists, who tend to read the biblical text through a modern lens. Certainly, a contemporary outlook can be strong, but if you are not as nearsighted about issues of faith as many modern people are, the extra strong lens may actually distort the picture. (Try looking at the world through the glasses of a highly nearsighted person; it gives you a headache unless you are just as nearsighted.) Modern atheists get angry with the Bible because they expect the ancients to have modern sensibilities: Why did not God teach Israel more physics, biology, et cetera? Why did God permit animal sacrifices or slavery? On the other hand, some biblical literalists build a career on seeing today's headlines in Bible prophecy: the Bible must be talking about my period of history, so I will make the prophetic oracles about Russia, the United States, England, and other nations that did not exist in ancient times. Both atheists and literalists may win adherents for a while, but history tends to leave them both in the dust, while the deeper meaning of Scripture continues to nourish the Church through the millennia. Such nourishment will be the goal of this book.

Lesson 1

ISAIAH 1–2

The call of the Prophet Isaiah in chapter 6 might seem out of place to many readers. As a result, some want to re-edit the text by placing this call narrative at the beginning. However, another way to make sense of the first six chapters is to see chapters 1 through 5 as Isaiah's first stage of prophetic ministry during the reign of King Uzziah (769–743 BC), followed by the vision in the Temple in chapter 6 that reaffirms an earlier call for the new situation in Judah that arises after the death of King Uzziah in 743 and the reign of Jotham (743–735 BC). This will be the approach we take here.

Uzziah, also known as Azariah, became king in 769 BC at age sixteen, when his father, Amaziah, died. Uzziah, like his father, "did what was right in the eyes of the Lord," and his reign was a time of prosperity and military strength, as seen in the reconquest of Edom (see 2 Kgs 14:10; 15:1–6). During his reign, Amos began his prophetic ministry, around 760 BC, Hosea started his ministry around 750 BC, and according to tradition, Rome was founded in 753 BC. However, around 750 BC, Uzziah became a leper at age thirty-five (see 2 Kgs 15:5). His son Jotham became his co-regent, performing the actual duties of government, since Uzziah was confined to his room because of the uncleanness of the leprosy.

Though Uzziah was assessed as a good king at a prosperous time, he neglected to remove the "high places" where the people offered illicit sacrifices and incense, primarily to Canaanite gods. The people were not wholehearted in their faith or in their moral lives, so Isaiah speaks against them in chapter 1 with a number of oracles of judgment that indict them for their sins.

1:1

> **[1]The vision of Isaiah the son of Amoz, which he saw concerning Judah and Jerusalem in the days of Uzziah, Jotham, Ahaz, and Hezekiah, kings of Judah.**

This verse is called a "superscription" because it comes at the beginning of the book. The sole family identification is Isaiah's father, Amoz, which appears in other verses (see Is 2:1; 13:1; 20:2; 37:2, 21 = 2 Kgs 19:2, 20; Is 38:1 = 2 Kgs 20:1; 2 Chr 26:22; 32:32; 32:20). Amoz means "strength," while Isaiah means "the Lord will save." The Bible mentions nothing about Amoz except his son the prophet, but a late and unverifiable Jewish tradition claims he was the brother of King Uzziah (Sota 10b).

The other important information is the list of kings: Uzziah (769–743), Jotham's co-regency with Uzziah (750–743) and sole reign (743–735), Ahaz (735–715), and Hezekiah (715–687). Hezekiah's twelve-year-old son, Manasseh, appears to have been appointed co-regent in 697, but he is not mentioned in Isaiah 1, leading to the conclusion that Isaiah finished prophesying by that time. In fact, no prophetic activity occurs during Manasseh's fifty-five year reign, perhaps because he thoroughly persecuted the prophets during the most wicked reign in Israel's history.

—— Isaiah 1:2–3 ——

The first verses use a law court accusation and a father's lament over his child's ignorant disobedience to communicate the Lord's initial displeasure with his people.

1:2

> **[2]Hear, O heavens, and give ear, O earth; for the LORD has spoken:**
> **"Sons have I reared and brought up, but they have rebelled against me.**

The form here is a legal summons, "Hear, O heavens, and give ear, O earth," in the style of Deuteronomy 32:1: "Give ear, O heavens, and I will speak; and let the earth hear the words of my mouth." The indictment is that the Lord has raised Israel like his own sons, "but they have rebelled against me." Though Israel is recognized as God's children, the text avoids calling the Lord their father, perhaps to maintain the distinction between the Lord and Israel. Israel's sonship was based on the Lord calling Israel from Egypt (see Ex 4:22; Hos 11:1; Jer 3:19) and not on some type of physical generation. Many of the ancient peoples thought that they were physical descendants of their gods, but Israel thought of itself as one people among many, all of whom traced themselves to the first parents created by God rather than physically generated by Him.

1:3

> **[3]The ox knows its owner, and the ass its master's crib; but Israel does not know, my people does not understand."**

The form of speech here changes to a lament over Israel's lack of understanding since the people are not as intelligent as an ox or ass, who at least know their owner. Israel does not know her Lord. When Saint Francis of Assisi made the first Christmas crèche in a cave with real people and animals, he added the ox and ass to display them recognizing their Master's crib, even though the Gospels do not mention them. This was his way to indicate that people who have faith in Jesus Christ can undo Isaiah's rebuke from this verse.

—— Isaiah 1:4–9 ——

This is a "woe" oracle that begins with the Hebrew word "hoy," translated here as "Ah." Woe was expressed in particular to someone who was about to die or suffer greatly and it assumed that the object of the woe was already doomed. Apart from its use at a burial (see 1 Kgs 13:30), it is found only in prophetic books, but most frequently in Isaiah, to indicate the inevitability of the doom and devastation that the person or nation was about to receive (see Is 1:24; 5:8, 11, 18, 20, 21, 22; 10:1, 5; 16:4; 17:12; 18:1; 28:1; 29:1, 15; 30:1; 31:1; 33:1; 45:9, 10; 55:1—twenty-two out of forty-nine uses in the Old Testament). This particular "woe" has several parts:

1:4

> **[4]Ah, sinful nation, a people laden with iniquity, offspring of evildoers, sons who deal corruptly! They have forsaken the LORD, they have despised the Holy One of Israel, they are utterly estranged.**

Woe to the disobedient people who have been punished greatly for their sin and corruption, especially that of forsaking the Lord.

First, the address of the "woe" is to a sinful nation that was born of sinners. They will not experience mere disaster as innocent victims but will be punished for sins. Their corrupt deeds are identified with forsaking the Lord and despising the Holy One. These willful acts of turning away from the Lord are the root of their other sins, which is why they are mentioned first.

1:5–6

> **5Why will you still be smitten, that you continue to rebel? The whole head is sick, and the whole heart faint. 6From the sole of the foot even to the head, there is no soundness in it, but bruises and sores and bleeding wounds; they are not pressed out, or bound up, or softened with oil.**

These verses describe the thorough punishment they have received from head to foot by beginning with a rhetorical question: why do you continue to rebel after such a beating? No one soothes the wounds, and the nation continues to suffer. The sensible reaction would be to repent by returning to the Lord.

1:7–8

> **7Your country lies desolate, your cities are burned with fire; in your very presence aliens devour your land; it is desolate, as overthrown by aliens. 8And the daughter of Zion is left like a booth in a vineyard, like a lodge in a cucumber field, like a besieged city.**

This is a description of the fate of the nation that results from their chastisement. The description of "burned" cities, enemy armies in the land, and Jerusalem remaining alone like a "booth" or "lodge" in a vineyard or field fits the situation of 701 BC when the Assyrian army of Sennacherib did precisely these things. The reason people set up little huts in fields and vineyards was to protect the crops from being eaten by animals at harvest time.

1:9

> **[9]If the Lord of hosts had not left us a few survivors, we should have been like Sodom, and become like Gomorrah.**

A concluding verse that recognizes a glimmer of hope: at least there are survivors of God's chastisement in Israel. Sodom and Gomorrah, who were unable to produce even ten righteous people to save it from God's wrath, were completely destroyed without any survivors except the foreigner, Lot and his two daughters.

—— Isaiah 1:10–17 ——

The form here is a prophetic instruction on sacrifice which criticizes the detestable worship in Jerusalem that is divorced from moral behavior.

1:10

> **[10]Hear the word of the Lord, you rulers of Sodom! Give ear to the teaching of our God, you people of Gomorrah!**

The summons to listen to God's instruction begins with a strong criticism of the people's moral character. Isaiah identifies the rulers as belonging to Sodom and the people as belonging to Gomorrah, the two cities doomed to destruction in Genesis 19:24–29. In Deuteronomy, any person, family, or tribe that turns away from the Lord to serve other gods will be punished like Sodom and Gomorrah (see Dt 29:18–28; 32:32–33), and Isaiah uses those cities as classic examples of evil places that deserve punishment (see 1:9, 10; 3:9; 13:19), as Scripture does elsewhere (see Jer 23:14; 49:18; 50:40; Lam 4:6; Ez 16:46, 48, 49, 53, 55, 56; Am 4:11; Zep 2:9; Mt 10:15; 11:23–24; Lk 10:12; 17:29; Rom 9:29, quoting Is 1:9; 2 Pt 2:5-6; Jude 7; Rv 11:8).

1:11–12

> **[11]"What to me is the multitude of your sacrifices? says the Lord; I have had enough of burnt offerings of rams and the fat of fed beasts; I do not delight in the blood of bulls, or of lambs, or of he-goats. [12]"When you come to appear before me, who requires of you this trampling of my courts?**

The Lord's message begins with rhetorical questions about the people's sacrifices not being necessary for the Lord. This contrasts with various pagan beliefs that the gods ate the sacrifices set before them for nourishment. For instance, in the Babylonian creation story, the *Enuma Elish,* the gods cry out to Marduk, the chief god who had defeated and killed Tiamat, the grandmother of all gods, "Who will feed us now?" He then cut her corpse in two, the long way, made the earth from the bottom half and the sky from the top, killed her monster ally Kingu, mixed his blood with the earth, and fashioned human beings as the slaves of the gods to feed them. When the first humans offered a sacrifice, the gods gathered around the smoke "like flies" (*Enuma Elish,* Tablets II, IV,VI, especially lines 1–40, 70–80). Isaiah's message about the Lord not needing animal sacrifice is present in Psalms 50:8–15, where the Lord says, also with a rhetorical question: "If I were hungry, I would not tell you; for the world and all that is in it is mine. Do I eat the flesh of bulls, or drink the blood of goats?" Isaiah asks who "requires" the "trampling" of his courts with animals, assuming the answer to be "no one."

1:13–15

> **13Bring no more vain offerings; incense is an abomination to me. New moon and sabbath and the calling of assemblies—I cannot endure iniquity and solemn assembly. 14Your new moons and your appointed feasts my soul hates; they have become a burden to me, I am weary of bearing them. 15When you spread forth your hands, I will hide my eyes from you; even though you make many prayers, I will not listen; your hands are full of blood.**

The Lord then commands the people not to bring "vain offerings," celebrate assemblies on Sabbath, new moon, and feasts, or even stretch out their hands in simple prayer and supplication because these weary Him as abominations. He will not listen or see their religious practices. Of course, since the Law of Moses commands sacrifices of different kinds in Leviticus, the people would be confused. However, the Lord makes His reasons clear: "iniquity and solemn assembly" are incompatible with each other, as is indicated by the very structure of the Law of Moses. The commandments begin with faith in God—only one God may be worshiped and His name may not be taken in vain—and then move to duties to fellow humans, from parents to neighbors and spouses. Many other moral laws are laid out (see Ex 20–23), and the people were required to accept these solemnly (see Ex 24:3) before offering a sacrifice that ratified the covenant in the blood of bulls (see Ex 24:5–8). Only after accepting the moral laws did the Lord reveal the laws of worship (see Ex 25–31, 35–40; Lv 1–17), after which moral laws are re-stated (see Lv 18–22), followed by liturgical laws again (see Lv 23–27). The very structure of Israelite legislation shows that the moral law sets the condition for the exercise of the liturgical laws; both must be integrated with each other. Therefore, in Isaiah 1:13, the Lord will not endure "iniquity" with their worship or, in 1:15, listen to hands lifted in prayer if they are full of the blood of murder.

1:16–17

> [16]**Wash yourselves; make yourselves clean; remove the evil of your doings from before my eyes; cease to do evil, [17]learn to do good; seek justice, correct oppression; defend the fatherless, plead for the widow.**

The logical conclusion from this criticism is the following command to make themselves morally clean and cease to do evil. In particular, the population must seek justice for the poor, the orphans, and widows, who were the most defenseless members of society. This is the precondition for worship, much as sacramental confession is a precondition for Catholics to receive Holy Communion at the Holy Sacrifice of the Mass.

—— Isaiah 1:18–20 ——

The Lord sets before the people two kinds of options and admonishes them to make basic choices.

1:18

> [18]**"Come now, let us reason together, says the LORD: though your sins are like scarlet, they shall be as white as snow; though they are red like crimson, they shall become like wool.**

The Lord invites the people to "reason together," as in a dialogue or even a courtroom setting. First, the people need to recognize that their sins are like scarlet or crimson. These red colors are chosen to imply that the sins are like shedding blood and discolor the clothing of the perpetrator. However, the Lord can transform the sins into a whiteness like snow or wool. Such a promise shows the power of the Lord's forgiveness in the soul of the sinner.

1:19–20

> **19If you are willing and obedient, you shall eat the good of the land;**
> **20But if you refuse and rebel, you shall be devoured by the sword; for the mouth of the LORD has spoken."**

Here the Lord lays out a fundamental moral decision for Israel: obey God and eat the fruit of the land; rebel against God and be eaten by the sword. This stark decision is similar to that which Moses offered, "I have set before you life and death, blessing and curse; therefore choose life" (Dt 30:19).

—— Isaiah 1:21–31 ——

The Hebrew meter of this section is recognized as a lament or funeral dirge for the dead. However, the content sets a choice before Jerusalem to accept the Lord's punishment for sin as a purification that will return the city to its heritage of righteousness or stay the immoral course and be destroyed.

1:21–23

> **21How the faithful city has become a harlot, she that was full of justice! Righteousness lodged in her, but now murderers. 22Your silver has become dross, your wine mixed with water. 23Your princes are rebels and companions of thieves. Every one loves a bribe and runs after gifts. They do not defend the fatherless, and the widow's cause does not come to them.**

A rebuke against Jerusalem that contrasts a faithful and righteous past with the present sinful state of society (v. 21). The backward change to immorality is compared to silver that reverts to the dross that had once been removed by smelting or to watered down wine that maintains some of the color but not the flavor (v. 22). Then the specific moral problems are identified as coming from the political leaders. They are thieves who seek bribes rather than defend the weak members of society—the widows and the fatherless children. Use of raw power for self-aggrandizement is the corruption the Lord laments in Israel (v. 23).

1:24–25

24Therefore the LORD says, the LORD of hosts, the Mighty One of Isra-
el: "Ah, I will vent my wrath on my enemies, and avenge myself on my
foes. 25I will turn my hand against you and will smelt away your dross
as with lye and remove all your alloy.

On account of such unrighteousness, the Lord threatens punishment in order to purify the city as smelting removes dross from pure metal or lye removes stains from clothing. These verses recognize that purification is possible and the Lord will accomplish it, even if it is a painful process to the recipients.

1:26

26And I will restore your judges as at the first, and your counselors as at the beginning. Afterward you shall be called the city of righteousness, the faithful city."

Since the princes, who were the main candidates for judging legal cases, are the primary perpetrators, they will be the ones who are purified and restored to moral rectitude, thereby allowing the city to be restored to its original righteous and faithful standing, as in the lament of verse 21.

1:27–28

27Zion shall be redeemed by justice, and those in her who repent, by
righteousness. 28But rebels and sinners shall be destroyed together,
and those who forsake the LORD shall be consumed.

The Lord lays out the basic choice for justice and righteousness by repenting or to continue rebelling and forsaking the Lord until complete destruction takes place. This is not addressed directly to anyone but is stated as a basic principle for sinners and rebels to choose. These verses simply make it clear that the stakes are very high.

1:29–31

> **29For you shall be ashamed of the oaks in which you delighted; and**
> **you shall blush for the gardens which you have chosen. 30For you shall**
> **be like an oak whose leaf withers, and like a garden without water.**
> **31And the strong shall become tow, and his work a spark, and both of**
> **them shall burn together, with none to quench them.**

This section is a threat of vengeance because the people have changed their commitment to the Lord to a worship of the Canaanite gods. Those nature deities were worshiped under the oak trees and in gardens, often with orgiastic rites. The Lord will destroy those rebels and sinners because they have forsaken the Lord. As a result, they will be ashamed of the oaks under which they held their pro-Baal orgies.

Verses 30–31 present images of destruction because the choice to turn away from the Lord to other deities is inherently self-destructive. The wicked deeds of the unfaithful people are like sparks that catch the trees on fire. Even though the Baal worshipers seem to be as strong as oaks, they will be destroyed by the flames that their wickedness sparks.

—— Isaiah 2:1–5 ——

This promise for a Jerusalem renewed as the religious center of the whole world also appears in Micah 4:1–5, nearly word for word. Micah came from Moresheth, a small town west of Jerusalem. As one expects from the prophets, Micah criticizes both Jerusalem and Samaria. Micah is partial to small towns. Scholars remain quite divided on which prophet actually composed this text and which borrowed it, but the heading in Isaiah explicitly ascribes it to him, while Micah makes no such claim to authorship, thereby pushing the argument in Isaiah's favor.

2:1

> **1The word which Isaiah the son of Amoz saw concerning Judah and Jerusalem.**

The heading identifies Isaiah son of Amoz as the author, giving the attribution a formal quality. This word is directed to Jerusalem and Judah.

2:2–3

[2]It shall come to pass in the latter days that the mountain of the house of the LORD shall be established as the highest of the mountains, and shall be raised above the hills; and all the nations shall flow to it [3]and many peoples shall come, and say: "Come, let us go up to the mountain of the LORD, to the house of the God of Jacob; that he may teach us his ways and that we may walk in his paths." For out of Zion shall go forth the law, and the word of the LORD from Jerusalem.

The first and decisive promise is that Zion, the mountain on which the house of the Lord—that is, the Temple—is located, will rise above all the mountains of the world. At present, even the Mount of Olives is higher than the Temple, which provides the best view of the site today. The miraculous rising of the Temple Mount will attract all the nations, much as the light of Israel will attract the nations who live in darkness to come to Jerusalem in Isaiah 60.

However, the physical change of the mountain will not be the main attraction. Rather, the nations will come so that the Lord "may teach us his ways." They will recognize the superiority of His wisdom, laws, and word, and they will want to "walk in his paths." Since the great majority of the people who read the Old Testament over the past centuries have been Christians of Gentile origin, this prophecy is already being fulfilled.

2:4

[4]He shall judge between the nations, and shall decide for many peoples; and they shall beat their swords into plowshares, and their spears into pruning hooks; nation shall not lift up sword against nation, neither shall they learn war any more.

After the nations arrive in Jerusalem, the Lord will judge them as He does Israel. The effect of His judgment will be to turn their weapons of war into farming tools that produce nourishment rather than shed blood. Without weapons, they will cease training for war and produce prosperity.

2:5

[5]O house of Jacob, come, let us walk in the light of the LORD.

This verse is the prophet's exhortation to Israel to walk in the Lord's light so that they might be worthy to be that city to which the nations come for the word of the Lord and instruction. If the residents do not walk in the Lord's ways, then the nations who stream toward Zion may take Israel's place.

—— Isaiah 2:6–22 ——

A lament (2:6–9) and a threat (2:10–19) and judgment (2:20–22) against the people for occultism and idolatry.

2:6–9

[6]For thou hast rejected thy people, the house of Jacob, because they are full of diviners from the east and of soothsayers like the Philistines, and they strike hands with foreigners. [7]Their land is filled with silver and gold, and there is no end to their treasures; their land is filled with horses, and there is no end to their chariots. [8]Their land is filled with idols; they bow down to the work of their hands, to what their own fingers have made. [9]So man is humbled, and men are brought low—forgive them not!

Here Isaiah addresses the Lord directly with a lament over the people's numerous religious sins.

The sin of consulting "diviners" and "soothsayers" was strongly condemned as an abomination in Deuteronomy 18:9–11. In fact, Deuteronomy 18:9 specifically warns that when Israel enters Canaan they are not to "learn to follow the abominable practices of those nations," but here Isaiah says they have learned them from various different nations.

The warning against having an abundance of silver, gold, horses, and chariots in Deuteronomy 17:14–17 is addressed to the future kings of Israel, but here Isaiah claims that the whole land is full of such luxuries (horses were for the rich, while average farmers might have a donkey or ox). The excavations at Megiddo (an ancient city in Northern Israel) contain the ruins of multiple horse stables and evidence for many luxury items. Such was likely the case for other cities as well.

The criticism of making idols is standard throughout the histories of Israel (Samuel, Kings, and Chronicles) and the prophets. Many examples of bronze and clay idols have been excavated from Jerusalem and other towns and cities in Israel.

Isaiah's conclusion is that these sins bring down the perpetrators to a low estate, and therefore he petitions the Lord not to forgive them. Presumably, he wants them to pay for their crimes.

2:10–19

> **[10]Enter into the rock, and hide in the dust from before the terror of**
> **the LORD, and from the glory of his majesty. [11]The haughty looks of**
> **man shall be brought low, and the pride of men shall be humbled; and**
> **the LORD alone will be exalted in that day. [12]For the LORD of hosts**
> **has a day against all that is proud and lofty, against all that is lifted up**
> **and high; [13]against all the cedars of Lebanon, lofty and lifted up; and**
> **against all the oaks of Bashan; [14]against all the high mountains, and**
> **against all the lofty hills; [15]against every high tower, and against every**
> **fortified wall; [16]against all the ships of Tarshish, and against all the**
> **beautiful craft. [17]And the haughtiness of man shall be humbled, and**
> **the pride of men shall be brought low; and the LORD alone will be**
> **exalted in that day. [18]And the idols shall utterly pass away. [19]And men**
> **shall enter the caves of the rocks and the holes of the ground, from**
> **before the terror of the LORD, and from the glory of his majesty, when**
> **he rises to terrify the earth.**

The preceding lament over sin prepares for this present threat against the day of the Lord on which all will be punished.

He begins with a command to hide from the Lord's terror and glory, which are two sides of the same coin, on the day of the Lord. Those who are righteous will see the Lord's glory; the same manifestation will terrorize the unrepentant sinner. The command to hide is similar to the warning of Revelation 6:15–17, where "the great day of their wrath has come, and who can stand before it?" (Rv 6:17).

The day will humble sinful, arrogant human beings. Only the Lord will be exalted on His day of judgment, and sinners will be cast down.

The day of the Lord will certainly exalt His majesty, but it will bring down all the mighty people and objects of this world, from mountains, cedars, and oaks to humanly manufactured towers, walls, and ships. However, as in verse 11, the main point will be the humbling of human "haughtiness" and "pride" while the Lord alone is exalted. How else can this be? The infinite Lord God will simply be seen for the majesty that He is, while people, who cannot be seen from the window of a passing jet airplane, will be shown for their own smallness from the perspective of almighty divine infinity.

As in verse 10, people will futilely attempt to hide in the caves and the ground from the "terror of the Lord and from the glory of his majesty," but they will not be able to. He rises to terrify the earth with His truthful and just judgment, and the sinners can only try to hide from Him.

2:20–22

> **20In that day men will cast forth their idols of silver and their idols of gold, which they made for themselves to worship, to the moles and to the bats, 21to enter the caverns of the rocks and the clefts of the cliffs, from before the terror of the LORD, and from the glory of his majesty, when he rises to terrify the earth. 22Turn away from man in whose nostrils is breath, for of what account is he?**

At the point of the final judgment, all people who see the Lord's majesty and glory will realize that their silver and gold idols are worse than useless, so they will toss them to the moles and bats that live in darkness under the ground or in caves. Again, they will try to hide from His terror and majesty, but they will fail to do so.

The prophet concludes with a petition for the Lord to turn away from the awful judgment of insignificant man. He is not worth the trouble. However, this petition seems weak and pale in the face of the vivid description of the coming judgment on the Day of the Lord. One does not have the impression that this petition will avail. God is too concerned with human sin to simply let it slide into obscurity.

Lesson 2

Isaiah 3–5

—— Isaiah 3:1–11 ——

This unit describes the Lord's judgment on Jerusalem and Judah because of the sins already described in the preceding oracles (2:6–22).

3:1–3

[1]For, behold, the Lord, the Lord of hosts, is taking away from Jerusalem and from Judah stay and staff, the whole stay of bread, and the whole stay of water; [2]the mighty man and the soldier, the judge and the prophet, the diviner and the elder, [3]the captain of fifty and the man of rank, the counselor and the skilful magician and the expert in charms.

The first stage of the judgment will be a series of losses: bread, water, soldiers, religious leaders, officers, and the various "magicians, charmers, and diviners" who had led the people into sin in the first place. Judges had become corrupt and prophets did not speak the hard words that would challenge people to repent. The military and political leaders sought to maintain their own power rather than sustain society's values and truths that God had bestowed upon them.

3:4

[4]And I will make boys their princes, and babes shall rule over them.

Since boys and babies cannot even govern their own lives and take care of their own needs, the nation will be punished through having such immature and incompetent children rule them.

3:5

[5]And the people will oppress one another, every man his fellow and every man his neighbor; the youth will be insolent to the elder, and the base fellow to the honorable.

The mutual oppression of neighbors is the logical consequence of letting the political leadership get away with oppression. Knowledge and application of moral, righteous principles eludes the people who forsake God's law. When society does not base itself on moral principle, then people use the principle that might makes right. Such is the beginning of the social acceptance of oppression.

3:6–7

[6]When a man takes hold of his brother in the house of his father, saying: "You have a mantle; you shall be our leader, and this heap of ruins shall be under your rule"; [7]in that day he will speak out, saying: "I will not be a healer; in my house there is neither bread nor mantle; you shall not make me leader of the people."

In the resulting societal chaos, people will become desperate for any kind of leadership and will accept the flimsiest qualifications for rulers, such as possessing a piece of clothing, a mantle. However, with society's circumstances in such dire straits, everyone will reject the offer of governing because they will see no hope either for success against horrible odds nor personal advantage in being a leader.

3:8–9

[8]For Jerusalem has stumbled, and Judah has fallen; because their speech and their deeds are against the LORD, defying his glorious presence. [9]Their partiality witnesses against them; they proclaim their sin like Sodom, they do not hide it. Woe to them! For they have brought evil upon themselves.

The inevitable judgment is explained as the consequence of Jerusalem and Judah turning both speech and action against the Lord's will. Their own sin will testify against them, and the inevitable punishment is due to the evils they themselves have done. No one else is to blame for the coming catastrophe, and the Lord wants them to accept their full responsibility for their coming doom.

3:10–11

> **[10]Tell the righteous that it shall be well with them, for they shall eat the fruit of their deeds. [11]Woe to the wicked! It shall be ill with him, for what his hands have done shall be done to him.**

This section is an explanatory note clarifying that the wicked are the segment of society that is doomed to the "woe" of coming destruction. However, the righteous shall do well, since the Lord can distinguish between the moral decisions that human beings make and give recompense that is appropriate to the righteous and the wicked.

—— Isaiah 3:12–15 ——
The Lord's Dispute

3:12

> **[12]My people—children are their oppressors, and women rule over them. O my people, your leaders mislead you, and confuse the course of your paths.**

The Lord addresses the people with a lament over the people because the leaders have so misled and confused them that the threats made in 3:4–5 about children oppressing them has come true. The ancients did not accept women as rulers because kings and other leaders were generally expected to lead in war—a frequent experience. Leaders gained the respect of the troops, in part, by their own ability to fight in battle, as well as in having enough battle experience to direct successful war strategies. Israel's experience of women in leadership was not positive. Jezebel in the northern Kingdom of Israel killed the Lord's prophets and promoted Baal worship (see 1 Kgs 18:4, 13; 19:1–3; 21:5–25). A generation later, Athaliah, in Judah, executed her husband's sons (from multiple wives) and ruled until the restoration of the surviving boy prince to the throne and her own murder (see 2 Kgs 11). They were no Margaret Thatcher.

3:13–14a

> **[13]The LORD has taken his place to contend, he stands to judge his people. [14a]The LORD enters into judgment with the elders and princes of his people:**

The prophet describes how the Lord enters into the courtroom to judge His people.

3:14b–15

> **[14b]"It is you who have devoured the vineyard, the spoil of the poor is in your houses. [15]What do you mean by crushing my people, by grinding the face of the poor?" says the LORD God of hosts.**

The Lord accuses the people of their sins of oppressing the poor. Many of the poor would have been tenant farmers whose crops were exacted by the rich landowners in payment. However, the attitude that focused so strongly on making a profit without concern for the labor's welfare is condemned. This type of practice crushed the poor, ignoring their legitimate needs. Employers ought to strike a balance between making a legitimate profit and the good of their workers, each of whom has a dignity from God and personal needs.

— Isaiah 3:16–26; 4:1 —
Judgment on the Women of Jerusalem

3:16–17

> **[16]The LORD said: Because the daughters of Zion are haughty and walk with outstretched necks, glancing wantonly with their eyes, mincing along as they go, tinkling with their feet; [17]the LORD will smite with a scab the heads of the daughters of Zion, and the LORD will lay bare their secret parts.**

The Lord accuses the women of Jerusalem for their haughtiness that is connected with various seductive activities (v. 16). Therefore, the Lord inflicts them with a skin disease to ruin their beauty. The punishment fits the crime.

3:18–23

> **[18]In that day the LORD will take away the finery of the anklets, the headbands, and the crescents; [19]the pendants, the bracelets, and the scarfs; [20] the headdresses, the armlets, the sashes, the perfume boxes, and the amulets; [21]the signet rings and nose rings; [22]the festal robes, the mantles, the cloaks, and the handbags; [23]the garments of gauze, the linen garments, the turbans, and the veils.**

On the day of the Lord, the punishment meted out to the women includes the loss of the luxury items listed here.

3:24

> **[24]Instead of perfume there will be rottenness; and instead of a girdle, a rope; and instead of well-set hair, baldness; and instead of a rich robe, a girding of sackcloth; instead of beauty, shame.**

These punishments will replace pleasant items with opposite experiences: the stench of rottenness instead of perfume; the rope of a slave instead of a fashionable girdle; rough sackcloth instead of fine clothes; shame, especially of nakedness and sexual use instead of beauty.

3:25–26

> **[25]Your men shall fall by the sword and your mighty men in battle. [26]And her gates shall lament and mourn; ravaged, she shall sit upon the ground.**

The men who once protected them and acquired their luxuries will die in battle, causing the women to lament and mourn at the city gates that the dead soldiers will leave defenseless.

4:1

> **[1]And seven women shall take hold of one man in that day, saying, "We will eat our own bread and wear our own clothes, only let us be called by your name; take away our reproach."**

The fate of the women is that after the enemy defeat, they can expect to be raped. In such a case, they would not be considered marriageable in that culture. Therefore, seven such abandoned women will take hold of one man, promising to provide for themselves if he will only marry them, give them his name to transfer them to the category of once more honorable women, and thereby remove the reproach of being shamed and unwanted. My father told us of large groups of such women and their children wandering North Africa begging for food during his deployment in World War II. He described it as a pathetic and pitiable sight.

—— Isaiah 4:2–6 ——

After the oracles of threats of judgment on the day of the Lord (2:6–4:1), the last section of Isaiah 4:2–6 is a prophecy of salvation on the day of the Lord for the survivors of Israel.

4:2

> **[2]In that day the branch of the LORD shall be beautiful and glorious, and the fruit of the land shall be the pride and glory of the survivors of Israel.**

In the preceding judgments, the Lord has condemned the people for their pride, arrogance, or haughtiness several times (2:11–17; 3:16), and many of the punishments He decrees are meant to humble the proud. This verse promises that the day of the Lord will witness the Lord's "branch" as the origin of the land's fruit. The image is one in which the Lord promises the prosperity of a rich harvest for the survivors of Israel. They will recognize that this branch will be "beautiful and glorious" because it comes from the Lord. The survivors will take pride in the fruit, not the way most farmers show for the work of their hands but rather in the fact that the origin of the fruit is from the Lord, not their own labor. In that way, they will live humbly as they honor the Lord's work.

4:3–4

> **[3]And he who is left in Zion and remains in Jerusalem will be called holy, every one who has been recorded for life in Jerusalem, [4]when the LORD shall have washed away the filth of the daughters of Zion and cleansed the bloodstains of Jerusalem from its midst by a spirit of judgment and by a spirit of burning.**

These verses describe the hope for the men and women of Jerusalem. The people will be holy, which has a sense of being set apart for the Lord. They will be "recorded for life" in the Lord's book and, therefore, like registered citizens, will be permitted to live in the holy city on the day of the Lord. The idea of the Lord having a book to record His people is not developed at length in the Bible, but it is first mentioned in Exodus 32:32–34, where the Lord says, "Whoever has sinned against me, him will I blot out of my book," and mentions this for the "day" He visits people's sins on them. (See also Ez 13:9; Lk 10:20 "your names are written in heaven"; the "book of life" is mentioned in Phil 4:3; Rv 3:5; 13:8; 17:8; 20:15; 21:27.)

These holy survivors are not without sin, but what distinguishes them from the previously mentioned doomed people is the fact that the Lord has "washed away" the filth of the women and the bloodstains from the men with His "spirit of judgment" and "burning." Naturally, Christians will see in this a promise of baptism that washes away sins and the purifying gift of the Holy Spirit. This prophecy adds to our understanding of Christ's saying, "Unless one is born of water and the Spirit, he cannot enter the kingdom of God" (Jn 3:5).

4:5–6

> **[5]Then the LORD will create over the whole site of Mount Zion and over her assemblies a cloud by day, and smoke and the shining of a flaming fire by night; for over all the glory there will be a canopy and a pavilion. [6]It will be for a shade by day from the heat, and for a refuge and a shelter from the storm and rain.**

Mount Zion, the site of the Temple, will have an experience like that of the Israelites walking through the Sinai desert, where a cloud protected them from the sun by day and a fire guided them at night (Ex 13:21–22; 14:19–20, 24; 40:34–38; Nm 9:15–22, where the cloud covered them at the time of the dedication of the desert temple). The day of the Lord will be a new beginning, as the Exodus experience was the old beginning for the people.

— Isaiah 5:1–7 —

This section is named the "song of the vineyard" because the prophet states that he will sing this poem. However, the content is a trial scene, in which the Lord is acquitted of any mistake but Judah is convicted of being in the wrong.

5:1–2

> **[1]Let me sing for my beloved a love song concerning his vineyard: [1b]My beloved had a vineyard on a very fertile hill. [2a]He dug it and cleared it of stones, and planted it with choice vines; he built a watchtower in the midst of it, and hewed out a wine vat in it; [2b]and he looked for it to yield grapes, but it yielded wild grapes.**

The request to sing the song is made to an unnamed audience.

The topic is a "love song" about his beloved friend's relationship with his vineyard. The word for "beloved" (dod) is from the same Hebrew root as the name David. Isaiah's use of "beloved" here certainly influenced the way later Jewish exegesis of the Song of Solomon's use of the same word (2:16; 5:2; 5:16; 6:3) applied it to the Lord, while Israel was the bride in that Song. This was also used by Christian commentators on the Song (Saint Gregory of Nyssa and Saint Bernard) to understand the Lord's relationship to the Church or to the individual soul.

Psalms 80:8–13 uses the image of a vineyard to describe Israel, but the psalm questions God for permitting enemies to break down its walls and have "boars" eat its fruit. Isaiah makes it clear in this passage that Israel has erred and will receive deserved punishment.

The singer presents the evidence of the great care His beloved (the Lord) had put into locating His vineyard on a fertile hill that was hoed, cleared of stones, planted with an excellent variety of vines, provided with a vat hewn into the stone (examples of which can still be seen in Israel), and protected with a watchtower. Everything was completely ready for an excellent harvest of wine.

However, it yielded "wild grapes." The word for "wild" better means "smelly, stinky," like certain foul-smelling berries that grow wild and cannot be eaten. This refers to the harvest of immorality and the lack of justice in Israel.

5:3–4

> **[3]And now, O inhabitants of Jerusalem and men of Judah, judge, I pray you, between me and my vineyard. [4]What more was there to do for my vineyard, that I have not done in it? When I looked for it to yield grapes, why did it yield wild grapes?**

Witnesses in Jerusalem and Judah are here summoned to judge between the owner, who is now speaking for himself as "I," and the vineyard (v. 3). He uses rhetorical questions to remind this jury of the facts of his case: there was nothing more he was able to do for his vineyard; why did it yield foul grapes (v. 4)?

5:5–6

> **[5]And now I will tell you what I will do to my vineyard. I will remove its hedge, and it shall be devoured; I will break down its wall, and it shall be trampled down. [6]I will make it a waste; it shall not be pruned or hoed, and briers and thorns shall grow up; I will also command the clouds that they rain no rain upon it.**

The verdict: the owner will remove its protecting wall and hedge so it can be trampled by the unappreciative and devoured by those who have no taste for good grapes (v. 5). The owner will personally turn it into a waste, and in a threat that reveals the owner's identity as the Lord, he will command the clouds to give it no rain.

5:7

> **[7]For the vineyard of the LORD of hosts is the house of Israel, and the men of Judah are his pleasant planting; and he looked for justice, but behold, bloodshed; for righteousness, but behold, a cry!**

With the identity of the owner already revealed in 6b, the Lord makes clear that the vineyard is Israel and the sought-after harvest was justice. However, the "stinky" grapes that Israel and Judah produced were bloodshed and the outcry of those who were oppressed.

— Isaiah 5:8–24 —

This next long section lists a series of "woes" against Israel for its sins. Recall Isaiah 1:4, where "woe" was said to someone doomed to die or suffer greatly. It is used most frequently in Isaiah, and this passage has the greatest concentration of woes in the Bible until Matthew 23, where there are seven woes against the Pharisees as opposed to six in this section of Isaiah.

5:8–10

> **8Woe to those who join house to house, who add field to field, until**
> **there is no more room, and you are made to dwell alone in the midst of**
> **the land. 9The LORD of hosts has sworn in my hearing: "Surely many**
> **houses shall be desolate, large and beautiful houses, without inhabi-**
> **tant. 10For ten acres of vineyard shall yield but one bath, and a homer**
> **of seed shall yield but an ephah."**

First, woe is against those who buy up the property of the poor when they go bankrupt and then evict them from their houses and land. These landowners may be rich in land and houses, but they end up being isolated as their neighbors leave. To this situation, the Lord will add the desolation of the houses by the removal of the inhabitants in war (v. 9). Without people to work the land, it will become nearly worthless, producing one "bath" (about three gallons) of wine from ten acres of vines, or a "homer" of seed (ten bushels) producing an ephah (one bushel).

5:11–17

> **11Woe to those who rise early in the morning, that they may run after**
> **strong drink, who tarry late into the evening till wine inflames them!**
> **12They have lyre and harp, timbrel and flute and wine at their feasts;**
> **but they do not regard the deeds of the LORD, or see the work of his**
> **hands. 13Therefore my people go into exile for want of knowledge;**
> **their honored men are dying of hunger, and their multitude is parched**
> **with thirst. 14Therefore Sheol has enlarged its appetite and opened its**
> **mouth beyond measure, and the nobility of Jerusalem and her multi-**
> **tude go down, her throng and he who exults in her. 15Man is bowed**
> **down, and men are brought low, and the eyes of the haughty are hum-**
> **bled. 16But the LORD of hosts is exalted in justice, and the Holy God**

shows himself holy in righteousness. [17]Then shall the lambs graze as in their pasture, fatlings and kids shall feed among the ruins.

The second and longest woe is directed against those who drink intoxicants throughout the whole day while people are without knowledge, food, or water.

First, Isaiah describes the constant state of intoxication, from early morning to late night with "strong drink," a type of beer (distilled liquor would not be discovered for another 1,600 years) and wine. They keep entertained in their stupor, since drunkenness does not suffice for them. In such an addled state, they are incapable of paying attention to God's deeds and work. Consequently, they cannot discern God's activity or will because they have renounced control of their minds in favor of alcohol.

Their inability to discern God's will because of their drunkenness had a destructive impact on the rest of society. The people do not have knowledge, and in their ignorance, they will end up in exile. People die of hunger and thirst while the rich leadership is drunk with wine and beer all day (v. 13). Because the people die of starvation and thirst, Sheol, the place of the dead, is more than sated with these dead people (v. 14). As was the case in the threats of the day of the Lord, this woe will also lead to the humiliation of the proud and arrogant, presumably those who think that they can live an intoxicated life while others starve.

The punishment of the evildoers becomes the occasion for the exaltation of the Lord because His justice, holiness, and righteousness are made clear in the contrast with evil. He demonstrates that evil cannot overcome goodness but righteousness defeats evil by showing its inherent tendency to the ultimate doom of its plans in death. The contrast with evil is made more clear when the humble and gentle lambs, fatlings, and kid goats (generally more playful than lambs) feed peacefully in the ruins of houses where the drunks and gluttons had lived in debauchery.

5:18–19

[18]Woe to those who draw iniquity with cords of falsehood, who draw sin as with cart ropes, [19]who say: "Let him make haste, let him speed his work that we may see it; let the purpose of the Holy One of Israel draw near, and let it come, that we may know it!"

The third woe is against sinners who speak falsehood and then treat faith in God with cynicism, demanding that God perform some sign or miracle so they can see it as proof. Similar arguments were frequently brought up to Jesus (Mt 12:28–41; 16:1–4; Mk 8:11–12; Lk 11:16; Jn 2:18–19; 4:48), even after He had just performed miracles. Scoffers were also criticized in 2 Peter 3:3–12. Psalm 73 describes cynical scoffers at length, though with the sense that the psalmist was himself tempted to imitate them—a danger Isaiah may implicitly have in mind.

5:20

> **[20]Woe to those who call evil good and good evil, who put darkness for light and light for darkness, who put bitter for sweet and sweet for bitter!**

The fourth woe is against those who refuse to accept authentic goodness and instead choose evil as their preferred "good." This criticism applies well in the relativistic world of redefined values that characterize modern moral discourse.

5:21

> **[21]Woe to those who are wise in their own eyes, and shrewd in their own sight!**

The fifth woe belongs to the arrogance of self-assured people who consider themselves intelligent when they are no longer able to understand the basic principles of determining right from wrong.

5:22–23

> **[22]Woe to those who are heroes at drinking wine, and valiant men in mixing strong drink, [23]who acquit the guilty for a bribe, and deprive the innocent of his right!**

The sixth woe combines the criticism of the intoxicated with that of the politically corrupt.

5:24

> **[24]Therefore, as the tongue of fire devours the stubble, and as dry grass sinks down in the flame, so their root will be as rottenness, and their**

blossom go up like dust; for they have rejected the law of the LORD of hosts, and have despised the word of the Holy One of Israel.

The whole list of woes concludes with a decree of punishment for all those against whom the woes were decreed. They are like mere dried grass or short stubble that burns quickly, or like a rot that lies in the root of a plant and makes its blossom turn to dust at the merest touch. The key to understanding the woes is that all of the sinners had turned against the Lord's law and word. Their personal opinions and their pleasure took precedence over the law and word of the Lord. However, in these woes, they are confronted by the word of the Lord that is based on the principles of His law, and as a result, they will be destroyed. While this primarily applied to the people of Isaiah's time, it will fit the drug culture, relativistic morality, and narcissism of the modern world that ignores true goodness and charity for the most vulnerable.

—— Isaiah 5:25–30 ——

This description of the Lord's final judgment is the conclusion of the first five chapters of Isaiah. Most of the preceding oracles have criticized the nation's social sins, and here the scene of God's judgment is presented.

5:25

25Therefore the anger of the LORD was kindled against his people, and he stretched out his hand against them and smote them, and the mountains quaked; and their corpses were as refuse in the midst of the streets. For all this his anger is not turned away and his hand is stretched out still.

The Lord appears in a theophany (a manifestation of God) with anger and outstretched hand to punish the sinners He has criticized throughout the first five chapters of Isaiah.

5:26–30

26He will raise a signal for a nation afar off, and whistle for it from the
ends of the earth; and lo, swiftly, speedily it comes! 27None is weary,
none stumbles, none slumbers or sleeps, not a waistcloth is loose, not

**a sandal-thong broken; [28]their arrows are sharp, all their bows bent,
their horses' hoofs seem like flint, and their wheels like the whirlwind.
[29]Their roaring is like a lion, like young lions they roar; they growl
and seize their prey, they carry it off, and none can rescue. [30]They will
growl over it on that day, like the roaring of the sea. And if one look
to the land, behold, darkness and distress; and the light is darkened
by its clouds.**

The Lord will use a distant foreign nation to effect the judgment in history. This nation was unknown in the lifetime of Uzziah, but at the time of his death, Tiglath-Pileser III will usurp the Assyrian throne and turn it into an empire that aggressively moves west to subdue the nations of western Asia, including Israel and Judah.

Verse 26 is the announcement of the summons of the distant nation who comes quickly to the Lord's signal. Like an animal trained to hunt prey, this nation will respond quickly to the Lord's summons because it wants to take part in the destruction of others.

The enemy is well prepared for the punitive battle—well rested, properly uniformed for a fight, with plenty of ammunition, and with proper chariots, which served as the equivalent of the tank in modern warfare.

The eagerness of the enemy's ferocity is compared to that of lions who are determined to take their prey with no one to stop them. This will not occur in King Uzziah's time (he died in 743 BC), but Assyria's aggression will dominate the rest of Proto-Isaiah up through chapter 33, plus the additions from 2 Kings in Isaiah 36–39. This passage is ominous indeed.

Lesson 3

Isaiah 6–7

—— Isaiah 6:1–13 ——

While in the Jerusalem Temple, Isaiah has a vision of the Lord and His seraphim in the "year King Uzziah died"—that is, 743 BC. Many people have considered this Isaiah's initial call to become a prophet, which does not explain why it is placed in chapter 6. In its present position, the vision assumes that the first five chapters were spoken during the reign of Uzziah. Most of those oracles criticized the people for their willingness to worship other gods, practice magic and occult arts, and especially for their haughtiness, injustice, and oppression of the poor and weak. If this vision did occur after Isaiah had delivered the oracles of the first five chapters, it seems more likely to be a recommissioning rather than an initial call since his words were rejected during his first years as a prophet. In this view, Isaiah understands the Lord's statements about the people's incomprehension of God's word.

6:1–4

In these verses, Isaiah describes his Temple vision.

> **[1]In the year that King Uzziah died I saw the Lord sitting upon a**
> **throne, high and lifted up; and his train filled the temple. [2]Above him**
> **stood the seraphim; each had six wings: with two he covered his face,**
> **and with two he covered his feet, and with two he flew. [3]And one called**
> **to another and said: "Holy, holy, holy is the Lord of hosts; the whole**
> **earth is full of his glory." [4]And the foundations of the thresholds shook**
> **at the voice of him who called, and the house was filled with smoke.**

1

While the Lord is seated up high on a throne, Isaiah does not describe His features, a reticence typical of the Bible. God is too far beyond human conception or explanation for anyone to truly describe Him; therefore, silence is appropriate. In fact, what Isaiah does see is the "train" of His garment. This word translated as "train" may be better understood as the fringes found on the edges or bottoms of royal clothing. Since the Lord is the great King seated in heaven, just the fringe of His garment is able to fill the whole Temple, which was the most magnificent building in the nation. Tiny humans like Isaiah can see no more than that fringe in the Temple.

2–3

Isaiah describes the seraphim, a word that means "burning ones," and is also the name of a type of poisonous snake. Some artists emphasize the flames, and others use images of a serpent for the seraphim, but they, too, are a mystery to humans. It is more important to note that only two wings are used for flight, while two cover their faces in humility before the Lord, and two wings modestly cover their "feet," a word frequently used in the Old Testament as a euphemism for sexual organs. Of course, angels do not generate, so they would have no true sexuality comparable to the animals, but this description modifies their power to fly with humility and modesty, two virtues absent from Israel, according to 2:11–18 and 3:16–26.

The seraphim called to each other in chorus, "Holy, holy, holy is the Lord of hosts; the whole earth is full of his glory," words that are the basis for Revelation 4:8–9 and subsequently the liturgies of the synagogues and Christian churches over the centuries. These seraphim recognize God's holiness, a term that has a double meaning to its root. First, it means to be "on fire" and carries the sense of purifying fire. This would be appropriate for seraphim, whose name means "burning ones." Second, "holy" means to be separate, as in set apart from secular uses and things for the sacred and holy use. Both attributes belong to the Lord's holiness, and even the mighty seraphim sing it aloud in praise of God.

4
This hymn causes the Temple foundations to shake, as in an earthquake. The house is filled with the smoke of incense because the smoke hides the presence of the Lord, as was the goal of the high priests burning finely ground incense upon entering the Holy of Holies on the Day of Atonement. The smoke would shield them from the dangerous presence of God, whose holiness would harm sinful humans that see it.

6:5

> **[5]And I said: "Woe is me! For I am lost; for I am a man of unclean lips, and I dwell in the midst of a people of unclean lips; for my eyes have seen the King, the LORD of hosts!"**

Isaiah responds to the vision by declaring a woe against himself, even as he had done against the sinners in Israel (1:4, 24; 5:8, 11, 18, 20, 21, 22). The closer the saints get to God, the more clearly they can recognize their sinfulness; conversely, the people more distant and unaccustomed to God's presence tend to feel more self-confidence despite their sins. That is because they cannot recognize the infinite gap between God's holiness and their own sinfulness the way Isaiah does in his vision. Similarly, when John saw Jesus in Revelation 1:16ff, he fell at His feet as though one dead until Jesus, the First and the Last, touches him and tells him to "Fear not" (1:17–18).

6:6–7

> **[6]Then flew one of the seraphim to me, having in his hand a burning coal which he had taken with tongs from the altar. [7]And he touched my mouth, and said: "Behold, this has touched your lips; your guilt is taken away, and your sin forgiven."**

Isaiah's self-description as a sinner with unclean lips was not false humility but a realistic self-knowledge that a seraph recognizes by purifying his mouth with a hot coal from the altar. Just as God's holiness has a root meaning in a word for being on fire, so also the hot coal can purify Isaiah's lips and make them holy by taking away his guilt, a guilt he shares with the whole people; indeed, with all of humanity.

6:8

> **[8]And I heard the voice of the LORD saying, "Whom shall I send, and who will go for us?" Then I said, "Here am I! Send me."**

Still, Isaiah does not see and describe the Lord, but he hears Him ask, "Whom shall I send, and who will go for us?" The use of the plural "us" in the Lord's question is usually understood as a *pluralis maiestatis*, as in Genesis 1:26, "Let us make man in our image, after our likeness." The plural of majesty was used by kings to show that they were speaking for the whole realm and not just as an individual person. Of course, the Fathers of the Church understood this type of expression as an early hint at the doctrine of the Trinity, particularly in connection with the threefold expression of "holy, holy, holy" in verse 3.

Several prophets tried to avoid the Lord's call. For instance, Moses gives the Lord five reasons why he should not be chosen (see Ex 3–4), and Jeremiah says he is "too young" to accept the call, but the Lord insists (Jer 1:4–10). Here, Isaiah volunteers and asks the Lord to send him.

6:9–10

> **[9]And he said, "Go, and say to this people: 'Hear and hear, but do not understand; see and see, but do not perceive.' [10]Make the heart of this people fat, and their ears heavy, and shut their eyes; lest they see with their eyes, and hear with their ears, and understand with their hearts, and turn and be healed."**

The Lord's acceptance of Isaiah's offer is indicated by His command, "Go and say to this people." However, the commission does not promise popular acceptance. In fact, His message to them is "Hear, but do not understand, see but do not perceive." This is a realistic message given the ways the leaders and people will focus on their own ideas rather than the word of the Lord. In fact, it is precisely the communication of the Lord's prophetic word that will make their hearts "fat." In their idea of persons, the heart was the organ of thought. Modern insults like the expressions "fat head" and "fat hearts" would be the Israelite equivalent. The experience of the people will be similar to Pharoah's: the more often Moses brought the word of the Lord to Pharaoh, the more frequently he hardened his heart, until finally widespread death made him change his mind. Even then he would not remain with his earlier decision to let Israel go free, and he pursued them into the sea for the destruction of his army. So too, in Isaiah's time, the kings, leaders, and people would harden their hearts as often as they heard Isaiah's prophecies, and their stubbornness kept them from having an understanding heart that was capable of repenting and being healed.

6:11–13

> **[11]Then I said, "How long, O LORD?" And he said: "Until cities lie**
> **waste without inhabitant, and houses without men, and the land**
> **is utterly desolate, [12]and the LORD removes men far away, and the**
> **forsaken places are many in the midst of the land. [13]And though a**
> **tenth remain in it, it will be burned again, like a terebinth or an oak,**
> **whose stump remains standing when it is felled." The holy seed is**
> **its stump.**

Isaiah realizes how daunting this mission doomed to failure will be, so he asks the Lord how long it will go on (v. 11a). The Lord answers that the prophetic word will continue until the cities and land are destroyed and desolate, with people removed far away in exile. Not even a tenth of the people will be left in the land, which will be as when a tree stump in the ground is all that is left of an oak or terebinth tree (which is also quite large) that then gets burned (vv. 11b–13a).

Finally, "The holy seed is its stump," appears as an explanatory note in light of the prophecy in 11:1 about the shoot that will come forth from the stump of Jesse. This means it is a messianic note of hope that the destruction of the nation still conceals within it.

Since 6:1 mentions the year of Uzziah's death (743 BC), we assume that he said nothing for the next nine years, since the next chapter occurs after Uzziah's son and successor, Jotham, died in 735 BC. He was replaced by his son, Ahaz, in a time of great danger.

International problems began in 783 BC with the death of King Adad-Nirari of Assyria. The empire entered a period of disorder and sudden weakness in which the transitions between reigns seem to have taken place by treachery and violence rather than orderly succession. In 782, Adad-Nirari was replaced by his oldest son, Shalmaneser IV. He died in

771 and was replaced by his brother, Ashur-dan III, the second son of Adad-nirari. A serious plague hit Assyria at this time, further weakening the empire. He died in 753, and his next younger brother, Ashur-nirari V, the third son of Adad-nirari, became the king of Assyria. He died in 745, two years before Uzziah died. Through a revolt, Tiglath-Pileser III (called Pul in the Bible), the fourth son of Adad-nirari, became king of Assyria, and he began a war against Arpad in northern Syria.

Meanwhile, in the northern kingdom of Israel, King Menachem paid Tiglath-Pileser one thousand talents of silver to keep the Assyrians from invading. Menachem forced the nobility of Israel to pay this tribute by taxing them, which of course, was very unpopular (2 Kgs 15:19–22).

In 742, Tiglath-Pileser razed Arpad to the ground and forced Damascus, Tyre, Carchemish, and other cities to pay tribute. The Assyrians then attacked Urartu in the north, so King Rezin of Damascus led a coalition against Assyria, but it failed, and Tiglath-Pileser required tribute from Rezin, Menahem of Israel, Hiram of Tyre, and even the Queen of Arabia, Zabibi.

A period of political chaos started in Israel at this point. In 739, Menachem died, and his son, Pekahiah, became king, continuing his father's pro-Assyrian policy. In 738, King Pekahiah was assassinated by Pekah, one of his generals, probably with the support of the nobles, who were tired of being taxed to pay Assyrian tribute. Pekah stopped paying the tribute, thereby commencing a revolt against Assyria (see 2 Kgs 15:25, 27–31). Meanwhile in Syria, Tiglath-Pileser defeated a coalition of nineteen cities near Hamath.

—— Isaiah 7:1–9 ——

Isaiah gives his first oracle to young King Ahaz of Judah in 734 BC.

7:1–2

> **1In the days of Ahaz the son of Jotham, son of Uzziah, king of Judah, Rezin the king of Syria and Pekah the son of Remaliah the king of Israel came up to Jerusalem to wage war against it, but they could not conquer it. 2When the house of David was told, "Syria is in league with Ephraim," his heart and the heart of his people shook as the trees of the forest shake before the wind.**

These introductory verses review the historical situation, which began in 735, when King Jotham of Judah died and was replaced by his twenty-year-old son, Ahaz (see 2 Kgs 16:1–4). The next year, 734, King Rezin of Syria and King Pekah of Israel, attacked Jerusalem to replace Ahaz with a Syrian named Tabeel in order to force Judah to join their anti-Assyrian coalition. In this period, Isaiah met King Ahaz at the Upper Pool and prophesied the collapse of Rezin and Pekah and offered the sign that a virgin would conceive and bear a son and call His name Immanuel, as this chapter of Isaiah records.

7:3–9

> **3And the LORD said to Isaiah, "Go forth to meet Ahaz, you and Shear-jashub your son, at the end of the conduit of the upper pool on the highway to the Fuller's Field, 4and say to him, 'Take heed, be quiet, do not fear, and do not let your heart be faint because of these two smoldering stumps of firebrands, at the fierce anger of Rezin and Syria and the son of Remaliah.' 5Because Syria, with Ephraim and the son of Remaliah, has devised evil against you, saying, 6"Let us go up against Judah and terrify it, and let us conquer it for ourselves, and set up the son of Tabeel as king in the midst of it," 7thus says the LORD God: It shall not stand, and it shall not come to pass. 8For the head of Syria is Damascus, and the head of Damascus is Rezin. (Within sixty-five years Ephraim will be broken to pieces so that it will no longer be a people.) 9aAnd the head of Ephraim is Samaria, and the head of Samaria is the son of Remaliah. 9bIf you will not believe, surely you shall not be established.'"**

The Lord commissions Isaiah to speak a message to Ahaz about having faith during the crisis of the attack on Judah by King Rezin of Syria and King Pekah of Israel.

3

Nine years after the Lord's commission to Isaiah during the Temple vision in chapter 6, the Lord gives Isaiah a specific commission to speak to King Ahaz, now twenty-one years old. He is told to bring his son, Shearjashub, a symbolic name meaning "a remnant will return." Like many good symbols, the name can have a variety of nuances: will merely a remnant return or is this a promise that at least a remnant will return? Given the pessimistic understanding of the inability of the people's willingness to hear and understand, or see and perceive the word of God (6:9–10), the boy's name could also mean that a remnant will repent, a common enough meaning for the Hebrew root *shub*. The instructions tell Isaiah to meet the king at the "upper pool," near the Fuller's Field. A "fuller" washed clothes, often by trampling dirty clothes in water with local cleaning agents, with the feet acting like an "agitator" in a washing machine. Such sites were away from the drinking water so as not to pollute it; therefore, the site is somewhere outside the city before the enemy armies arrive.

4–9

Verses 4 through 9 comprise the content of the message that Isaiah is to bring to Ahaz.

The key to the whole message is for King Ahaz to be quiet and have no fear of Rezin of Syria and Pekah the son of Remaliah. Note that Isaiah does not even pronounce Pekah's name but calls him the son of Remaliah, which was a more honorable name to mention.

The reason to be quiet and unafraid is that Syria and Ephraim (the name of the dominant tribe in the northern Kingdom of Israel) may have planned to conquer Jerusalem, but the Lord will not permit it (vv. 6–7). Not only will they fail, but they will be destroyed (vv. 8–9a). In fact, in 734, Tiglath-Pileser first attacked the nations to the west of Syria—Phoenicia, Philistia, and coastal towns in between. King Ahaz paid tribute and Pekah of Israel gave up resistance. Then, when Syria was without any allies, Tiglath-Pileser defeated Damascus.

The oracle closes with another aspect of the opening message to Ahaz to be quiet and fear not: if Ahaz does not believe, he will not stand, "be established." The English cannot convey the play on the Hebrew root *amn* (from which comes "amen"), which in one form means "believe," and in the second form means "stand, be firm, established."

—— Isaiah 7:10–17 ——

Isaiah invites Ahaz to choose some sign from God that the preceding oracle is true, but Isaiah will be the one to give the sign to him, since Ahaz is afraid to have faith.

7:10

[10]Again the LORD spoke to Ahaz,

The introduction to this oracle to Ahaz indicates a separate occasion.

7:11–12

[11]"Ask a sign of the LORD your God; let it be deep as Sheol or high as heaven." [12]But Ahaz said, "I will not ask, and I will not put the LORD to the test."

Isaiah takes this initiative to invite Ahaz to choose any sign of the Lord's fulfillment that he can think of. However, he refuses to do so out of a false piety that claims he does not want to "test" the Lord. Certainly, Moses taught in Deuteronomy 6:16, "You shall not put the Lord your God to the test," but Ahaz unquestionably tested the Lord in various ways, such as sacrificing one of his sons to a pagan deity in the Valley of Hinnom (Aramaic "Gehenna") to avoid an attack (2 Chr 28:1–4).

7:13–17

[13]And he said, "Hear then, O house of David! Is it too little for you to weary men, that you weary my God also? [14]Therefore the LORD himself will give you a sign. Behold, a young woman shall conceive and bear a son, and shall call his name Immanuel. [15]He shall eat curds and honey when he knows how to refuse the evil and choose the good. [16]For before the child knows how to refuse the evil and choose the good, the land before whose two kings you are in dread will be deserted. [17]The LORD will bring upon you and upon your people and upon your father's house such days as have not come since the day that Ephraim departed from Judah—the king of Assyria."

Isaiah then chooses the sign: Immanuel.

13

Isaiah uses rhetorical questions to recognize Ahaz's hypocrisy regarding the request for a sign. While he had used "you" singular in his first address to Ahaz, here he uses a more formal "you" plural to "hear" and "you (pl) weary." Ahaz wearied men by taking silver and gold from the Temple to pay King Tiglath-Pileser tribute to bribe him to attack Syria and Israel (2 Kgs 16:7–9); now he wearies God by not accepting His offer of a sign.

14–16

Isaiah's frustration with Ahaz does not prevent him from taking the initiative of delivering the message that the Lord has a sign (v. 14a).

14b

A "young woman shall conceive and bear a son." The Hebrew word *almah* can refer to any young woman before she gives birth to a child, as in Genesis 24:43; Song of Songs 6:8, and Proverbs 30:19. However, it is important to note that the Greek Septuagint translation (probably second century BC) uses the word *parthenos*, specifically meaning a "virgin," and the Aramaic Targum also uses the word meaning "virgin." These translations indicate that Jewish readers understood *almah* in the sense of "virgin," and this is the background for citing this verse in Matthew 1:23, where it shows that Mary's virginal conception of Jesus by the power of the Holy Spirit was the fulfillment of this prophecy.

"Immanuel" is simply "God (*El*) is with us (Hebr. *immanu*). The child will indicate through his name that God is present with the people during this grave political crisis, so neither the king nor the people need fear.

15–16

A further expansion of the sign of Immanuel is that the defeat of the kings of Syria and Israel will be complete before He has enough use of His reason to refuse evil and choose good, an ability He will have by the time He is weaned and can eat curds (yogurt) and honey. Certainly, the Assyrians had defeated Syria and killed Rezin and had invaded Israel by 732 BC, two years after the prophecy.

17

This prophecy ends ominously for Ahaz, who is himself threatened with days of threat that will be the worst since the northern Kingdom of Israel, led by Jeroboam ben Nebat, revolted against Solomon's son Rehoboam around 933 BC (see 1 Kgs 12:1–24). The instrument of this threat will be the king of Assyria, but Isaiah does not name which king. Ahaz himself will build an altar to the Assyrian gods inside the Jerusalem Temple, displeasing the Lord greatly (see 2 Kgs 16:10–16). After his death, his son Hezekiah would experience much devastation of the land under King Sennacherib of Assyria, and this may be the object of this prophecy.

Isaiah 7:18–25

This is a series of four oracles threatening the "day of the LORD" on Judah. Just as the Lord had warned Isaiah in 6:9–10, the people, including King Ahaz, would be unwilling to comprehend the Lord's words and do them. Therefore, they will suffer the dire consequences laid out in the following oracles of threat for the day of the Lord.

7:18–19

> **18In that day the LORD will whistle for the fly which is at the sources of the streams of Egypt, and for the bee which is in the land of Assyria. 19And they will all come and settle in the steep ravines, and in the clefts of the rocks, and on all the thornbushes, and on all the pastures.**

On that day, the two superpowers of the era—Egypt and Assyria—will be summoned by the Lord. The "fly" from Egypt may refer to the Egyptian use of flies carved from stone on a necklace as the insignia of an Egyptian general. Also, the large flies in Egypt bite quite aggressively and form a parallel to the sting of the attacking Assyrian bee. This confrontation between Assyria and Egypt will take place in the territories of western Asia, including Judah, for the decades preceding the final defeat of Egypt by King Esarhaddon's army in 671 BC.

7:20

> **20In that day the LORD will shave with a razor which is hired beyond the River—with the king of Assyria—the head and the hair of the feet, and it will sweep away the beard also.**

This prophesies that the king of Assyria will "hire" a razor—that is, mercenary soldiers—to shave all the hair on the head and beard and the feet—a euphemism for the genitals. Shaving off the hair of Semites brought great shame, as when David's ambassadors to Ammon Rabbah (modern Amman, Jordan) were shaved to insult them and him (see 2 Sm 10:4), an act sufficiently insulting to cause a war.

7:21–22

[21]In that day a man will keep alive a young cow and two sheep; [22]and because of the abundance of milk which they give, he will eat curds; for every one that is left in the land will eat curds and honey.

That day will devastate the crops grown on farms, so the curds from a cow and two sheep would have to suffice for nourishment. Everyone in the land will eat curds and honey because there will be no bread after the grain harvests are devastated by the invading armies.

7:23–25

[23]In that day every place where there used to be a thousand vines, worth a thousand shekels of silver, will become briers and thorns.
[24]With bow and arrows men will come there, for all the land will be briers and thorns; [25]and as for all the hills which used to be hoed with a hoe, you will not come there for fear of briers and thorns; but they will become a place where cattle are let loose and where sheep tread.

On that day, the armies will also ruin valuable vineyards, which will revert to useless and painful briars and thorns. Because the briers and thorns will be too thick to permit fighting with the sword, archers will shoot at enemies fleeing into them, thus avoiding getting caught in the briars. The lack of people to tend the plowed, sown, and hoed fields will also turn them to briars and thorns that will be good only for cattle to graze in. The once rich and fertile sown land will become dangerous, painful, and useful only for the bare existence grazing of cattle. Their milk will be turned into the curds on which the population would have to survive during the foreign invasions.

Lesson 4

Proto-Isaiah 8–9

The material in these chapters belongs to the reign of Ahaz and the ongoing crises of the Assyrian moves to subject western Asia and the danger of attack from Syria and the northern Kingdom of Israel against the southern Kingdom of Judah.

—— Isaiah 8:1–4 ——

At this point, the Lord commissions Isaiah to write a symbolic action about the future of Damascus and Samaria.

8:1

> **1Then the Lord said to me, "Take a large tablet and write upon it in common characters, 'Belonging to Mahershalalhashbaz.'"**

The Lord orders the first stage: write the name Mahershalalhashbaz, which means in Hebrew, "one who hastens to spoil, is speedy to prey." This name describes how Assyria will attack Syria and Damascus and Israel quickly in order to take many spoils of war. Historically, Assyria became dependent on taking booty in war to maintain its economy. The empire kept expanding to attract more peoples and nations whose work would support the large and well-equipped army who served their chief god Asshur, the god of war.

8:2–3a

> **2And I got reliable witnesses, Uriah the priest and Zechariah the son of Jeberechiah, to attest for me. 3And I went to the prophetess, and she conceived and bore a son.**

Then Isaiah took two practical steps: he obtained two witnesses to his written word and then has relations with "the prophetess," presumably his wife, who conceived and bore the son whose name will bear the sign of coming destruction.

8:3b–4

> **[3b] Then the LORD said to me, "Call his name Mahershalalhashbaz; [4]for before the child knows how to cry 'My father' or 'My mother,' the wealth of Damascus and the spoil of Samaria will be carried away before the king of Assyria."**

After the boy's birth, the Lord orders Isaiah to name him Mahershalal-hashbaz and predicts the destruction of Damascus and Samaria before he can say his first words, "Abi," "My father," "Imi" "My mother."

The Historical Background for 8:5–18

King Ahaz apparently did not pay much attention to the oracles or signs given to him by Isaiah. Instead of trusting in the word of the Lord, he took steps that he considered practical in order to secure help from the Assyrians. First, he sent silver and gold taken from the Temple and his own treasury to bribe Tiglath-Pileser III to attack Damascus and Israel to get them out of Judah (see 2 Kgs 16:7–9). Isaiah condemned this tactic as a lack of faith in the Lord in 8:6–8,12–15. Far worse, Ahaz sacrificed one of his sons to a pagan deity to win his favor and prevent the attack (see 2 Kgs 16:3; 2 Chr 28:1–4). Third, after the defeat of Damascus, he went there to pay homage to Tiglath-Pileser. When he saw the Assyrian altar there, he had a model made and ordered the building of such an altar in the Jerusalem Temple (see 2 Kgs 16:10–18).

In this war, Tiglath-Pileser did not directly confront Syria but indirectly attacked by subduing the nations west of Syria—Phoenicia, Philistia, and coastal towns in between. At that point, Pekah of Israel gave up resistance. Syria, without allies, was defeated by Assyria, Rezin died of "insanity", and his successor, Rukibtu, son of Mitinti, sued for peace with Tiglath-Pileser (ANET, p. 283).

—— Isaiah 8:5–8 ——

The Lord threatens the people of Judah who fear Rezin and Pekah instead of trusting in the Lord that they themselves will be overwhelmed by a river of an Assyrian army.

8:5

> **5The LORD spoke to me again:**

The introduction of the Lord speaking to Isaiah.

8:6

> **6"Because this people have refused the waters of Shiloah that flow gently, and melt in fear before Rezin and the son of Remaliah;**

The Lord accuses the people of Jerusalem of being afraid of Rezin, king of Damascus, and Pekah, "the son of Remaliah," the king of Israel. The gently flowing waters of Shiloah are those that flow from the Gihon Spring, which is just south of the Temple Mount, at the base of the hill on which the ancient city of Jerusalem was built, and in fact the very reason for the existence of a city at that location—water. While this water from a spring is small, it is a reliable source of water and life. This symbolizes their faith in the Lord, which they have rejected in favor of treaties with mighty Assyria.

8:7–8

> **7therefore, behold, the LORD is bringing up against them the waters of the River, mighty and many, the king of Assyria and all his glory; and it will rise over all its channels and go over all its banks; 8and it will sweep on into Judah, it will overflow and pass on, reaching even to the neck; and its outspread wings will fill the breadth of your land, O Immanuel."**

Because of their lack of faith in the Lord, he threatens them with a flood by a river—namely, Assyria, whose empire is between the two great rivers, the Tigris and Euphrates. This Assyrian river will flood Judah and overwhelm the land with destruction. Interestingly, he addresses the nation as "Immanuel," an ironic name meaning "God is with us," addressed to a people that trusts more in treaties and other gods than in its Lord.

— Isaiah 8:9–10 —

9Be broken, you peoples, and be dismayed; give ear, all you far countries; gird yourselves and be dismayed; gird yourselves and be dismayed. 10Take counsel together, but it will come to nought; speak a word, but it will not stand, for God is with us.

Isaiah warns those nations that seek to attack Jerusalem, reminding them that their plans would fail so badly that they would be "broken" and "dismayed." Isaiah boldly asserts his most basic act of faith: "God is with us" (Hebrew: "Immanu-el"). Therefore, their "word" of threat will not prevail over the Lord's word and presence. Isaiah has in mind the protection of the city of Jerusalem, whose Temple is the Lord's sacred place and will be protected. This idea becomes especially important during the Assyrian invasion under Sennacherib in 705–701.

Such faith also appears in Romans 8:31: "If God is for us, who is against us?" However, Saint Paul does not apply this to the physical city of Jerusalem but to everyone who believes in Jesus Christ.

— Isaiah 8:11–15 —

Here the Lord admonishes the people not to fear but rather to take advice that builds up their faith in the Lord.

8:11

11For the LORD spoke thus to me with his strong hand upon me, and warned me not to walk in the way of this people, saying:

Isaiah describes his experience of receiving this oracle in terms of "his strong hand upon me," probably a reference to a type of shaking of Isaiah caused by the Lord's presence.

8:12

12"Do not call conspiracy all that this people call conspiracy, and do not fear what they fear, nor be in dread.

The Lord gives three admonitions: do not call the Syrian-Ephraimite conspiracy a real conspiracy, since God has doomed it to failure, do not fear Assyria, which is what they fear, and do not dread Syria and Ephraim either. This is all consistent with Isaiah's messages.

8:13–15

> **[13]But the LORD of hosts, him you shall regard as holy; let him be your fear, and let him be your dread. [14]And he will become a sanctuary, and a stone of offense, and a rock of stumbling to both houses of Israel, a trap and a snare to the inhabitants of Jerusalem. [15]And many shall stumble thereon; they shall fall and be broken; they shall be snared and taken."**

The advice is meant to increase the people's faith. First, regard the Lord as holy, much as the seraphim did during Isaiah's vision in 6:3, recognizing that He is the powerful purifying flame who is completely other from sinful and weak humanity. He is the one they should legitimately fear (v. 13).

Since the Lord is holy, He can become the "sanctuary," which means "holy place." As such, He will be a stumbling stone, trap, and snare for many people in Jerusalem. Those who have faith will be able to stand firmly on Him, but those who reject faith in the Holy One will stumble and become ensnared. Recall here Isaiah's words to King Ahaz in 7:9: "If you will not believe, surely you shall not be established." This verse is cited to make the same point about the need for faith in 1 Peter 2:7–8: "To you therefore who believe, he is precious, but for those who do not believe. . . . 'A stone that will make men stumble, a rock that will make them fall'; for they stumble because they disobey the word, as they were destined to do."

—— Isaiah 8:16–18 ——

Isaiah presents his personal reflection at the conclusion of the oracles of chapters 7 and 8.

8:16

> **[16]Bind up the testimony, seal the teaching among my disciples.**

First, he binds and seals these words among his disciples, an important verse that indicates he was not a lone ranger prophet but had the support of a whole school. This has been understood by many scholars as the basis for considering an ongoing school that continued to add materials to the scroll Isaiah left in their keeping. As in this commentary, this school added much material in the sixth through fifth centuries BC in response to the Babylonian exile, Cyrus the Persian's release of the exiles, and the return to Jerusalem. This Isaian school would have been responsible for the historical additions (chapters 36 to 39), chapters 34 and 34, Deutero- and Trito-Isaiah, and the Isaiah Apocalypse.

8:17–18

> **17I will wait for the LORD, who is hiding his face from the house of Jacob, and I will hope in him. 18Behold, I and the children whom the LORD has given me are signs and portents in Israel from the LORD of hosts, who dwells on Mount Zion.**

Isaiah personally takes a twofold response. First, he is determined to "wait for the Lord" and "hope in him," no matter how hidden He seems. Second, he and his children, particularly Shearjashub (a Remnant will return) and Mahershalalhashbaz (Hastens to the spoil and is quick to prey), will be signs and portents from the Lord. They will remain as signs in hope of fulfillment, no matter what the king, his successor, or the people might choose to do.

— Isaiah 8:19–9:1a —

A threat of famine and gloom to those who consult occult sources.

8:19–20

> **19And when they say to you, "Consult the mediums and the wizards who chirp and mutter," should not a people consult their God? Should they consult the dead on behalf of the living? 20To the teaching and to the testimony! Surely for this word which they speak there is no dawn.**

Isaiah continues speaking to his disciples, here addressed as "you." He warns them that people will want to turn them to consulting the mediums and wizards, for which he would criticize the Egyptians in 19:3 and Israel in 29:4. Instead, he tells them to consult the Lord God and go to the "teaching and testimony" in Scripture, as he himself does (see v. 16). He references prohibitions against all occult practices, such as Deuteronomy 18:9–11, which calls occult practices, such as mediums and wizards, "abominations," or Leviticus 20:6: "If a person turns to mediums and wizards, playing the harlot after them, I will set my face against that person, and will cut him off from among his people." Leviticus 20:27 threatens occultists with a death penalty by stoning.

8:21–9:1a

[21]They will pass through the land, greatly distressed and hungry; and when they are hungry, they will be enraged and will curse their king and their God, and turn their faces upward; [22]and they will look to the earth, but behold, distress and darkness, the gloom of anguish; and they will be thrust into thick darkness.

[9:1a]But there will be no gloom for her that was in anguish.

The declaration of punishment for those who ignored the Lord will be distress and famine. The pain will induce them to sin further by cursing king and God, crimes that were punishable by death (see Lv 24:15–16; 1 Kgs 21:10). They may turn to the earth, but earth cannot help them any more than the mediums and wizards. Their refusal to seek God means destruction for them.

—— Isaiah 9:1b–7 ——

This is a prophetic hymn that promises messianic hope for the people of northern Israel who were conquered by Assyria in 732 BC after Pekah's defeat by Tiglath-Pileser III. He confiscated two-thirds of Israel as an Assyrian province, leaving Samaria as the capital of one-third of northern Israel. After this debacle, Hoshea, son of Elah, assassinated Pekah to appease Tiglath-Pileser and stop him from destroying all of Israel. Hoshea made himself king and paid tribute to Assyria (see 2 Kgs 16:30; 17:1–2), though Tiglath-Pileser claims to have set Hoshea on the throne (ANET, p. 283).

9:1b

[1b]In the former time he brought into contempt the land of Zebulun and the land of Naphtali, but in the latter time he will make glorious the way of the sea, the land beyond the Jordan, Galilee of the nations.

The opening line of the prophecy begins with the sad situation of Zebulun and Naphtali, two tribal territories just west of the Sea of Galilee which were part of the territory annexed by Assyria. The verse predicts that it will be a glorious "way of the sea" in the latter times that contrast with the events that had just occurred. The "way of the sea" refers to the road that connects Egypt along the Mediterranean coast and then moves inland through a pass in the Carmel mountain range, near Megiddo, and goes past the Sea of Galilee to Damascus and the rest of Asia. This route, along with the equally ancient King's Highway in modern Jordan, that connects land travel between Africa, Asia, and Europe may be seen as a reason for Israel to be the Promised Land. Because it straddled both land routes in its history, and had contact with coastal territory along the Mediterranean, Israel was an ideal location for spreading a message to the three continents of the "Old World."

This verse is cited in Matthew 4:13–16 when Jesus left Nazareth to begin His preaching ministry in Capernaum and the Galilee region. As is still true today, the route from Nazareth to Galilee crosses the Zebulun valley and comes into Naphtali. As Jesus walks through the territory, He makes the way glorious and is the "light" that the people see in their darkness (9:2).

9:2–7

**[2]The people who walked in darkness have seen a great light; those who
dwelt in a land of deep darkness, on them has light shined. [3]Thou hast
multiplied the nation, thou hast increased its joy; they rejoice before
thee as with joy at the harvest, as men rejoice when they divide the
spoil. [4]For the yoke of his burden, and the staff for his shoulder, the
rod of his oppressor, thou hast broken as on the day of Midian. [5]For
every boot of the tramping warrior in battle tumult and every garment
rolled in blood will be burned as fuel for the fire. [6a]For to us a child
is born, to us a son is given; [6b]and the government will be upon his
shoulder, [6c]and his name will be called "Wonderful Counselor, Mighty
God, Everlasting Father, Prince of Peace." [7a]Of the increase of his government and of peace there will be no end, upon the throne of David,
and over his kingdom, to establish it, and to uphold it with justice and
with righteousness from this time forth and for evermore. [7b]The zeal of
the LORD of hosts will do this.**

The prophetic hymn of hope promises a relief from foreign oppression and a messianic king who will transform society for the better.

2–3

The people who "walked" and "dwelt" in darkness are those living in the territories annexed from Israel by Assyria in 732 BC. The great light that shines on them is the Lord, as indicated by the direct address to him in verse 3: "thou" multiplied the people, "thou" increased joy. Even though they are now ruled by the mighty Assyrians, the people rejoice in the Lord as if they were at the harvest instead of being divided as the spoils of war. This is a remarkable promise of hope given the real political situation of misery at the time.

4–5

The reason for their joy is that the Lord has broken the yoke, staff, and rod that the enemy used to enslave the people with forced labor and oppression. The model for this victory is the "Day of Midian," when Gideon was ordered by the Lord to dismiss all but three hundred men out of thirty thousand troops to defeat the Midianites by God's power rather than by human force (see Jgs 6–8). The boots and garments of the enemy soldiers, which made it possible for them to leave their country and invade Israel, will be burned as a way to indicate their defeat.

6–7a

The next reason to rejoice is the birth of a messianic king.

6a

The first element of this good news is that he is born and given "for us." The prophet counts himself among the people who will benefit from the birth of this king, even though he is speaking about the northern territories in verses 1b–5.

6b

The attention now shifts to the child, who will have the power to rule or have dominion. The translation "government" sounds too bureaucratic for the Hebrew *misrah*, whose root is not well understood, but may come from the unused verb *srr*, from which is derived the word for "prince" (*sar*). Placing "the government" on his shoulder refers to a coronation ceremony of placing a scepter on the new king's shoulder as a symbol of authority similar to the crown on the head.

6c

Four names are given him, much the way kings, particularly in Egypt, received "throne names" once they were inaugurated into authority. Each name conveys a desired characteristic of the king. The "Wonderful Counselor" refers to his ability to give wise counsel and conveys the idea that his counsel is both wonderful and will cause wonders to occur, like God who does wonders (cf. Ps 77:11–12, 14–15; 78:12; 89:5).

He is "Mighty God," or "God the Warrior," possessed of power to save people from distress. Psalm 45 is a song from northern Israel that was composed for the king's wedding. Interestingly, it addresses the royal bridegroom as both "mighty"—"Gird your sword upon your thigh, O mighty one, in your glory and majesty!" (Ps. 45:3)—and God—"Your throne, O God (Hebrew *Elohim*) endures for ever and ever" (Ps 45:6). Of course, Christians understand this title in terms of Jesus Christ, who is God made flesh.

"Everlasting Father" treats the king as a father to the nation and wishes him an everlasting reign, similar to modern cries, "Long live the king!" In Daniel, the kings were frequently addressed "May you live forever" (Dn 2:4; 3:9; 5:10; 6:6, 21; Neh 2:3), and it was said to David in 1 Kings 1:31, though not Saul (see 1 Sm 10:24) or David's son Adonijah, who tried to take the throne without David's permission (see 1 Kgs 1:25).

The title "Prince of Peace" anticipates the hope for the king expressed in the royal psalm 72, "In his days may righteousness flourish, and peace abound, till the moon be no more!" (72:7).

7a

This verse describes various aspects of the newborn king's reign at which the four throne names hint—the increase of his rule and never ending peace. However, he states explicitly that the king will come from David's family, a lineage which the northern kingdom explicitly rejected when they established themselves under a new king, Jeroboam ben Nebat (see 1 Kgs 12). The north will be returned to the Davidic kingdom which the newborn king will establish and uphold with the justice and righteousness that were prayed for in royal Psalms 72 and 89, but were absent in Solomon's foolish son, Rehoboam, at the time of the division of the two kingdoms of Israel and Judah, and in later centuries.

7b

Isaiah concludes with a promise that the "zeal" of the Lord will accomplish this, indicating that the Lord has enthusiasm to accomplish this salvation. Isaiah also attributed the salvation of Judah to the Lord's zeal in 37:32, which is part of an addition from 2 Kings 19:31 that had been edited into the Isaiah scroll.

—— Isaiah 9:8–10:4 ——

A poem about the "outstretched arm of the Lord" is used as a refrain in verses 9:12, 17, 21, 10:4 and helps mark off four stanzas of seven lines each. The first line indicates that the poem is directed to the Northern Kingdom of Israel after the Assyrian victory over them.

9:8–12

> **[8]The LORD has sent a word against Jacob, and it will light upon Israel; [9]and all the people will know, Ephraim and the inhabitants of Samaria, who say in pride and in arrogance of heart: [10]"The bricks have fallen, but we will build with dressed stones; the sycamores have been cut down, but we will put cedars in their place." [11]So the LORD raises adversaries of Rezin against them, and stirs up their enemies. [12]The Syrians on the east and the Philistines on the west devour Israel with open mouth. For all this his anger is not turned away and his hand is stretched out still.**

The first stanza is the Lord's word against the northerners in Israel who think they will be able to undo the punishment inflicted by the Assyrians by building better structures than the ones that Assyria destroyed.

8–9

The word of the Lord is directed against the people in Ephraim, the main tribal territory in the northern kingdom, and its capital, Samaria, who make plans in arrogance rather than in repentance.

10

Their plan is to replace fallen brick buildings with buildings of stone, and cheaper local sycamore wood with expensive cedar imported from Lebanon, the leading source of cedar in the ancient Near East for millennia.

11–12

The Lord responds with the threat of raising the "adversaries of Rezin" (whose name is in the Hebrew but absent from the RSV translation) and his enemies—namely, the Assyrians—against the arrogant people of the north. Even Syria and Philistia, their former allies in the anti-Assyrian rebellion, will turn against them to "devour" them. Yet, this is not a mere human act but the result of the Lord's anger, whose arm is stretched out to punish them with destruction.

9:13–17

> **13The people did not turn to him who smote them, nor seek the LORD of hosts. 14So the LORD cut off from Israel head and tail, palm branch and reed in one day – 15the elder and honored man is the head, and the prophet who teaches lies is the tail; 16for those who lead this people lead them astray, and those who are led by them are swallowed up. 17Therefore the LORD does not rejoice over their young men and has no compassion on their fatherless and widows; for every one is godless and an evildoer, and every mouth speaks folly. For all this his anger is not turned away and his hand is stretched out still.**

Because the people did not repent and turn to the Lord who had punished them, he now threatens the whole people, from leaders to youths, children and widows.

The Lord lays out the accusation that the people did not repent after their punishment, but as in 9:9–10, they made arrogant plans to rebuild their lives.

The Lord lays out the first threats, which are against the leadership, whether elders and "honored" rich men who counseled the people or the prophets who teach lies.

The second group of threats are against those who follow the leaders. The young men who fought the battles, the orphans, and the widows will not receive compassion from the Lord because they are all guilty too. The term "godless" does not mean "atheist" but is a Hebrew word (*hanef*) that is derived from the idea of being inclined away from what is good and right, and therefore it came to mean ritually "polluted," "profane," or "irreligious." All of the people choose to be profane, do evil, and speak "folly" (Hebrew *nebalah*, a word for willful folly that makes one a lout or boor). Therefore, all will suffer because of the Lord's anger and outstretched arm.

9:18–21

> **[18]For wickedness burns like a fire, it consumes briers and thorns; it
> kindles the thickets of the forest, and they roll upward in a column of
> smoke. [19]Through the wrath of the LORD of hosts the land is burned,
> and the people are like fuel for the fire; no man spares his brother.
> [20]They snatch on the right, but are still hungry, and they devour on the
> left, but are not satisfied; each devours his neighbor's flesh, [21]Manasseh
> Ephraim, and Ephraim Manasseh, and together they are against Judah.
> For all this his anger is not turned away and his hand is stretched
> out still.**

18

This is a proverbial statement describing the reality of the power of wickedness to destroy everything around it, despite the intentions of the perpetrators of the evil. Modern examples would include the destruction of Germany during the Third Reich. Also, tens of millions of citizens in Communist countries were killed by their own governments.

19–21

Though the preceding proverb sets out the principle of the self-destructive quality of evil, here the prophet explains that the wrath of the Lord of hosts is ultimately behind that principle. People may try to "snatch" and "devour" what they can grab out of the destructive fire, but they will never satisfy their hunger. In fact, they will devour each other's flesh, as in fact often happened during long sieges of cities (v. 20). Manasseh was another northern tribe, descended from Jacob's second youngest son, Joseph. These tribes survived the initial occupation of Israel by the Assyrians, but because of their own wickedness, they attacked each other and then turned against Judah, who also had survived Tiglath-Pileser's war. The Lord's anger and outstretched arm will accomplish this.

10:1–4

> **10:1 Woe to those who decree iniquitous decrees, and the writers who keep writing oppression, 2 to turn aside the needy from justice and to rob the poor of my people of their right, that widows may be their spoil, and that they may make the fatherless their prey! 3 What will you do on the day of punishment, in the storm which will come from afar? To whom will you flee for help, and where will you leave your wealth? 4 Nothing remains but to crouch among the prisoners or fall among the slain. For all this his anger is not turned away and his hand is stretched out still.**

The fourth stanza is a woe, as in Isaiah 1 and 5, decreeing the doom of the north.

1–2

The reasons for the woe is that the leaders decree immoral laws that are "iniquitous," and the government scribes continue to issue the decrees of injustice. The needy, poor, widows, and fatherless children are all deprived of the justice that is their due. This would refer to attempts by the powerful and wealthy people in the government to confiscate the land and other property of these vulnerable people through ruinous taxation, foreclosures on loans, or acts of fraud.

3–4

In the face of the Lord's anger and outstretched arm, the prophet poses rhetorical questions to the oppressors: What will you do on the day of God's punishment? Where will you get help? The answer is, "Nowhere!" No escape will be possible, not even if they play dead among the corpses of the fallen, or try to hide their prominence by taking a place among the poor prisoners. They will be found out and duly punished by the Lord's wrath and outstretched arm.

Lesson 5

PROTO-ISAIAH 10:5–12:6

While God used Assyria as His instrument to punish Israel and her allies during their rebellion according to Isaiah, Assyria's power was limited. They, too, are humans subject to moral standards that belong to the whole human race under the natural law. At this point, Isaiah threatens Assyria with punishment because of the evil things it did in its arrogance.

—Isaiah 10:5–15 —

This is the first oracle against Assyria, a woe oracle that decrees their doom from the Lord for having pursued their role as people who punish with arrogance and without mercy.

10:5

5Ah, Assyria, the rod of my anger, the staff of my fury!

"Ah" translates Hebrew *hoy*, meaning "woe." In this opening address to Assyria, the Lord addresses it as His instruments of punishment and discipline. Since they were doing God's will, a listener would wonder why a woe would be directed to them.

10:6

6Against a godless nation I send him, and against the people of my wrath I command him, to take spoil and seize plunder, and to tread them down like the mire of the streets.

This verse states the mission God had given Assyria: attack the "godless," (*hanef* as in 9:17) or irreligious people of God's wrath, plunder them, and trample them down like mire, an image of humiliation here and in Job 30:19. Had Assyria stayed within these limits, God would have no complaint against them.

10:7–11

> **[7]But he does not so intend, and his mind does not so think; but it is in his mind to destroy, and to cut off nations not a few; [8]for he says: "Are not my commanders all kings? [9]Is not Calno like Carchemish? Is not Hamath like Arpad? Is not Samaria like Damascus? [10]As my hand has reached to the kingdoms of the idols whose graven images were greater than those of Jerusalem and Samaria, [11] shall I not do to Jerusalem and her idols as I have done to Samaria and her images?"**

However, Assyria decided to destroy, not merely chastise, many nations, including Samaria and Jerusalem, which had both made peace with Tiglath-Pileser in 732 BC.

Verses 8 through 11 are a series of Assyrian boasts. In Akkadian (the language used in Assyria), "king" referred to the ruler of a city-state. The Assyrians permitted them to keep their titles if they joined the Assyrian side, so having numerous "kings" in the army was itself a war trophy. Carchemish, a Hittite city on the Euphrates River located near the modern border of Syria and Turkey, was conquered by Assyria many times over the centuries, and Tiglath-Pileser mentions it as a city that brought him tribute. As far as he was concerned, Calno, a city in northern Syria, was no different. Interestingly, Carchemish was destroyed by Sargon in 717 BC as the last Hittite territory but would be the site of the final destruction of the Assyrian Empire in 609 BC.

Hamath and Arpad, always mentioned together in the Bible, were both in northern Syria. Arpad (now a ruin on Tel Erfad) surrendered to Tiglath-Pileser after a three-year siege, and Hamath (modern Hama on the Orontes River) also surrendered to him and paid tribute. Later, Hamath rebelled against Sargon and was destroyed in 720 BC.

Tiglath-Pileser destroyed Damascus but let Samaria survive. However, in his arrogance, he claims to be able to conquer it too. In fact, he would die during a war with Samaria, but his son, Shalmaneser V, would take the city in 722 BC, and his grandson, Sargon II, would take credit for it, since he returned to further destroy the country in 720 after his conquest of Hamath. Sargon mentions that he took 27,290 Samaritan inhabitants captive and then settled people of Hamath in Samaria.

Finally, Assyria threatens to take Jerusalem and its idols as Sargon had taken the pagan cities and Samaria's idols. This is an insult to the Lord of hosts, since He is not an idol but is the God who created the world and saves Israel. He cannot be taken by Assyria or anyone else.

10:12–14

> **12 When the LORD has finished all his work on Mount Zion and on**
> **Jerusalem he will punish the arrogant boasting of the king of Assyria**
> **and his haughty pride. 13 For he says: "By the strength of my hand I**
> **have done it, and by my wisdom, for I have understanding; I have re-**
> **moved the boundaries of peoples, and have plundered their treasures;**
> **like a bull I have brought down those who sat on thrones. 14 My hand**
> **has found like a nest the wealth of the peoples; and as men gather eggs**
> **that have been forsaken so I have gathered all the earth; and there was**
> **none that moved a wing, or opened the mouth, or chirped."**

The Lord decrees a verdict against Assyria.

The Lord will punish Assyria for its sins of "arrogant boasting" and "haughty pride," even though it had been His chosen instrument to punish others. Being God's instrument does not give permission to sin.

The Lord cites quotations of the Assyrian boasts about acting by their own hand—that is, power, wisdom, and understanding. These are faulty if they are not congruent with the Lord's moral principles. Since Assyria went too far in destroying others, they are guilty. Assyria also boasts of its accomplishments in taking the land of other countries by removing their boundaries, plundering their wealth, and removing their kings by brute strength like a willful bull.

10:15

> **15 Shall the axe vaunt itself over him who hews with it, or the saw magnify itself against him who wields it? As if a rod should wield him who lifts it, or as if a staff should lift him who is not wood!**

Using a proverbial statement about the power of an ax to boast as if it were superior to the hand that wielded it, or of a rod or staff to move themselves, the Lord rhetorically questions Assyria's pride. Of course, the answer is that no ax, rod, or staff has any power to do anything on its own, and neither does Assyria have power apart from the Lord. Therefore, for its foolish pride that is bereft of wisdom or understanding of the reality of God's lordship, it will be punished.

—— Isaiah 10:16–19 ——

Continuing from the preceding woe oracle and its decree of guilt against Assyria, the Lord now announces the punishment in two parts for two stages of chastising Assyria.

10:16

> **16 Therefore the Lord, the LORD of hosts, will send wasting sickness among his stout warriors, and under his glory a burning will be kindled, like the burning of fire.**

First, the Lord will send "wasting sickness" against the Assyrian soldiers. This refers to the plague brought by the angel of the Lord that decimated the Assyrian army besieging Jerusalem in 701 BC, during the reign of King Hezekiah, the son of Ahaz (see 2 Kgs 19:35). This part of the punishment protects Jerusalem from an Assyrian attack.

10:17–19

> **17 The light of Israel will become a fire, and his Holy One a flame; and it will burn and devour his thorns and briers in one day. 18 The glory of his forest and of his fruitful land the LORD will destroy, both soul and body, and it will be as when a sick man wastes away. 19 The remnant of the trees of his forest will be so few that a child can write them down.**

Psalms 27:1 declares, "The Lord is my light and my salvation; whom shall I fear?" In this second part of the announcement of punishment, the Lord's saving light becomes a flame that will burn the thorns, briars, forests, and orchards of the Assyrian homeland. They may have boasted about the damage they had done to other nations and threatened to do to Jerusalem, but now the "Holy One" is a flame (recall that the root of holy also means to burn) that will do to Assyria what their armies have done to other nations.

10:20–23

This oracle of salvation for the remnant of Israel plays on the meaning of the name of Isaiah's older son Shearjashub—"a remnant will return."

10:20–21

> [20]**In that day the remnant of Israel and the survivors of the house of Jacob will no more lean upon him that smote them, but will lean upon the Lord, the Holy One of Israel, in truth. [21]A remnant will return, the remnant of Jacob, to the mighty God.**

The "survivors" of the Assyrian war of 734–732 BC had depended on making a pact to offer tribute to Tiglath-Pileser, the very person who had attacked ("smote") them. However, the real means of survival will be their faith, when they "lean" on the Lord, the Holy One of Israel, in truth and not in the hypocrisy shown by Ahaz in 7:10–13 when he refused to ask for a sign.

Therefore, the remnant will return (Hebrew Shear jashub as in the name of Isaiah's son) primarily to the mighty God (Hebrew El Gibbor, the same phrase used as one of the four names of the messianic king in 9:6.)

10:22–23

> [22]**For though your people Israel be as the sand of the sea, only a remnant of them will return. Destruction is decreed, overflowing with righteousness. [23]For the Lord, the Lord of hosts, will make a full end, as decreed, in the midst of all the earth.**

At the same time that the Lord offers a promise of hope for the remnant, He reminds the nation here that it will be merely a remnant, no matter how large the nation might be. The Lord intends to bring about a full judgment on everyone in the world, and all will be judged by His righteous norms. The Assyrians' verdict and punishment were decreed in 10:5–19, and Israel will also be judged, with only a remnant coming through the judgment because of their faith. This is not unlike Jesus Christ's warning in the Sermon on the Mount in Matthew 7:13–14: "Enter by the narrow gate; for the gate is wide and the way is easy, that leads to destruction, and those who enter by it are many. For the gate is narrow and the way is hard, that leads to life, and those who find it are few" (see also Mt 22:14; Lk 13:23–24).

—— Isaiah 10:24–27a ——

Condemning and punishing Assyria for their wickedness, the Lord gives oracles of salvation to Zion, the mount in Jerusalem where the Temple was built.

10:24–26

> **24Therefore thus says the LORD, the LORD of hosts: "O my people,**
> **who dwell in Zion, be not afraid of the Assyrians when they smite**
> **with the rod and lift up their staff against you as the Egyptians did.**
> **25For in a very little while my indignation will come to an end, and my**
> **anger will be directed to their destruction. 26And the LORD of hosts**
> **will wield against them a scourge, as when he smote Midian at the**
> **rock of Oreb; and his rod will be over the sea, and he will lift it as he**
> **did in Egypt.**

The first oracle speaks directly to the people who dwell in Zion. This was the name of the hill on which was built the original settlement of Jerusalem; later, the name became attached to the Temple Mount.

24

The Lord tells the people of Jerusalem not to fear the Assyrians when they smite with their rod and staff. In 10:15, the Lord called Assyria the rod and staff in His hand and condemned them for thinking that they wielded the Lord rather than recognizing that they were the instruments in His hand. Since they are merely His rod and staff, Jerusalem need not fear them when the Lord, who truly wields Assyria, tells them not to worry. The Egyptians had beaten Israel with rods before the Lord liberated them from slavery; therefore, Israel need not fear Assyria either.

25–26

Although the Lord was indignant with Jerusalem for its lack of trust in Him and for their other sins, they still can count on His indignation coming to an end as He turns His anger against Assyria to destroy them. As in 9:4, where He brought up the "Day of Midian" when the Lord defeated the Midianites through Gideon and his 300 men with lamps and horns, so again the Lord brings up the "rock of Oreb (meaning "raven"), where the Ephraimites killed King Oreb and King Zeeb of Midian (see Jgs 7:24–25). He also mentions the power of His rod over sea, as when Moses raised it to divide the sea to let Israel walk through but drowned the Egyptians. If the Lord can save Israel in those dangerous situations, He can save Zion from Assyria.

10:27a

> [27]**And in that day his burden will depart from your shoulder, and his yoke will be destroyed from your neck."**

The day of the Lord is usually portrayed in terms of the destruction and punishment of His enemies, but it will also be a day when oppressive Assyria will depart from Jerusalem, thereby freeing the people from the burden of tribute and the yoke of slavery to the Assyrians

—— Isaiah 10:27b–34 ——

10:27b–29

> [27b]**He has gone up from Rimmon, [read Pne-Shamen according to the Hebrew]** [28]**he has come to Aiath; he has passed through Migron, at Michmash he stores his baggage;** [29]**they have crossed over the pass, at Geba they lodge for the night; Ramah trembles, Gibeah of Saul has fled.**

The Assyrians march across the country, taking town after town in an unstoppable path of conquest. The Revised Standard Version's "Rimmon" is not in the Hebrew text, but instead is, "Pne Shamen" (lit. "Face of oil"). However, in Numbers 21:20 and 23:28, it is "Pne hayshimon" (lit. "face of the desert;" RSV, "the desert") as the last site mentioned as an Israelite stopping place on the east side of the Jordan River.

"Aiath" is a later name for Ai, a city just northwest of Jericho, which Joshua conquered (see Jo 7–8). Migron is a bit south of Ai and on the outskirts of Gibeah (see 1 Sm 14:2); Michmash was near Bethel (see 1 Sm 13:2) and is mentioned with Geba here and in 1 Samuel 14:5. Ramah and Gibeah are now contiguous with modern Jerusalem. These places are listed in the order of their proximity to Jerusalem. Obviously the Assyrians are on the march to the city.

10:30–31

**[30]Cry aloud, O daughter of Gallim! Hearken, O Laishah! Answer her,
O Anathoth! [31]Madmenah is in flight, the inhabitants of Gebim flee
for safety.**

As the Assyrians approach, the villages near Jerusalem are ordered to cry out in fear. Verses 27b through 29 dispassionately list the towns through which the Assyrians march; these other towns cry out because it has become the time for panic and terror, since the army will camp nearby and inevitably pillage the unwalled towns nearby. Of the cities mentioned here, only Anathoth, which was just north of the city, is otherwise known.

10:32

[32]This very day he will halt at Nob, he will shake his fist at the mount of the daughter of Zion, the hill of Jerusalem.

Nob, an ancient site of worship (see 1 Sm 21:1; 22:9–11), was located within eyesight of the city of Jerusalem (near "French Hill" in modern Jerusalem). Assyria shakes his fist in warning to the city. This recalls the embassies of the Assyrian Rabshakeh (Akkadian for "cup-bearer"), who threatened Jerusalem in the siege of 701 BC (see Is 36:2–22; 37:4, 8; 2 Kgs 18:17–37; 19:4, 8).

10:33–34

**[33]Behold, the Lord, the LORD of hosts will lop the boughs with terrifying power; the great in height will be hewn down, and the lofty will be
brought low. [34]He will cut down the thickets of the forest with an axe,
and Lebanon with its majestic trees will fall.**

In the face of the Assyrian advance and threatening shaking of the fist, the Lord threatens to go far beyond shaking a fist: He will cut down the trees and forest thickets. That is a poetic way to say He will destroy the Assyrian army.

This image fits a pattern in Isaiah: The Lord punishes the leaders of northern Israel whom He "cut off from Israel head and tail, palm branch and reed in one day" (Is 9:14); "wickedness burns like a fire, it consumes briers and thorns; it kindles the thickets of the forest" (Is 9:18); He describes Assyria as an ax while He is the one who wields it (see Is 10:15); Israel's light, the Holy One, "will burn and devour his thorns and briers in one day. The glory of his forest and of his fruitful land the Lord will destroy" (Is 10:17–19). So also here in 10:33–34, He cuts down the Assyrian army as if it were trees and brush.

— Isaiah 11 —
The Hope for the Messiah

The Lord promises to destroy the great Assyrian Empire in chapter 10, with hope for Jerusalem to be saved and a remnant of people to survive. The Lord's protection of Jerusalem was a great theme in Proto-Isaiah, despite its sins and failings.

Isaiah 11 takes up another great theme of salvation: the renewal of the Davidic kingship. In Isaiah 7:14, hope was hinted via the virgin giving birth to Immanuel; more explicit hope for the newborn son of David's line was expressed after the Assyrian defeat of the Northern Kingdom in 9:1b–7. Here, 11:1–9 and 11:10–16 speak of a much fuller hope for the Davidic Messiah.

— Isaiah 11:1–9 —

The promise of the Davidic Messiah will transform creation itself into a renewal of paradise.

11:1

[1]There shall come forth a shoot from the stump of Jesse, and a branch shall grow out of his roots.

This opening verse contains both hope and disappointment. Jesse was David's father (see Ru 4:17, 22; 1 Sm 16:11–13) and therefore is the root of David's line. However, the Davidic kings of Isaiah's time were so disappointing, and after Hezekiah, his son Manasseh would be the worst in Judah's history. He was so bad that his sins are described as the reason for the destruction of Jerusalem and the Temple, according to 2 Kings 21:1–17 and 2 Chronicles 33:1–20. For that reason, the Davidic family tree will be cut down, with only a "stump of Jesse" remaining.

However, olive tree stumps are quite capable of having new shoots come from them and become new branches as large as the old trunk that had been cut down. Eight olive trees in the present Garden of Gethsemane are said to have root systems that date back 2,500 years, though their trunks have certainly been cut down, particularly in various wars. This verse announces that the stump of Jesse (the name of David is not mentioned because the present kings were so bad) will be the source of a new shoot.

The Hebrew word for "shoot" is *netzer*. This is the root of the name "Nazareth," and it explains why Matthew 2:23 says Jesus will be called a "Nazarene," since He is the shoot that fulfills this prophecy.

11:2–3a

[2]And the Spirit of the LORD shall rest upon him, the spirit of wisdom and understanding, the spirit of counsel and might, the spirit of knowledge and the fear of the LORD. [3a]And his delight shall be in the fear of the LORD.

When the prophet Samuel anointed David as king to replace Saul, "the Spirit of the Lord came mightily upon" him (1 Sm 16:13). Since the promised Messiah of David's line will be a new beginning, he, too, will be filled with the same Spirit of the Lord.

It is worth noting that the Spirit of the Lord will transform the Messiah interiorly with wisdom, understanding, counsel, might, knowledge, and fear of the Lord. Normally, these are studied and learned in the royal schools that trained princes for leadership. The book of Proverbs collected poetic essays to motivate the students to seek wisdom and understanding (1–9) and then presented collections of proverbs that provided the content of wisdom and knowledge about the way life truly is. Memorization, reflection, and pondering the meaning of such wisdom was the normal process for acquiring these gifts. Here, the messiah will receive the Spirit of the Lord who bestows these gifts supernaturally, thereby transforming Him far beyond the abilities of the normal human mind.

11:3b–5

> **3bHe shall not judge by what his eyes see, or decide by what his ears hear; 4but with righteousness he shall judge the poor, and decide with equity for the meek of the earth; and he shall smite the earth with the rod of his mouth, and with the breath of his lips he shall slay the wicked. 5Righteousness shall be the girdle of his waist, and faithfulness the girdle of his loins.**

Isaiah considers justice and righteousness essential virtues which are present in the Lord God (5:16; 30:18) and should be present in people (1:17, 27; 9:7; 16:3–5; 28:5–6,17; 32:1–2, 16; 33:5). He criticizes the king, leaders, and people when they do not live them out (1:23–27; 5:7; 10:1–2).

Here, the messianic Davidic king who is filled with the wisdom gifts of the Spirit of the Lord, will possess justice, righteousness, and faithfulness with full authenticity. He will not judge on the basis of external knowledge but on the basis of righteousness and equity. The link between God's gifts of wisdom and the virtues of righteousness and justice also appear in Isaiah 33:5–6: "The Lord is exalted, for he dwells on high; he will fill Zion with justice and righteousness; and he will be the stability of your times, abundance of salvation, wisdom, and knowledge; the fear of the Lord is his treasure."

For the poor and the meek, who can expect true equity from the Messiah, this is good news. At the same time, it is bad news for the wicked because God also knows them and will punish them with the rod of His mouth and His breath. This last image appears in Revalation 1:16, 2:16, and 19:15, where a sword and (in 19:15) a rod comes from the mouth of Jesus Christ to punish the wicked, whether they are unfaithful Christians (2:16) or the nations (19:15).

The king will wear righteousness and faithfulness as his girdle, wrapping the lower part of the trunk of the body where the kidneys and intestines are found, the organs in which the free will and decision making are located, according to the Hebrew understanding of the human person (they considered the heart the organ of understanding).

11:6–9

> **6The wolf shall dwell with the lamb, and the leopard shall lie down with the kid, and the calf and the lion and the fatling together, and a little child shall lead them. 7The cow and the bear shall feed; their young shall lie down together; and the lion shall eat straw like the ox. 8The sucking child shall play over the hole of the asp, and the weaned child shall put his hand on the adder's den. 9They shall not hurt or destroy in all my holy mountain; for the earth shall be full of the knowledge of the LORD as the waters cover the sea.**

The effects of having a Messiah endowed with the Spirit of the Lord who gives wisdom and understanding that produce justice and righteousness include a transformation of nature. Animals that normally live in a predator-prey relationship will now dwell together in peace and harmony. Such an idea lies behind Isaiah 32:16: "Then justice will dwell in the wilderness, and righteousness abide in the fruitful field." Another related passage is Hosea 2:18–20, where the Lord will make "a covenant on that day with the beasts of the field, the birds of the air, and the creeping things of the ground; and I will abolish the bow, the sword, and war from the land; and I will make you lie down in safety" (Hos 2:18). Later, Trito-Isaiah (Is 56–66) will use the picture of "the wolf and the lamb shall feed together, the lion shall eat straw like the ox; and dust shall be the serpent's food. They shall not hurt or destroy in all my holy mountain, says the Lord" (Is 65:25).

The reason underlying this transformation of nature is that the knowledge of the Lord will overflow the earth like a tremendous flood, and that knowledge will bring peace and gentleness to all of God's creatures.

— 11:10–16 —
Expanded Images of the Time of Salvation

11:10

> **10In that day the root of Jesse shall stand as an ensign to the peoples; him shall the nations seek, and his dwellings shall be glorious.**

On the day of the Lord, the Messianic King that comes forth from the root of Jesse (11:1) will become a signal for all the nations of the earth. He is not merely a ruler for Israel, nor is He meant to conquer and subdue other peoples in war. The peaceful images of 11:1–9, particularly 6–9, contradict such political hopes. Rather, due to His Spirit-given wisdom, understanding, knowledge, and fear of the Lord, with its consequent justice and righteousness, the nations will seek Him out and His glorious dwellings. Such international appeal and mission comes from the very roots of the call of Abram in Genesis 12:1–3, where He is to become a blessing for all the families of nations in the world. Through the Davidic Messiah, ultimately descended from Abraham, this blessing will be bestowed on the whole world.

11:11–14

> **11In that day the LORD will extend his hand yet a second time to recover the remnant which is left of his people, from Assyria, from Egypt, from Pathros, from Ethiopia, from Elam, from Shinar, from Hamath, and from the coastlands of the sea. 12He will raise an ensign for the nations, and will assemble the outcasts of Israel, and gather the dispersed of Judah from the four corners of the earth. 13The jealousy of Ephraim shall depart, and those who harass Judah shall be cut off; Ephraim shall not be jealous of Judah, and Judah shall not harass Ephraim. 14But they shall swoop down upon the shoulder of the Philistines in the west, and together they shall plunder the people of the east. They shall put forth their hand against Edom and Moab, and the Ammonites shall obey them.**

The day of the Lord will also be the day on which the Lord gathers the people of Israel who had been scattered throughout the ancient world.

11–12

They will come from Assyria, which had conquered northern Israel and had exiled many of its people. Then he mentions Egypt (referring to Lower Egypt in the north) and Pathros (a name for Upper Egypt in the south) and Ethiopia, furthest south. Elam is in southern Iran today, and Shinar refers to the plains around Babylon. Hamath is in northern Syria. The Israelite remnant will come from all directions and from the most distant lands Isaiah could locate in his day. Some of these will be mentioned again in the oracles against the nations in Isaiah 13–22 that were written later in his career, but here they are places that the Israelites will give up to come home.

13

Peace will exist between formerly feuding Ephraim (northern Kingdom) and Judah (southern Kingdom). They will not even entertain the vices, such as jealousy, that instigate disputes.

14

However, together they will take power over the Philistines on the Mediterranean coast in the southwest, on Edom (southern Jordan), Moab (central Jordan), and the Ammonites (settled near Amman, Jordan). These were formerly part of the empire established by King David, so it seems appropriate to bring them back into the fold after the Davidic Messiah takes power.

11:15–16

> **15And the LORD will utterly destroy the tongue of the sea of Egypt; and will wave his hand over the River with his scorching wind, and smite it into seven channels that men may cross dryshod. 16And there will be a highway from Assyria for the remnant which is left of his people, as there was for Israel when they came up from the land of Egypt.**

Here the transformation of nature is meant to bring unity to formerly enemy peoples, which is the true goal of the day of the Lord. The "tongue of Egypt" refers to the Red Sea east of Egypt, which will be dried up so that a highway can connect Assyria and Egypt as they go through Israel.

No longer will the two superpowers try to destroy each other or anyone else. Rather, peace will make commerce between them possible for the remnant of all three nations after the day of the Lord has judged and destroyed the wicked.

—— Isaiah 12:1–6 ——

This is a hymn of thanksgiving that the redeemed will sing on the day of the Lord.

12:1

> **[1]You will say in that day: "I will give thanks to thee, O LORD, for though thou wast angry with me, thy anger turned away, and thou didst comfort me.**

The people are instructed here to sing this hymn of thanksgiving on the day of the Lord. It recognizes that they suffered judgment and punishment on that day because of their wickedness and sins, but by this point, the Lord has turned away His anger and comforts them. A similar picture of the Lord's comfort after the final judgment appears in Revelation 7:17 and 21:4.

12:2

> **[2]"Behold, God is my salvation; I will trust, and will not be afraid; for the LORD GOD is my strength and my song, and he has become my salvation."**

Their thanksgiving takes the form of a confession of faith in God as their salvation, strength, and song. Isaiah often prophesied that their lack of faith and trust in the Lord was the reason they sinned, as with Ahaz in 7:9–13.

12:3–4

> **[3]With joy you will draw water from the wells of salvation. [4]And you will say in that day: "Give thanks to the LORD, call upon his name; make known his deeds among the nations, proclaim that his name is exalted.**

Because the people have turned to the Lord in trusting faith that He personifies salvation, the following will result.

First, they will continue to draw out salvation like water from a deep well. The image of water as a symbol of God's new life appears in Deutero-Isaiah 55:1–2, and the "fountain of life" (Ps 36:9). God calls Himself the fountain of living water (see Jer 2:13). Jesus Christ promises He can give living water (see Jn 4:10–14) and that if anyone "believes in me, as the scripture has said, 'Out of his heart shall flow rivers of living water,'" which was a promise of the Holy Spirit flowing from within him (Jn 7:37–39). Revelation also promises that the living water will be present in the New Jerusalem (see 7:17; 21:1; 22:17).

Second, they will continue to give thanks to the Lord, call upon Him, and tell the remnant people from the other nations about the Lord and His deeds. At the time of Isaiah, Israelites did not proselytize the Gentiles. By the first century, they had begun to do so. However, major evangelization of the Lord's deeds to the nations would take place after Pentecost, when the Church was endowed with the Holy Spirit that Jesus had promised. At that point, they were empowered to "teach all nations" as Jesus had commanded them to do (see Mt 28:19; Mk 16:15; Lk 24:47–48; Acts 1:8).

12:5–6

> **5"Sing praises to the LORD, for he has done gloriously; let this be known in all the earth. 6Shout, and sing for joy, O inhabitant of Zion, for great in your midst is the Holy One of Israel."**

The hymn concludes with a series of imperatives to sing praises, shout, and sing for joy because the Lord is great in the midst of Zion. These commands to praise God in song are described in great detail in the book of Revelation, where God and the Lamb are on a throne in the midst of heaven, the New Jerusalem, and everyone there sings hymns of praise (see Rv 4:8–11; 5:9–14; 11:16–19; 12:10–12; 15:3–4; 16:5–7; 19:1–3, 6–8).

Lesson 6

Proto-Isaiah 13–16: Oracles Against Israel's Enemy Nations

A whole new section of Isaiah's writings extend from chapter 13 to 23. Like other prophets (Amos, Jeremiah, and Ezekiel), sections of the book are devoted to oracles against other nations, particularly the small states of western Asia that surrounded Israel and the great empires of Egypt, Assyria, and Babylon. A theological key to these oracles was that the Lord God ruled not only Israel but also the whole world. Typically the peoples had national gods—Asshur, god of war in Assyria (after whom they named themselves), Marduk in Babylon, Haddad in Syria, Baal in Canaan, and Chemosh in Moab—who ruled their lands but may not have power over other countries unless their worshipers conquered them, as was the policy of devotees of Asshur and Marduk. However, Israel believed that the Lord God was the only God, a hard lesson they learned through history, and that He created the universe. Therefore, the Lord ruled over other nations, judged their behavior by His laws and not theirs, and frequently acted among the nations with a focus on Israel's historical purpose—either to punish or to save Israel, depending on the people's faithfulness to their covenant with Him.

In addition to this theological point, these oracles mostly occurred during the first years of King Hezekiah of Judah's reign. His father, Ahaz, died in 715, and Hezekiah became king that year. The international scene was in great turmoil, largely because of the Assyrian policy of expansion that Tiglath-Pileser III had begun in the 740s and was continued by his successors Shalmaneser V, Sargon II, Sennacherib, Esarhaddon, and Ashurbanipal.

— Isaiah 13:1–22 —

This oracle against Babylon and the taunt that follows in Isaiah 14 form the first and the longest foreign criticism in Isaiah 13–23.

Understanding Babylon's history is important. The year 732 BC saw the beginning of chaos in Babylon, when King Nabu-nadin-zer died and was replaced by the short-lived Nabu-shum-ukin, the last king of the Ninth Dynasty. When he died that year, Nabu-ukin-zer became king, thereby beginning the Tenth Dynasty of Babylon.

The following year, 731, Aramean tribes led by a certain Nabu-mukinzeri, abbreviated as Ukinzer or Kinzer, took control of Babylon from Nabu-ukin-zer. Tiglath-Pileser III found that situation unacceptable, so he attacked Babylon, killed King Nabu-ukin-zer, and called himself the "king of Babylon." This showed Assyrian respect for Babylon as the source of Assyrian culture. Interestingly, the Babylonians called the Assyrian king Pulu or Pul, as is seen in 2 Kings 15:19 and 1 Chronicles 5:26. In 727, Tiglath-Pileser died and Ululai became the king of Babylon until he died in 722. In 721, Merodach-Baladan II became the king of Babylon. He was the son of Iakina, the king of Sealand (the marshes) or the king of Kaldu—that is, Chaldea (according to Sargon II). With the help of king Humbanigash of Elam, Merodach-Baladan II revolted against Assyria. Sargon II attacked them but was defeated in battle at Der, freeing Babylon from Assyria until 711. That year, Sargon attacked and conquered the Chaldean king, Merodach-Baladan of Babylon, who fled to his allies in Elam. Sargon claimed to liberate the native Babylonians from the Chaldeans, but he did not take the title "king of Babylon" for himself.

Babylon's complicated history of turmoil lies behind the following text.

13:1

1 The oracle concerning Babylon which Isaiah the son of Amoz saw.

The heading identifies Isaiah son of Amoz as the prophet who "saw" these events, therefore dating this oracle to his lifetime, presumably the events after King Hezekiah ascended the throne.

13:2–5

[2]On a bare hill raise a signal, cry aloud to them; wave the hand for them to enter the gates of the nobles. [3]I myself have commanded my consecrated ones, have summoned my mighty men to execute my anger, my proudly exulting ones. [4]Hark, a tumult on the mountains as of a great multitude! Hark, an uproar of kingdoms, of nations gathering together! The LORD of hosts is mustering a host for battle. [5]They come from a distant land, from the end of the heavens, the LORD and the weapons of his indignation, to destroy the whole earth.

The renewal of Assyrian war against the Chaldean rulers of Babylon in 711 BC is the immediate occasion of this oracle, but Isaiah begins to lay out his vision of the judgment that will come upon the world because of it.

2–3

The Lord summons "my consecrated ones," "my mighty men" (the Assyrians) to the battle of 711 in which He executes His anger against Babylon.

4–5

Since Mesopotamia is a flat region, the "tumult on the mountains" and uproar of kingdoms alludes to the Elamites, who lived in the mountainous region of modern Iran. This battle was meant to have a major impact on the whole earth in a great cataclysm of war that would end the Elamite kingdom and bring down Chaldean power in Babylon. It would also affect the other nations, such as Philistia, Edom, Moab, and Judah, who would use the occasion to rebel against Assyria (4–5).

13:6–13

[6]Wail, for the day of the LORD is near; as destruction from the Almighty it will come! [7]Therefore all hands will be feeble, and every man's heart will melt, [8]and they will be dismayed. Pangs and agony will seize them; they will be in anguish like a woman in travail. They will look aghast at one another; their faces will be aflame. [9]Behold, the day of the LORD comes, cruel, with wrath and fierce anger, to make the earth a desolation and to destroy its sinners from it. [10]For the stars of the heavens and their constellations will not give their light; the sun will be dark at its rising and the moon will not shed its light. [11]I will punish the world for its evil, and the wicked for their iniquity; I will

put an end to the pride of the arrogant, and lay low the haughtiness of the ruthless. [12]I will make men more rare than fine gold, and mankind than the gold of Ophir. [13]Therefore I will make the heavens tremble, and the earth will be shaken out of its place, at the wrath of the LORD of hosts in the day of his fierce anger.

This war against Assyria spread from the Mediterranean coast to Elam (modern day southern Iran), and here Isaiah identifies it as "the day of the Lord" (vv. 6, 9, 13) with horrible consequences for the peoples. Frequently, kings and other political leaders predict that an ensuing war will end the nation's problems and result in peace, but Isaiah sees a dreadful day of the Lord in which suffering for all is inevitable.

6

The command to "wail" (Hebrew helilu, plural imperative) is from the root *yalal*, which is always used in its causative (*hiphil*) form, bears a resemblance to *hallelu*, from the root *halal*, meaning "praise," as in "hallelujah." The command to "wail" over what God is about to do on His day is quite contrary to praising God for what the political leaders want Him to do for their side. The order to wail is directed to all peoples who hear of the coming catastrophe of the nearness of the day of the Lord with its destruction that is ultimately caused by God.

7–8

Normally, soldiers train for battle by strengthening themselves, and leaders try to fire them up with patriotism in order to inspire courage on the battlefield. However, the Lord will make hands feeble and the soldiers will lose heart with interior "pangs and agony" that take the fight out of them.

9–10

This second announcement of the "day of the Lord" describes it as cruel and fierce with wrath. The earth will be desolate and the stars, sun, and moon will not shine. Astrology was invented in Babylon in order to understand the destiny of the nation—individual horoscopes were not made until Alexander the Great democratized this occult practice in the late fourth century. Here, the point is that Babylon's destiny will not be known through the darkened heavenly lights because it is the Lord, not they, who will determine the outcome of the war.

11–13

Here the Lord lays out His reasons for declaring His destructive day against the world: the world is evil and wicked in its iniquity, arrogance, and haughtiness—the same sins for which he had condemned Israel in 2:11–17 and 3:16. The punishment will be to "make men rare" as fine gold, since so many will die in battle. The Lord's wrath will affect not only human lives, but even the heavens will tremble and earth will shake on the day of the Lord's fierce anger. These far-reaching effects show that He is not merely some national deity for Israel but is the Lord of all nations, the whole earth and the heavens above.

13:14–16

> **14 And like a hunted gazelle, or like sheep with none to gather them,**
> **every man will turn to his own people, and every man will flee to his**
> **own land. 15 Whoever is found will be thrust through, and whoever is**
> **caught will fall by the sword. 16 Their infants will be dashed in piec-**
> **es before their eyes; their houses will be plundered and their wives**
> **ravished.**

These verses return to a description of war's effects on human beings. The men will flee to their own countries after the chaos of defeat. When they are caught, they will be killed, and at home, their children will be killed, wives will be raped, and houses plundered. The men will no longer be able to defend their own property, let alone defeat the Assyrian Empire.

13:17–18

> **17 Behold, I am stirring up the Medes against them, who have no re-**
> **gard for silver and do not delight in gold. 18 Their bows will slaughter**
> **the young men; they will have no mercy on the fruit of the womb;**
> **their eyes will not pity children.**

The Lord is stirring the Medes, a people who came from the northern Iranian plateau. Their lack of regard for silver and gold means they will not be distracted by opportunities for plunder. Rather, they will kill youths, children, and infants without mercy so as to bring about a thorough destruction of peoples on the day of the Lord.

13:19–22

[19]And Babylon, the glory of kingdoms, the splendor and pride of the Chaldeans, will be like Sodom and Gomorrah when God overthrew them. [20]It will never be inhabited or dwelt in for all generations; no Arab will pitch his tent there, no shepherds will make their flocks lie down there. [21]But wild beasts will lie down there, and its houses will be full of howling creatures; there ostriches will dwell, and there satyrs will dance. [22]Hyenas will cry in its towers, and jackals in the pleasant palaces; its time is close at hand and its days will not be prolonged.

The focus of these verses is the future destruction of Babylon, modeled on the devastation of Sodom and Gomorrah from a millennium prior to this time. In historical fact, Babylon was not destroyed in 711. However, in a later Babylonian revolt against Assyria in 652 BC, again with Elamite help, failed by 648 and led to much destruction in Babylon. However, the city was rebuilt and became the focal point for yet another rebellion by the Chaldean general, Nabopolassar, in 626 BC. This led to the establishment of the Neo-Babylonian Empire that eventually defeated the Assyrians with the help of the Medes and left the Assyrian capital, Nineveh, in total ruins in 609 BC. The total destruction and abandonment of Babylon began after the Arab conquests and the establishment of Baghdad as a more defensible capital. That abandonment left it to the wild animals and has lasted until the present time.

Isaiah 14:1–4a

[1]The LORD will have compassion on Jacob and will again choose Israel, and will set them in their own land, and aliens will join them and will cleave to the house of Jacob. [2]And the peoples will take them and bring them to their place, and the house of Israel will possess them in the LORD's land as male and female slaves; they will take captive those who were their captors, and rule over those who oppressed them. [3]When the LORD has given you rest from your pain and turmoil and the hard

service with which you were made to serve, [4a]you will take up this taunt against the king of Babylon:

As a response to the threat of the day of the Lord during the Babylonian revolt against Assyria, these verses offer four promises to Israel from the Lord. First, the Lord will have compassion on them and return them to their land from exile. Second, foreigners will join them and cling to the house of Jacob. Third, other peoples will bring them back home to Israel, at which point these foreigners will become Israel's slaves. Fourth, once they are at rest, they will sing a taunt against Babylon, a taunt which follows in verses 4b–21.

—— Isaiah 14:4b–21 ——

This section is a lament that taunts the king of Babylon as he falls from power.

14:4b–8

[4b]"How the oppressor has ceased, the insolent fury ceased! [5]The LORD has broken the staff of the wicked, the scepter of rulers, [6]that smote the peoples in wrath with unceasing blows, that ruled the nations in anger with unrelenting persecution. [7]The whole earth is at rest and quiet; they break forth into singing. [8]The cypresses rejoice at you, the cedars of Lebanon, saying, 'Since you were laid low, no hewer comes up against us.'

The world is at rest and rejoices in song that the wicked, oppressive rule is over. While the Babylonian revolt had brought about a war that ravaged many nations on "the day of the Lord," now the peoples, nations, and the earth itself can enjoy enough peace and quiet to sing in exultation at the end of the oppression. Even the cypresses and cedars of Lebanon, which had been cut down to make temples and other great buildings in Mesopotamia, can now rejoice because no one is coming to hew them down.

14:9–11

[9]Sheol beneath is stirred up to meet you when you come, it rouses the shades to greet you, all who were leaders of the earth; it raises from their thrones all who were kings of the nations. [10]All of them will

speak and say to you: `You too have become as weak as we! You have become like us!' [11]Your pomp is brought down to Sheol, the sound of your harps; maggots are the bed beneath you, and worms are your covering.

Sheol, the place of the dead, rouses the shades of all dead people to greet this king with a taunt that he is now as weak as all preceding rulers. His arrogant pomp is brought down to Sheol, where maggots and worms form the bedding of the dead.

14:12–15

[12]"How you are fallen from heaven, O Day Star, son of Dawn! How you are cut down to the ground, you who laid the nations low! [13]You said in your heart, 'I will ascend to heaven; above the stars of God I will set my throne on high; I will sit on the mount of assembly in the far north; [14]I will ascend above the heights of the clouds, I will make myself like the Most High.' [15]But you are brought down to Sheol, to the depths of the Pit.

The shades in Sheol continue their taunt with the theme of his great fall from a heaven which he was in fact unable to climb. The fallen king is called "Day Star," a translation of a Hebrew word whose root means "to shine," and "son of Dawn," which Saint Jerome translated into his Vulgate as Lucifer, "light bearer." The taunt identifies him with names associated with heavenly beings because he wanted to "ascend to heaven above the stars of God." This idea may relate to various pagan myths in which a younger god wants to take over from the reigning god, who was usually his father. For instance, Baal had to fight his brother Mot (meaning "death") in order to take the throne of his father, Il Elyon (meaning "God Most High"), after his father's retirement as king and father of the gods. This king is accused of having similar ambitions to make himself "like the Most High" (Hebr. *Elyon*). However, his hope is futile and he is brought down to Sheol, the place of the shades of the dead.

14:16–19

[16]Those who see you will stare at you, and ponder over you: 'Is this the man who made the earth tremble, who shook kingdoms, [17]who made the world like a desert and overthrew its cities, who did not let his

> **prisoners go home?' [18]All the kings of the nations lie in glory, each in his own tomb; [19]but you are cast out, away from your sepulchre, like a loathed untimely birth, clothed with the slain, those pierced by the sword, who go down to the stones of the Pit, like a dead body trodden under foot.**

The people still alive on earth also taunt the dead ruler.

Their first taunt is in the form of rhetorical questions about whether such a man as they now see dead was able to have so much power as to trouble the earth and its cities.

The living then contrast the glory of great kings in richly adorned tombs with this king, who is among the corpses on the battlefield, like a common soldier, far away from the tomb he had prepared.

14:20–21

> **[20]You will not be joined with them in burial, because you have destroyed your land, you have slain your people. "May the descendants of evildoers nevermore be named! [21]Prepare slaughter for his sons because of the guilt of their fathers, lest they rise and possess the earth, and fill the face of the world with cities."**

The king is denied burial with his soldiers because his policies had been a catastrophe for his own people and they will not even bury him (v. 20). The final insult is the plans of his own people to slaughter his sons because of their father's guilt. The people fear that the dynasty could continue their father's policies and destroy them even further, so they kill his children. All is lost for this king, even after his death.

Isaiah 14:22–23

> **[22]"I will rise up against them," says the Lord of hosts, "and will cut off from Babylon name and remnant, offspring and posterity, says the Lord. [23]And I will make it a possession of the hedgehog, and pools of water, and I will sweep it with the broom of destruction, says the Lord of hosts."**

In a first-person oracle, the Lord of hosts says He will cut off name, remnant, offspring, and posterity from Babylon—a thorough removal of a future life. The Lord promises the thorough destruction that is sung about in the preceding taunt. Of course, anyone who visits Babylon today or for the past centuries will see sand among its ruins.

— Isaiah 14:24–27 —

The Lord of hosts swears an oath to destroy Assyria in the mountains of Israel.

14:24–25

> **24The Lord of hosts has sworn: "As I have planned, so shall it be, and as I have purposed, so shall it stand, 25that I will break the Assyrian in my land, and upon my mountains trample him under foot; and his yoke shall depart from them, and his burden from their shoulder."**

This prophecy of Assyria's destruction in the land of Israel is presented in the most solemn form of an oath from the mouth of the Lord. He adds to the sureness of the oath by saying, "As I have planned, so it shall be." His word and plan convey no doubt at all, as in Numbers 33:56: "I will do to you as I thought to do to them." His thoughts inevitably lead to action.

This threat to break Assyria within Israel would take place in 701 BC, when the angel of the Lord strikes the Assyrian army besieging Jerusalem (see Is 37:36–38; 2 Kgs 19:35–37; see Lesson 11 in this book).

14:26–27

> **26This is the purpose that is purposed concerning the whole earth; and this is the hand that is stretched out over all the nations. 27For the Lord of hosts has purposed, and who will annul it? His hand is stretched out, and who will turn it back?**

No longer is the Lord speaking in the first person. Rather, the prophet makes his own comment that the Lord has decreed His purpose for the whole earth and no one can change it. This is an important comment because it recognizes that the Lord is sovereign over all the earth, and therefore, he can decree these oracles against the nations with full authority.

—— Isaiah 14:28–32 ——

The Lord addresses an oracle against Philistia after King Iamani of Ashdod started a revolt against Assyria in 713 BC, which Egypt, Edom, Moab, and Judah joined until Iamani's defeat in 712 and the abandonment of the revolt in 711.

14:28

28In the year that King Ahaz died came this oracle:

The introduction to the oracle dates it to Ahaz' death, which occurred in 715 BC.

14:29

29"Rejoice not, O Philistia, all of you, that the rod which smote you is broken, for from the serpent's root will come forth an adder, and its fruit will be a flying serpent.

First, the Lord orders Philistia not to rejoice over the "broken" rod that used to smite the land. This may refer to the removal of Pharaoh Bakenrenef, the second, though last pharaoh of the Twenty-Fourth Dynasty at Sais, a city in the western Nile Delta. Pharaoh Shabaka, of the Twenty-Fifth Dynasty, was Ethiopian and replaced the native Egyptian Bakenrenef with an Ethiopian governor at Sais and extended his control over the western oases. While the "serpent" Bakenrenef was gone, an adder, Shabaka, took his place. The flying serpent could be Shebitku, who became the next Ethiopian pharaoh. The snake imagery was appropriate since the pharaohs' crowns always had a serpent on them.

14:30

30And the first-born of the poor will feed, and the needy lie down in safety; but I will kill your root with famine, and your remnant I will slay.

The content of the prophecy is an oracle of doom: the Lord will kill the root of Philistia and slay its remnant. However, the "first-born of the poor" and the needy will eat and be safe, a reference to Judah being secure.

14:31

31 Wail, O gate; cry, O city; melt in fear, O Philistia, all of you! For smoke comes out of the north, and there is no straggler in his ranks."

Philistia is ordered to "wail" and "melt in fear" because of a smoke coming from the north. This is a reference to the Assyrians, who were to attack Philistia after King Iamani of Ashdod revolted against Sargon II. In 713 BC, Sargon defeated Ashdod, but King Iamani escaped and took refuge in Egypt. Then Pharaoh Shabaka captured King Iamani, put him in chains, and sent him to Sargon II as a prisoner to avoid an Assyrian invasion. In this, he proved himself to be a snake.

14:32

32 What will one answer the messengers of the nation? "The LORD has founded Zion, and in her the afflicted of his people find refuge."

This verse is confusing because it leaves much unsaid. However, the scene shifts from Philistia to Jerusalem, where messengers from Philistia were waiting for an answer, perhaps to a request for Judah to join the rebellion against Sargon. Isaiah gives the advice that he always does: trust in the Lord who founded Zion and provides its refuge. In each of the political crises, he warns the kings to stay out of alliances with weak humans and to trust solely in the Lord.

In fact, young King Hezekiah did join the Philistine's rebellion, along with Moab and Egypt, who are the subjects of Isaiah 15–16, 18–20. However, when King Iamani was so easily defeated, they all backed out of the rebellion.

Isaiah 15:1–16:14

This complex oracle against Moab is difficult to understand, though it was presumably clear enough to the people of that period. Not much of the history of Moab is known, except for references in Israel's history and oracles by various prophets, such as Jeremiah 27:3; 40:11; 48:1–47 (verses from Isaiah 15–16 are found in Jeremiah 48); Ezekiel 25:8–11.

A few references occur in the Assyrian histories from Isaiah's era and later. Tiglath-Pileser III of Assyria mentions receiving tribute from King

Salamanu of Moab in 728 BC. Later, when Ashdod revolted against Sargon II in 711 BC, Moab joined the rebellion but then quit it. In 701, Sennacherib included King Kammusunadbi of Moab in a list that paid him tribute willingly, and his son Esarhaddon received tribute from King Musurri. Musurri also gave mercenary troops to Ashurbanipal's army in Egypt. In 652 BC, Ashurbanipal's older brother, Shamash-shum-ukin, the king of Babylon, revolted against Ashurbanipal with the help of the Elamite princes. During this war, Arabs attacked Moab and killed King Kamashalta and took many captives.

It is difficult to assign the events of the oracle to these historical records; rather, it seems more likely that the events were known only to Isaiah and the people of Judah. These events did not matter to anyone else.

15:1–9

> **[1]An oracle concerning Moab. Because Ar is laid waste in a night Moab is undone; because Kir is laid waste in a night Moab is undone. [2]The daughter of Dibon has gone up to the high places to weep; over Nebo and over Medeba Moab wails. On every head is baldness, every beard is shorn; [3]in the streets they gird on sackcloth; on the housetops and in the squares every one wails and melts in tears. [4]Heshbon and Elealeh cry out, their voice is heard as far as Jahaz; therefore the armed men of Moab cry aloud; his soul trembles. [5]My heart cries out for Moab; his fugitives flee to Zoar, to Eglathshelishiyah. For at the ascent of Luhith they go up weeping; on the road to Horonaim they raise a cry of destruction; [6]the waters of Nimrim are a desolation; the grass is withered, the new growth fails, the verdure is no more. [7]Therefore the abundance they have gained and what they have laid up they carry away over the Brook of the Willows. [8]For a cry has gone round the land of Moab; the wailing reaches to Eglaim, the wailing reaches to Beerelim. [9]For the waters of Dibon are full of blood; yet I will bring upon Dibon even more, a lion for those of Moab who escape, for the remnant of the land.**

This section is a funeral lament for Moab after a night raid by some unnamed enemy against two cities but causes grief throughout the Moabite cities.

1

Ar was a city near the border of Moab and Ammon in northern Moab, not far from the Arnon River: the "valleys of the Arnon, and the slope of the valleys that extends to the seat of Ar, and leans to the border of Moab" (Nm 21:14–5); "Ar of Moab, the lords of the heights of the Arnon" (Nm 21:28); "the boundary of Moab at Ar . . . the frontier of the sons of Ammon" (Dt 2:18–19). The meaning of "Ar" is unknown.

Kir of Moab, named Kirhareseth in 16:7, is different from the Kir mentioned in Isaiah 22:6 and Amos 1:5 and 9:7, which was as a town in Syria. Kir of Moab was the capital, whose location may have been at modern Kerak in central Moab. "Kir" means "wall" in Hebrew.

2–3

The towns of Dibon (twenty miles north of Kir/Kerak), Nebo, Medeba (both are just east of the north end of the Dead Sea; they had been conquered from Israel by King Mesha of Moab around 840-830 BC), Heshbon, Elealeh (a bit farther northeast), and Jahaz (another town taken from Israel by Mesha and attached to Dibon's region) are in mourning over the loss of Ar and Kir, perhaps because they know they will be attacked if the border outpost of Ar and the capital of Kir have fallen. Standard customs of lament, including shaving the head and beard, sackcloth, and weeping are expressions of grief over the disaster.

5–7

The prophet expresses his personal grief for the destruction in Moab, the plight of the refugees, and sadness that the enemies have stolen much plunder. Such empathy is proper and prepares the way for the Judahite expressions of empathy (16:6–12) and willingness to shelter the refugees (16:1–5). Among the places to which they flee, only Zoar is mentioned as one of the "cities of the plain" (Gn 13:10; 14:2), while Deuteronomy 34:3 says it was opposite Jericho, placing it north of the Dead Sea. The other places are completely unknown.

8–9

The Byzantines identified Eglaim with a site southeast of Kerak, and Beerelim was over twenty miles northeast of Kerak. The news of the attacks on Ar and Kir (Kerak) traveled throughout the land, causing grief everywhere. Refugees fled north to Dibon and were pursued by the enemy, who continued to slay them and pollute the water with their blood. Those who did escape the attackers became the prey of lions (some of which lived in the region well into the twentieth century).

16:1–5

**[16:1]They have sent lambs to the ruler of the land, from Sela, by way of
the desert, to the mount of the daughter of Zion. [2]Like fluttering birds,
like scattered nestlings, so are the daughters of Moab at the fords of
the Arnon. [3]"Give counsel, grant justice; make your shade like night
at the height of noon; hide the outcasts, betray not the fugitive; [4]let
the outcasts of Moab sojourn among you; be a refuge to them from
the destroyer. When the oppressor is no more, and destruction has
ceased, and he who tramples under foot has vanished from the land,
[5]then a throne will be established in steadfast love and on it will sit in
faithfulness in the tent of David one who judges and seeks justice and
is swift to do righteousness."**

The Moabites turn to Judah for help.

1–2

Some of the Moabites fled to Jerusalem for refuge, showing their vulnerability as they fluttered like helpless birds and nestlings.

3–5

The Moabites plead to Judah for help and "justice," the Hebrew term referring to pleading or arbitration. They want shelter after their capital is destroyed so they might live in Jerusalem until the destructive oppressor is gone from their land. For their part, they promise that when they reestablish their kingdom, their king will be faithful to Judah and sit "in the tent of David" to seek justice and righteousness. The inclusion of David is interesting, since he had taken refuge from King Saul in Moab (1 Sm 22:3–5), so this would be recompense for that hospitality. Later, David conquered Moab (2 Sm 8:2–12; 1 Chr 18:11), so this action would also introduce Moab's fealty to the family of David.

16:6–12

**[6]We have heard of the pride of Moab, how proud he was; of his arro-
gance, his pride, and his insolence—his boasts are false. [7]Therefore let**

Moab wail, let every one wail for Moab. Mourn, utterly stricken, for the raisin-cakes of Kirhareseth. 8For the fields of Heshbon languish, and the vine of Sibmah; the lords of the nations have struck down its branches, which reached to Jazer and strayed to the desert; its shoots spread abroad and passed over the sea. 9Therefore I weep with the weeping of Jazer for the vine of Sibmah; I drench you with my tears, O Heshbon and Elealeh; for upon your fruit and your harvest the battle shout has fallen. 10And joy and gladness are taken away from the fruitful field; and in the vineyards no songs are sung, no shouts are raised; no treader treads out wine in the presses; the vintage shout is hushed. 11Therefore my soul moans like a lyre for Moab, and my heart for Kirheres. 12And when Moab presents himself, when he wearies himself upon the high place, when he comes to his sanctuary to pray, he will not prevail.

The people of Jerusalem raise a lament on the destruction of Moab.

6

Of course, they begin with a rehearsal of Moab's past sins of arrogance, pride, insolence, and false boasting, all of which had led to Moab separating itself from Judah's rule over them after David's conquest.

7–8

Nonetheless, everyone joins the lament over Moab and Kir, now called "Kirhareseth" which means "wall of pottery." They describe the situation in agricultural terms, by which the fields and vines "languish," that is, wither throughout the whole land.

9–11

These verses are another lament over Moab, but they are said by an individual, probably Isaiah, as a response to the community lament in verses 7–8. The same towns and cities are included as objects of grief, though Kir is here called Kirheres, meaning "wall of pottery," as in Kirhareseth, which is a synonymous form. The lack of food and harvests, the absence of joy, gladness, and wine, cause Isaiah to "moan like a lyre" in the depths of his soul.

12

The Mesha Stele mentions that Mesha's father had built a high place, but such sanctuaries will be useless and Moab's prayers will not be answered.

16:13–14

> **[13]This is the word which the LORD spoke concerning Moab in the past.**
> **[14]But now the LORD says, "In three years, like the years of a hireling, the glory of Moab will be brought into contempt, in spite of all his great multitude, and those who survive will be very few and feeble."**

The first line states that the preceding lament was the Lord's word at some past time, indicating that these two verses are a later addition to the unit (v. 13). That is why the Lord says "now"—that is, at a later period—that another disaster will hit Moab. Apparently "the glory of Moab" has returned, and the people have rebuilt their country. However, for a reason that is not stated, though the contemporary listeners may have understood it, Moab's glory will be in contempt and the survivors will be very few. This may refer to the time when the Moabites sided with Sennacherib's army when they attacked Judah in 701 BC. The laments that preceded these verses would have reminded the people of Judah of the ways they grieved for the Moabites and helped them in the past. The Moabites' promise to remain faithful to "David" would be understood as a hollow promise (see 16:5–6) so they would be punished within three years of the prophecy. However, since we are not positive about the date of the prophecy, we cannot determine the precise year they received punishment from the Lord.

Lesson 7

PROTO ISAIAH 17–20: ORACLES AGAINST THE NATIONS

—— Isaiah 17:1–8 ——

The oracle against Damascus, the capital of Syria, and Ephraim, which is the name of the dominant tribe of the northern Kingdom of Israel, makes sense in the context of their alliance against Assyria in 734 BC. To force Judah to join that alliance, they invaded Judah and tried to replace King Ahaz with Tabeel, whose name indicates he was an Aramean.

17:1–3

> **[1]An oracle concerning Damascus. Behold, Damascus will cease to be a city, and will become a heap of ruins. [2]Her cities will be deserted for ever; they will be for flocks, which will lie down, and none will make them afraid. [3]The fortress will disappear from Ephraim, and the kingdom from Damascus; and the remnant of Syria will be like the glory of the children of Israel, says the LORD of hosts.**

The oracle first gives a warning to Damascus (vv. 1–2) and then to Ephraim (v. 3).

1–2

The threat is that Damascus would cease to be a city and the surrounding towns will become deserted ruins. Damascus is the second oldest city in world history—only after Jericho. However, the Assyrians did attack and conquer it under Tiglath-Pileser III, who first attacked the nations to the west of Syria—Phoenicia, Philistia, and coastal towns in between. King Ahaz of Judah paid him tribute, and Pekah of Israel gave up resistance, so Syria was without any allies. In 732 BC, Tiglath-Pileser captured Damascus, deported its people, and executed Rezin (see 2 Kgs 16:0).

3

This verse threatens the disappearance of a fortress from Ephraim (northern Israel) and of the whole kingdom from Damascus. Only a remnant from Damascus will survive, though they will become like the "glory of the children of Israel." Ultimately, this would not be a great future since Israel would eventually be wiped off the map in 722 BC by Sargon. However, in the immediate aftermath of the war of 734 BC, Tiglath-Pileser invaded Israel in 732, set up a provincial headquarters at Megiddo and Dor, and took two-thirds of Israel as an Assyrian province, leaving Samaria as the capital of one-third of its former territory. Hoshea, son of Elah, assassinated King Pekah as a way to appease Tiglath-Pileser and stop him from destroying all of Israel. Hoshea then made himself king and paid tribute to Assyria (see 2 Kgs 16:30, 17:1–2).

17:4–6

> **[4]And in that day the glory of Jacob will be brought low, and the fat of his flesh will grow lean. [5]And it shall be as when the reaper gathers standing grain and his arm harvests the ears, and as when one gleans the ears of grain in the Valley of Rephaim. [6]Gleanings will be left in it, as when an olive tree is beaten—two or three berries in the top of the highest bough, four or five on the branches of a fruit tree, says the LORD God of Israel.**

The threat that Jacob/Israel will be humbled and "grow lean" was fulfilled in 732, as described above. The image for the people was to become like gleaning a few ears of grain after the harvest or beating the last olives from the top of a tree. They would become a small remnant, especially after Sargon destroyed the capital Samaria in 722 BC. Some people fled from Israel to Judah and survived, but it was a small remnant that formed a neighborhood on the northwest side of Jerusalem, in what is today the

Jewish Quarter, as seen by remnants of the city walls King Hezekiah built to enclose them.

17:7–8

> **[7] In that day men will regard their Maker, and their eyes will look to the Holy One of Israel; [8]they will not have regard for the altars, the work of their hands, and they will not look to what their own fingers have made, either the Asherim or the altars of incense.**

"That day" is the day of judgment, at which point both apostate Israel and the pagans of Damascus will realize that their Maker is the "Holy One of Israel" and the idols they have made for themselves are useless. Therefore, after the disasters described in verses 1–6, the day of the Lord may be an opportunity of repentance for both Israel and Syria if they "look to" the Holy One instead of unholy idols.

—— Isaiah 17:9–11 ——

This section is another oracle against the northern kingdom of Israel.

17:9

> **[9]In that day their strong cities will be like the deserted places of the Hivites and the Amorites, which they deserted because of the children of Israel, and there will be desolation.**

A prose section informing the Israelites that their cities will become deserted and desolate, just as the cities of the previous Canaanite inhabitants, the Hivites and Amorites were. The Hivites were also known as Hurrians, a non-Semitic people related to the ancestors of the Armenians, who had lived in Shechem, Kiriath-jearim, Beeroth, Chephirah, and the Gibeon area. Amorites were Semitic peoples who migrated from Mesopotamia to Canaan, like Abraham.

17:10–11

> **[10]For you have forgotten the God of your salvation, and have not remembered the Rock of your refuge; therefore, though you plant pleasant plants and set out slips of an alien god, [11]though you make them**

grow on the day that you plant them, and make them blossom in the morning that you sow; yet the harvest will flee away in a day of grief and incurable pain.

These two verses are the prophecy, directed to the people who have forgotten the "God of your salvation . . . the Rock of your refuge." They worship the Canaanite deities of fertility instead of the Lord. Therefore, they may see some initial growth, and perhaps they will credit Baal, but the Lord they have forgotten will take away their harvest and they will experience the grief and pain of hunger.

—— Isaiah 17:12–14 ——

12Ah, the thunder of many peoples, they thunder like the thundering of the sea! Ah, the roar of nations, they roar like the roaring of mighty waters! 13The nations roar like the roaring of many waters, but he will rebuke them, and they will flee far away, chased like chaff on the mountains before the wind and whirling dust before the storm.
14At evening time, behold, terror! Before morning, they are no more! This is the portion of those who despoil us, and the lot of those who plunder us.

This section is a threat against the many nations that "thunder" and "roar" against Jerusalem, probably in 701 BC when the Assyrian army was besieging the city. Isaiah promises that the Lord ("he") will rebuke these nations and they will flee (v. 13). They will experience terror one evening and run away before the next morning (v. 14). This fits the description of Isaiah 37:36 and 2 Kings 19:35, that the Assyrians were struck by the angel of the Lord one night and fled the next morning.

—— Isaiah 18:1–7 ——

A prophecy against the Ethiopian Twenty-Fifth Dynasty of Egypt, which had been founded by Pharaoh Shabaka after his defeat of Pharaoh Bakenrenef, the last pharaoh of the Twenty-Fourth Dynasty, in 715 BC. This was the same year Hezekiah became the king of Judah after his father Ahaz died.

18:1–2

**[1]Ah, land of whirring wings which is beyond the rivers of Ethiopia;
[2]which sends ambassadors by the Nile, in vessels of papyrus upon the waters! Go, you swift messengers, to a nation, tall and smooth, to a people feared near and far, a nation mighty and conquering, whose land the rivers divide.**

The "whirring wings" refers to the sailing ships that traveled the Nile from Ethiopia to Egypt and then to Judah. Pharaoh Shabaka's successor, Shebitku, sent ambassadors to Judah to persuade Hezekiah to join a revolt against the Assyrians in 705 BC. The Ethiopian officials are described as tall, smooth (without facial hair and with shaved heads), and much feared because of their ability to conquer Egypt.

18:3

[3]All you inhabitants of the world, you who dwell on the earth, when a signal is raised on the mountains, look! When a trumpet is blown, hear!

The various nations are summoned to pay attention to the signals sent out by the Egyptian ambassadors, in this case, regarding the revolt against Assyria.

18:4–6

**[4]For thus the LORD said to me: "I will quietly look from my dwelling like clear heat in sunshine, like a cloud of dew in the heat of harvest.
[5]For before the harvest, when the blossom is over, and the flower becomes a ripening grape, he will cut off the shoots with pruning hooks, and the spreading branches he will hew away. [6]They shall all of them
be left to the birds of prey of the mountains and to the beasts of the earth. And the birds of prey will summer upon them, and all the beasts of the earth will winter upon them.**

The Lord speaks to Isaiah with a clear confidence about the upcoming situation and a willingness to bide his time (v. 4). Just as the keeper of a vineyard knows when to prune the shoots and branches that stop light from reaching the ripening grapes (v. 5), so will the Lord know when to hew down the nations that rebel. Then Isaiah turns to the scene of a battlefield where the fallen soldiers are left for the vultures and other birds of prey and predicts that the armies that rebel against Assyria will lose the war and end up as carrion for the birds (v. 6).

18:7

> **7At that time gifts will be brought to the LORD of hosts from a people tall and smooth, from a people feared near and far, a nation mighty and conquering, whose land the rivers divide, to Mount Zion, the place of the name of the LORD of hosts.**

This defeat will demonstrate that the Lord of hosts is the one who really understands what is happening in politics and history, and therefore the "tall and smooth" Ethiopians ruling Egypt (the land divided by rivers refers to the Nile Delta and its tributaries, as well as the split between the White Nile and the Blue Nile that leads to Ethiopia), the mighty conquering nation, will bring gifts to the Lord at Zion, where the Lord is worshiped in His Temple.

—— Isaiah 19:1–15 ——

The Lord will pass judgment on Egypt and destroy their power and social structure. The historical allusions fit the seventh-century crises that led to the conquest of Egypt by Assyria.

19:1–4

> **1An oracle concerning Egypt. Behold, the LORD is riding on a swift cloud and comes to Egypt; and the idols of Egypt will tremble at his presence, and the heart of the Egyptians will melt within them.**
> **2And I will stir up Egyptians against Egyptians, and they will fight, every man against his brother and every man against his neighbor, city against city, kingdom against kingdom; 3and the spirit of the Egyptians within them will be emptied out, and I will confound their plans; and they will consult the idols and the sorcerers, and the mediums and the wizards; 4and I will give over the Egyptians into the hand of a hard master; and a fierce king will rule over them, says the LORD, the LORD of hosts.**

The Lord comes to Egypt and stirs up a civil war that causes society to collapse.

1

The Lord rides on the clouds, as in Deuteronomy 33:26: "There is none like God who rides through the heavens to your help, and in his majesty through the skies," as well as in other poetic passages (see Ps 18:10–12; 68:4, 33–34). He not only rules Israel but Egypt, and at His presence, the idols tremble and the people's hearts melt.

2

This verse describes the Lord as stirring up the Egyptians into a civil war that deprives them of national spirit, as happened between 672 and 663 BC.

At the city of Sais in the western Nile Delta, Necho I, a native Egyptian, became king in 672 BC. The next year, 671, the Assyrians invaded and defeated the Egyptians, taking the capital at Memphis, with many royal prisoners. Pharaoh Taharqa (Tirhakah) escaped to Ethiopia, so the Assyrian king, Esarhaddon, expelled all Ethiopian officials from Egypt and established native Egyptian princes throughout the Nile Delta region (ANET, 293), including Necho I in Sais. In 669, the Ethiopians incited a rebellion in Lower Egypt, causing the Assyrians to return under General Sha-nabushu. King Esarhaddon died on his way to Egypt, and his younger son, Ashurbanipal, became king in 668. Ashurbanipal remained in Nineveh while the army in Egypt defeated Taharqa (Tirhakah) at Memphis, making him flee south to Thebes and then to Napata in Ethiopia. The Ethiopian officials remaining in Upper Egypt surrendered to Ashurbanipal, but the kings of Lower Egypt rebelled against him and sought Taharqa's help. Ashurbanipal defeated and executed all those kings but Necho I, giving him control of Lower Egypt.

In 665, Taharqa appointed his cousin, Tantamani, as the heir of the throne of Napata, in Ethiopia. When Taharqa died in 664, Tantamani reconquered Egypt and defeated and killed Necho I. Necho's son, Psamtik, or Psammetichus I, became the king of Sais with Assyrian support. The Assyrians returned in 663 to defeat Tantamani at Memphis and Thebes, whose temples, especially Karnak, the largest and most sacred in Egypt, were pillaged. The world was shocked. This is the background to verse 2.

3

No matter how they consult the mediums and wizards, they will remain confused. Of course, this recalls the failures of the Egyptian magicians and sorcerers before the exodus (see Ex 7–9, but especially 9:11 when they get the boils on their skin and can no longer appear before Moses). The pillage of the temple at Karnak in Thebes in 663 devastated the Egyptian spirit, showing that their idols could not save themselves at the most sacred place in their world.

4

The Lord's plan is to hand them over to another ruler, a reference to the Assyrian King Esarhaddon, who began the Assyrian conquest of Egypt, but even more clearly to his son, Ashurbanipal, who completed the conquest and brought the Assyrian Empire to its greatest territorial extension.

19:5–10

> **[5]And the waters of the Nile will be dried up, and the river will be**
> **parched and dry; [6]and its canals will become foul, and the branches of**
> **Egypt's Nile will diminish and dry up, reeds and rushes will rot away.**
> **[7]There will be bare places by the Nile, on the brink of the Nile, and all**
> **that is sown by the Nile will dry up, be driven away, and be no more.**
> **[8]The fishermen will mourn and lament, all who cast hook in the Nile;**
> **and they will languish who spread nets upon the water. [9]The workers**
> **in combed flax will be in despair, and the weavers of white cotton.**
> **[10]Those who are the pillars of the land will be crushed, and all who**
> **work for hire will be grieved.**

The Nile and the water system, on which life in Egypt depends, will be dried up (vv. 5–8) and cause the ruin of the flax and cotton farming (v. 9), as well as the crushing and grief of all society, from the leaders (the pillars) to the hired hands that do day labor (v. 10). Herodotus's famous line "Egypt in the gift of the Nile," pointed out to his readers the absolute dependence on the success of the rains at the Nile's sources that made the annual flooding possible. Without the flood's nourishing deposits of mud on the otherwise desert land, Egypt languished.

19:11–15

[11]The princes of Zoan are utterly foolish; the wise counselors of Pharaoh give stupid counsel. How can you say to Pharaoh, "I am a son of the wise, a son of ancient kings"? [12]Where then are your wise men? Let them tell you and make known what the Lord of hosts has purposed against Egypt. [13]The princes of Zoan have become fools, and the princes of Memphis are deluded; those who are the cornerstones of her tribes have led Egypt astray. [14]The Lord has mingled within her a spirit of confusion; and they have made Egypt stagger in all her doings as a drunken man staggers in his vomit. [15]And there will be nothing for Egypt which head or tail, palm branch or reed, may do.

This stanza decries the foolishness of the Pharaohs and their advisers between 672 and 663 BC. Zoan was a city in the northeast Nile Delta, earlier known as Avaris under the Hyksos kings of the 1700s, as Pi-Rameses in the 1200s (see Gn 47:11; Ex 12:37; Nm 33:3, 5, where this is the name of the city where the Israelites settled in Egypt), as Tanis after 1100 BC, and then Zoan. Taharqa (Tirhakah) made it his capital at which he decided to rebel against the Assyrians, a foolish decision that drove him back to his Ethiopian homeland, brought war and destruction to Egypt, and thereby made Egypt "stagger" with a "spirit of confusion" (v. 14). Neither head nor tail, the palm branches on the farms, or the reeds along the Nile will do the Egyptians any good in the face their political folly and misguided ambitions.

—— Isaiah 19:16–25 ——

This section is a series of prophecies about the day of judgment, each of which begins with the expression "on that day." The main theme is the conversion of Egypt to worshiping the Lord.

19:16–17

[16]In that day the Egyptians will be like women, and tremble with fear before the hand which the Lord of hosts shakes over them. [17]And the land of Judah will become a terror to the Egyptians; every one to whom it is mentioned will fear because of the purpose which the Lord of hosts has purposed against them.

The first step will be the Egyptians' fear when "the hand of the Lord of hosts shakes over them." Even little Judah will become a terror. Such a picture is a contrast to the general confidence that Egypt felt throughout its history, both because of the strength of its population and its relative isolation as a river kingdom in the middle of great deserts.

19:18

[18]In that day there will be five cities in the land of Egypt which speak the language of Canaan and swear allegiance to the LORD of hosts. One of these will be called the City of the Sun.

The text mentions five cities in Egypt that will speak the language of Canaan—presumably either Hebrew or Aramaic. This would have been ironic, since Egypt had ruled Canaan for at least three centuries before the Israelites arrived, and often considered it under Egyptian hegemony after Israel became a kingdom (see Pharaoh Shishak's invasion of Israel during the reign of Rehoboam 1 Kgs 14:25; 2 Chr 12:2). "On that day" five cities will speak the language of Israel, indicating their rise in importance as Egypt fades. Jeremiah 41 addressed a warning against participating in Egyptian worship to Jews already living in four Egyptian cities Migdol, Tahpanhes, Memphis, and the land of Pathros after 587 BC (see Jer 41:1). Isaiah 19:18 adds "City of Destruction" (according to the Hebrew text), "City of the Sun" (according to fifteen manuscripts and some early translations), or the "City of Righteousness" in the Septuagint.

19:19–22

[19]In that day there will be an altar to the LORD in the midst of the land of Egypt, and a pillar to the LORD at its border. [20]It will be a sign and a witness to the LORD of hosts in the land of Egypt; when they cry to the LORD because of oppressors he will send them a savior, and will defend and deliver them. [21]And the LORD will make himself known to the Egyptians; and the Egyptians will know the LORD in that day and worship with sacrifice and burnt offering, and they will make vows to the LORD and perform them. [22]And the LORD will smite Egypt, smiting and healing, and they will return to the LORD, and he will heed their supplications and heal them.

"That day" will mean the conversion of the Egyptians to the Lord both in worship and morals. The pillar at the border indicates possession of the land by the Lord, much as farmers set up small pillars of rock to mark off the property lines of their fields. The rather astonishing prophecy is of an altar to the Lord in the middle of Egypt. Israel could have only one altar, the one in the Temple at Jerusalem. All other temples and altars were considered unacceptable to the Lord and were usually places where false worship was offered. In this passage, the altar, along with the pillar, will be a "sign and witness" to the Lord that He should send them a savior when they need defense and deliverance. This promise stands in clear distinction to the chaos Egypt brought upon itself in the period of rebellion described in the preceding passage.

Equally amazing is the promise of mutual knowledge between the Egyptians and the Lord. They will be able to offer sacrifices and make vows to the Lord, even as the Israelites do (v. 21). Of course, in later centuries, the Christian community of Egypt understood their own altars and the offering of the Eucharist as the fulfillment of this passage.

Finally, knowledge of the Lord will open them to a relationship with the Lord by which He smites and heals them. This refers to the kind of moral discipline that a father gives to a wayward son, followed by healing that flows from the other side of the father's love of the son. Such moral discipline belongs to a parental love relationship, "For the Lord disciplines him whom he loves, and chastises every son whom he receives" (Heb 12:6, citing Prv 3:12; see also Dt 8:5; Prv 13:24; Sir 30:2).

19:23

> **23In that day there will be a highway from Egypt to Assyria, and the Assyrian will come into Egypt, and the Egyptian into Assyria, and the Egyptians will worship with the Assyrians.**

In contrast to the devastating rebellions by Egypt and invasions by Assyria, "that day" will bring a highway that allowed easy access between the two great nations, not for military advantage but to make possible worship of the Lord together.

19:24–25

[24]In that day Israel will be the third with Egypt and Assyria, a blessing in the midst of the earth, [25]whom the LORD of hosts has blessed, saying, "Blessed be Egypt my people, and Assyria the work of my hands, and Israel my heritage."

Finally, that day will make Israel, Egypt and Assyria equal to each other in significance, and all three will be a blessing in the middle of the earth for all other peoples to receive. Israel had been called to be a blessing to all the families of the nations since the call of Abram from Mesopotamia (see Gn 12:1–3). When Egypt is converted, followed by Assyria, they will all be a blessing precisely because of their relationship to the Lord.

— Isaiah 20:1–6 —

Isaiah is told to walk through Jerusalem barefoot and naked as a sign that the Assyrians will take the Egyptians and Ethiopians who rule them as naked and barefoot prisoners to Assyria.

20:1–2a

[1]In the year that the commander in chief, who was sent by Sargon the king of Assyria, came to Ashdod and fought against it and took it,— [2a]at that time the LORD had spoken by Isaiah the son of Amoz, saying,

The prose introduction dates this prophecy to 713 BC, when King Iamani of Ashdod revolted against the Assyrian King Sargon II. The Ethiopian Pharaoh Shabaka of the Twenty-Fifth Dynasty and King Hezekiah of Judah joined the rebellion, as did Edom and Moab (see the oracles against this revolt in Is 14:28–32).

20:2b–5

[2b]"Go, and loose the sackcloth from your loins and take off your shoes from your feet," and he had done so, walking naked and barefoot—[3]the LORD said, "As my servant Isaiah has walked naked and barefoot for three years as a sign and a portent against Egypt and Ethiopia, [4]so shall the king of Assyria lead away the Egyptians captives and the Ethiopians exiles, both the young and the old, naked and barefoot, with buttocks uncovered, to the shame of Egypt. [5]Then they shall

> **be dismayed and confounded because of Ethiopia their hope and of Egypt their boast.**

The Lord first orders Isaiah to walk naked and barefoot through Jerusalem (v. 2b), an act that would be particularly shameful in a culture that rejected nudity very strongly. Then the Lord explains Isaiah's symbolic action as "a sign and a portent" that Assyria will lead Egyptian and Ethiopian prisoners to Assyria, walking the deserts without covering or shoes. This would be an extremely painful and long journey that predicts the failure of their rebellion.

20:6

> **6And the inhabitants of this coastland will say in that day, 'Behold, this is what has happened to those in whom we hoped and to whom we fled for help to be delivered from the king of Assyria! And we, how shall we escape?'"**

The conclusion that the other rebels make: if the Egyptians are taken captive, then the other nations in the rebellion have no chance to defeat Assyria.

Lesson 8

Proto-Isaiah 21–23: Visions of Catastrophe

—— Isaiah 21:1–10 ——

A confusing and obscure oracle about the attack of the Elamites and Medes against Babylon.

21:1–5

> **[1]The oracle concerning the wilderness of the sea. [1b]As whirlwinds in the Negeb sweep on, it comes from the desert, from a terrible land. [2]A stern vision is told to me; the plunderer plunders, and the destroyer destroys. Go up, O Elam, lay siege, O Media; all the sighing she has caused I bring to an end. [3]Therefore my loins are filled with anguish; pangs have seized me, like the pangs of a woman in travail; I am bowed down so that I cannot hear, I am dismayed so that I cannot see. [4]My mind reels, horror has appalled me; the twilight I longed for has been turned for me into trembling. [5]They prepare the table, they spread the rugs, they eat, they drink. Arise, O princes, oil the shield!**

A vision of armies approaching Babylon (vv. 1–2, 5) and the speaker's reaction to it.

1a

The title addresses this oracle to "the wilderness of the sea," which means "swamp." While Assyrian King Sargon identified the Babylonian ruler Marduk-apal-ippine (Merodach-Baladan in the Bible) as "Kaldu"—that is, Chaldean—his predecessor Tiglath Pileser III said that they were from

"Sealand"—that is, the swamps. Southern Mesopotamia still has swamp areas, which connects the oracle with Babylon, addressed explicitly in verse 9.

1b–2

A stern vision sweeps into the prophet's minds, like a whirlwind in the Negeb desert. Elam and Media are ordered to go up to lay siege. King Humbanigash of Elam (located in the south of modern Iran) helped the Chaldean King Marduk-apal-ippine II (Merodach-Baladan) take Babylon away from the Assyrians in a war in 721–720 BC. However, while young King Hezekiah of Judah was allied with Pharaoh Shabaka in the revolt against Assyria between 713 and 711, the Assyrian King Sargon attacked Babylon in 711, and the Elamites refused to help Babylon. In verse 2, the prophet urges Elam and Media (also a kingdom in modern Iran) to the attack, but they did not help in 711. Such failure would leave the rebels in Judah vulnerable to Sargon's retaliations too.

3–4

The prophet reacts with anguish that is as painful as a woman in childbirth, indicating his agony at Babylon's fate, since it kept the Assyrians occupied in Mesopotamia and distracted them from the western part of the empire, where Israel was located. He is so dismayed that he cannot hear or see; his mind is overwhelmed throughout the night. Though he awaits dawn, the gray twilight causes more trembling.

5

He sees the armies (Assyria) preparing their camp with a table and rugs in their tents to eat before the battle. They prepare to meet the enemy by oiling their shields.

21:6–10

6For thus the LORD said to me: "Go, set a watchman, let him announce what he sees. 7When he sees riders, horsemen in pairs, riders on asses, riders on camels, let him listen diligently, very diligently." 8Then he who saw cried: "Upon a watchtower I stand, O LORD, continually by day, and at my post I am stationed whole nights. 9And, behold,

here come riders, horsemen in pairs!" And he answered, "Fallen, fallen is Babylon; and all the images of her gods he has shattered to the ground." [10]O my threshed and winnowed one, what I have heard from the LORD of hosts, the God of Israel, I announce to you.

This section presents the oracle ("thus says the Lord") and its effects.

6–7

The Lord orders the prophet to set a watchman to report exactly what he sees, and then pay attention to the kind of cavalry that approaches, whether horse, asses, or camels. The watchman on the tower does not understand the meaning of each type of cavalry, and does not need to, since his job is merely to announce what he sees.

8–9

The watchman announces "horsemen in pairs," indicating that "fallen, fallen is Babylon" and her gods, particularly the chief god Marduk after whom the king was named, are smashed.

10

The "threshed and winnowed one" refers to Judah, which has been suffering under the Assyrians during Hezekiah's first revolt of 713–711. The prophet announces his message in full, confirming Isaiah's teaching that the king should never have joined the revolt but rather trusted in God, not in Egypt.

—— Isaiah 21:11–12 ——

[11]The oracle concerning Dumah. One is calling to me from Seir, "Watchman, what of the night? Watchman, what of the night?" [12]The watchman says: "Morning comes, and also the night. If you will inquire, inquire; come back again."

This short oracle on Dumah is confusing. Seir is the mountain range southeast of the Dead Sea, and is another name for Edom, which is the name of the bedouin people who conquered Seir from the Horites in the fourteenth or thirteenth centuries BC. For that reason, the Septuagint translated "Dumah" as "Edom." The name also appears among the Arab descendants of Ishmael (see Gn 25:14; 1 Chr 1:30) and was the name of an oasis in Arabia that Sennacherib defeated (called Adumatu in Akkadian, Prism B iv 1, ANET 291). Finally, the word also means "silence" (see Ps 94:17; 115:17). The explanations include seeing these two verses as a criticism of Edom (Septuagint and Vulgate and some moderns), or the Arab tribe of Dumah (Adumatu).

However, the meaning "silence" may use the name as a pun on Dumah the place in order to give an oracle on the silence in which the watchman (who is the prophet) says that nothing more than morning and night are passing. Otherwise all is silent, so come another time to see if there is any news. This belongs to the anxiety people feel when great danger is approaching, and they do not know what to do next because they hear silence.

—— Isaiah 21:13–15 ——

[13]The oracle concerning Arabia. In the thickets in Arabia you will lodge, O caravans of Dedanites. [14]To the thirsty bring water, meet the fugitive with bread, O inhabitants of the land of Tema. [15]For they have fled from the swords, from the drawn sword, from the bent bow, and from the press of battle.

This oracle concerning Arabia mentions the Dedanites, bedouin who traded in caravans (Ez 27:20) and Dedan is mentioned in association with Arabian locations, such as Sheba (Gn 10:7; 25:3; 1 Chr 1:9, 32; Ez 38:13) and, as here, Tema (Ez 25:13). This message instructs them to give water and bread to the fugitives of war that hide in Arabian oases, such as Tema (v. 14).

—— Isaiah 21:16–17 ——

[16]For thus the LORD said to me, "Within a year, according to the years of a hireling, all the glory of Kedar will come to an end; [17]and the remainder of the archers of the mighty men of the sons of Kedar will be few; for the LORD, the God of Israel, has spoken."

Kedar is another Arabian tribe (see Gn 25:13; 1 Chr 1:29) descended from Ishmael who receives advanced warning that within a year their glory will end, particularly their archers. This, along with the defeat of Babylon, intimates troubles for Judah, who had joined the revolt against king Sargon of Assyria.

—— Isaiah 22:1–14 ——

Isaiah criticizes Jerusalem for the city's inappropriate celebration at the withdrawal of the Assyrian army of Sennacherib in 701 BC. The Assyrians had besieged the city, but after exacting more tribute from King Hezekiah (2 Kgs 18:14–16 says that Hezekiah paid three hundred talents of silver and thirty talents of gold which he took from the Temple's decorations), they withdrew. Isaiah 37:36 and 2 Kings 19:35 credit the departure of the Assyrian army from Jerusalem to the Lord's angel slaying them, apparently by a plague. After the Assyrians leave, Isaiah gives this highly critical oracle.

22:1a

> **1The oracle concerning the valley of vision.**

The introduction of the oracle names it after the "valley of vision" mentioned in verse 5 as a place of confusion and violence.

22:1b–4

> **1bWhat do you mean that you have gone up, all of you, to the housetops,**
> **2you who are full of shoutings, tumultuous city, exultant town? 2bYour**
> **slain are not slain with the sword or dead in battle. 3All your rulers**
> **have fled together, without the bow they were captured. All of you**
> **who were found were captured, though they had fled far away. 4There-**
> **fore I said: "Look away from me, let me weep bitter tears; do not labor**
> **to comfort me for the destruction of the daughter of my people."**

The Lord reprimands the people of Jerusalem for rejoicing on "the housetops" exultantly when, in fact, their situation is a military catastrophe.

1b–2a

The Lord uses a rhetorical question to reprimand the people for rejoicing prematurely.

2b–3

The reality of the situation is that troops have died, the leaders had fled or were captured, no matter how far they had fled.

4

Isaiah speaks in the first person as he alone understands the reality of the catastrophe and weeps because of the destruction of the people.

22:5–6

> **5For the LORD God of hosts has a day of tumult and trampling and confusion in the valley of vision, a battering down of walls and a shouting to the mountains. 6And Elam bore the quiver with chariots and horsemen, and Kir uncovered the shield.**

The Assyrians had camped in the valleys surrounding Jerusalem, but in verse 5, a vision of the future "tumult, trampling, confusion" and "a battering down of walls" may look to the later destruction of Jerusalem that would take place in 587 under the Babylonians. If so, that would explain the threat of the Elamite archers, who were allies of Babylon, and Kir, which was the ancestral home of the Aramean people (see Am 9:7).

22:7–11

> **7Your choicest valleys were full of chariots, and the horsemen took their stand at the gates. 8aHe has taken away the covering of Judah. 8bIn that day you looked to the weapons of the House of the Forest, 9and you saw that the breaches of the city of David were many, and you collected the waters of the lower pool, 10and you counted the houses of Jerusalem, and you broke down the houses to fortify the wall. 11aYou made a reservoir between the two walls for the water of the old pool. 11bBut you did not look to him who did it, or have regard for him who planned it long ago.**

This is a description of the Assyrian invasion in 701 and of Judah's preparations that lacked one key component.

7–8a

Addressing Jerusalem in describing the invasion, Isaiah shows how the Assyrians took control of the "choicest valleys," which were the main lines of communication and travel, with their own chariots and cavalry.

8b–11a

The city's preparations included taking weapons from the "House of the Forest," a storage place for weapons built by Solomon (see 1 Kgs 7:2–5), gathering water of the lower pool. (2 Kgs 20:20 describes that Hezekiah dug a "conduit" from the Gihon Spring to the "old pool" This is "Hezekiah's Tunnel," which still exists and people can walk through, wading in the water that continues to flow through it.) They broke down the houses to use the stones to fortify the breaches in the wall.

11b

However, despite all their preparations, they did not look to the Lord, who is the real source of strength and who had His own plans to preserve Judah. Their main mistake was aligning themselves with Pharaoh Shebitku, who initiated the revolt against Sennacherib of Assyria. Judah's true strength came from trusting the Lord and in remaining quiet, but they preferred war preparations and revolt.

22:12–13

> **12In that day the LORD God of hosts called to weeping and mourning, to baldness and girding with sackcloth; 13and behold, joy and gladness, slaying oxen and killing sheep, eating flesh and drinking wine. "Let us eat and drink, for tomorrow we die."**

After the plague drove away the Assyrian army, the people's reaction should have been "weeping, mourning," and penitential acts, such as shaving their heads and wearing sackcloth. Instead, they celebrated with eating meat (generally a rare treat for most people of those times) and drinking wine, with the fatalistic motto that runs through the centuries and the cultures, "Eat, drink, and be merry, for tomorrow we die." Such action and attitude gives no place to God's role in their lives.

22:14

> **[14]The LORD of hosts has revealed himself in my ears: "Surely this iniquity will not be forgiven you till you die," says the LORD God of hosts.**

The Lord judges the people's reactions, telling Isaiah that they will not be forgiven throughout the whole of their lives. This is a harsh conclusion to a very critical oracle.

—— Isaiah 22:15–25 ——

Oracles for two members of Jerusalem's royal court—Shebna and Eliakim.

22:15–19

> **[15]Thus says the LORD God of hosts, "Come, go to this steward, to Shebna, who is over the household, and say to him: [16]What have you to do here and whom have you here, that you have hewn here a tomb for yourself, you who hew a tomb on the height, and carve a habitation for yourself in the rock? [17]Behold, the LORD will hurl you away violently, O you strong man. He will seize firm hold on you, [18]and whirl you round and round, and throw you like a ball into a wide land; there you shall die, and there shall be your splendid chariots, you shame of your master's house. [19]I will thrust you from your office, and you will be cast down from your station.**

Shebna is one of the three Judahite officials who met with the Assyrian Rabshakeh (Akkadian for "chief cupbearer," an important royal official) for negotiations during the revolt from 703 to 701 BC (see Is 36:2–3; 2 Kgs 18:17–18).

15

The introduction to the oracle ("thus says the Lord God of hosts") marks Shebna, who is over Hezekiah's household as the equivalent to a prime minister in Judah.

16

The prophet confronts Shebna, the prime minister, "here" where he was carving a tomb into the rock for himself as his permanent "habitation." A key to understanding the Lord's outrage is that Shebna helped convince

Hezekiah to join the rebellion against Assyria, which led to the city being under Assyrian siege and in great danger. While everyone else is preparing the city for attack (see 22:8b–11a above), Shebna is preparing a tomb, as if he fully expects to die but wants a fine burial place. One instigator of this danger appears to have lost hope.

Archaeologists have discovered a tomb cut into the rock at Jerusalem's Silwan neighborhood, where the ancient city was located. The inscription reads, "the one who is over the house," but the name is not included. Scholars debate whether it was Shebna's tomb.

17–19

Therefore, the Lord's judgment is that he will be thrown out to a wide land where he will be buried, rather than in his tomb. Furthermore, he will be removed from his office of prime minister (v. 19), which certainly did happen, since Isaiah 36:3 and 2 Kings 18:18 list Shebna as a scribe.

22:20–25

> **20In that day I will call my servant Eliakim the son of Hilkiah, 21and I**
> **will clothe him with your robe, and will bind your girdle on him, and will commit your authority to his hand; and he shall be a father to the inhabitants of Jerusalem and to the house of Judah. 22And I will place**
> **on his shoulder the key of the house of David; he shall open, and none shall shut; and he shall shut, and none shall open. 23And I will fasten**
> **him like a peg in a sure place, and he will become a throne of honor to his father's house. 24And they will hang on him the whole weight of**
> **his father's house, the offspring and issue, every small vessel, from the cups to all the flagons. 25In that day, says the LORD of hosts, the peg**
> **that was fastened in a sure place will give way; and it will be cut down and fall, and the burden that was upon it will be cut off, for the LORD has spoken."**

Eliakim was another of the three Judahite officials who met with the Assyrian Rabshakeh for negotiations (see Is 36:2–3; 2 Kgs 18:17–18).

20–24

Eliakim is here designated as Shebna's successor as prime minister, a point that is verified in Isaiah 36:3 and 2 Kings 18:18, where he is designated as the "one over the house"—that is, the prime minister—while Shebna is a scribe. The external signs of office include his robe and sash, and the placing of the key of the house of David on his shoulders with authority to shut or open, an authority no one else can countermand (vv. 21–22). The latter sign is very helpful in understanding Jesus's bestowal of the "keys of the kingdom of heaven" on Peter, the Rock (Mt 16:19) as a sign of placing him "over the house" as Eliakim had been. The idea is that Peter is like the prime minister, while Jesus, of course, is king.

Even more important, Eliakim will be "a father to the inhabitants of Jerusalem and to the house of David," taking authentic care of the people without rashly advising King Hezekiah to join alliances foolishly (v. 21b).

In addition to having the king's authority and to serving the people well, Eliakim will bring honor to his father's house, in contrast to the shame that Shebna brought down on himself (v. 18). The "peg" is a tent peg, which secures a tent from falling; so also will he secure his family and its place in society.

25

This verse appears to be a later addition that contradicts the previous promises of making Eliakim a sure peg. Here the peg will fall down and everything depending on it will collapse too. It seems from Isaiah 36:2ff. and 2 Kings 18:17ff. that Eliakim did not learn from Shebna's mistakes and supported the foolish anti-Assyrian policies. For that reason, the Lord will remove him too.

—— Isaiah 23:1–14 ——

The oracle against Tyre and Sidon comes because its king, Luli, also joined Pharaoh Shebitku in the rebellion against Assyria and, for a while, controlled the highway between Syria and Israel. However, Sennacherib successfully attacked Phoenicia from the north and appointed Ethbaal as his replacement, while Luli escaped to Cyprus. The revolt was a failure for Phoenicia too. The oracle is a prophetic lament over their fate.

23:1–4

> **[1]The oracle concerning Tyre. Wail, O ships of Tarshish, for Tyre is laid waste, without house or haven! From the land of Cyprus it is revealed to them. [2]Be still, O inhabitants of the coast, O merchants of Sidon; your messengers passed over the sea [3]and were on many waters; your revenue was the grain of Shihor, the harvest of the Nile; you were the merchant of the nations. [4]Be ashamed, O Sidon, for the sea has spoken, the stronghold of the sea, saying: "I have neither travailed nor given birth, I have neither reared young men nor brought up virgins."**

Tyre and Sidon formed a trade empire, with colonies around the Mediterranean basin, including Tarshish and Gadir (modern Cadiz) in Spain, Carthage in North Africa, and Kition (modern Larnaca) in Cyprus. The summons for the "ships of Tarshish" to wail at Tyre's defeat is due to the loss of the trade empire's home base. The same applies to Sidon's summons to be still, since their wealth came from trading grain from Egypt. ("Shihor" is one of the tributaries of the Nile and means "Water of Hor" an Egyptian deity.) However, now the cities do not have young people to populate them, since they have been defeated.

23:5–7

> **[5]When the report comes to Egypt, they will be in anguish over the report about Tyre. [6]Pass over to Tarshish, wail, O inhabitants of the coast! [7]Is this your exultant city whose origin is from days of old, whose feet carried her to settle afar?**

Phoenicia's Egyptian allies will grieve the loss and grimly ask the rhetorical question over the cities' ruins whether it is the ancient city that had founded distant colonies?

23:8–9

> **[8]Who has purposed this against Tyre, the bestower of crowns, whose merchants were princes, whose traders were the honored of the earth? [9]The LORD of hosts has purposed it, to defile the pride of all glory, to dishonor all the honored of the earth.**

Having observed the disaster, the question arises as to who could have done this. The prophet answers that the Lord of hosts did this to bring down the arrogant.

23:10–12

[10]Overflow your land like the Nile, O daughter of Tarshish; there is no restraint any more. [11]He has stretched out his hand over the sea, he has shaken the kingdoms; the LORD has given command concerning Canaan to destroy its strongholds. [12]And he said: "You will no more exult, O oppressed virgin daughter of Sidon; arise, pass over to Cyprus, even there you will have no rest."

The Lord's decrees about the future of Sidon and the whole land of Canaan. The people are to overflow the land "like the Nile"—that is, flee the capital city and settle in the hinterland. The sea, which is the force of chaos, is frequently portrayed as the Lord's enemy. He will defeat the sea and all the kingdoms, including the strongholds of Canaan. Again, the issue is to bring down the people's pride. Even if the Sidonians flee to their colony Kition on Cyprus, they will still not find safety or rest. Their trade empire is over, and Carthage, one of its colonies, will eventually take its place, at least until Rome destroys Carthage in 146 BC, at the end of the third Punic War.

23:13–14

[13]Behold the land of the Chaldeans! This is the people; it was not Assyria. They destined Tyre for wild beasts. They erected their siegetowers, they razed her palaces, they made her a ruin. [14]Wail, O ships of Tarshish, for your stronghold is laid waste.

The people of Tyre are told to look at what happened to the Chaldeans who revolted against Assyria: their cities were also destroyed. For that reason, the ships of Tarshish, which were a class of large cargo ships, are told to wail and lament because the home cities are destroyed.

— Isaiah 23:15–18 —

These verses are another oracle against Tyre, apparently referring to a different period of time. Since the Assyrians wrote on clay in cuneiform script, a "book" is a solid piece of clay with six facets and a hole in the center so that it can be placed on a stick and rotated in order to turn the "pages;" this is called a prism. Prism B tells the history of the reign of Esarhaddon, the son of Sennacherib who succeeded him as king after his two oldest sons assassinated him in 681 BC (see 2 Kgs 19:36–37; 2 Chr 32:21, the Babylonian Chronicles and Nabonidus Inscription). Prism B also relates that four years later, in 677, Phoenicia rebelled against Assyria. Sidon was captured and razed; King Abdimilkutte was beheaded as punishment. The people were deported, and Phoenicia became an Assyrian province with a new capital, Kar-Esarhaddon (Prism B, ii 65-82, ANET 291). King Ba'lu of Tyre also rebelled but then submitted to Esarhaddon, paid heavy tribute plus back tribute, gave Esarhaddon his daughters, with dowries, and lost a number of surrounding towns to Assyrian ownership (Prism B reverse 2-10, ANET 291).

23:15–16

> **15In that day Tyre will be forgotten for seventy years, like the days of one king. At the end of seventy years, it will happen to Tyre as in the song of the harlot: 16"Take a harp, go about the city, O forgotten harlot! Make sweet melody, sing many songs, that you may be remembered."**

Tyre would be forgotten for seventy years, a human life span (see Ps 90:10), like an old prostitute whose beauty is gone. She sings a "sweet melody" to attract her customers back to her. This would refer to attempts to regain the city's trade relationships with former colonies, like Carthage, which Esarhaddon now claimed to control (Prism B, v 54-vi 1 ANET 291).

23:17–18

> **17At the end of seventy years, the LORD will visit Tyre, and she will return to her hire, and will play the harlot with all the kingdoms of the world upon the face of the earth. 18Her merchandise and her hire will be dedicated to the LORD; it will not be stored or hoarded, but her merchandise will supply abundant food and fine clothing for those who dwell before the LORD.**

These verses offer hope that Tyre's vital trade industry with the Mediterranean world will return. On one hand, this trade is derisively called prostitution. On the other hand, her profits and wealth will be dedicated to the Lord to provide "abundant food and fine clothing" for those who dwell before the Lord," a reference to the people of Jerusalem as a whole, and possibly a particular reference to the priests who dwell before the Lord (Ps 134:1; 135:1–2). The possibility of including all the inhabitants as well as the priests in the category of "those who dwell before the Lord" may stem from the Lord's promise to the nation that "you shall be to me a kingdom of priests and a holy nation" (Ex 19:6).

The promise that foreign nations would bring tribute to Jerusalem appears frequently in the Old Testament (see Ps 72:10, which mentions Tarshish, Tyre's colony in Spain; Isaiah 18:7; plus later texts such as Isaiah 45:14; 49:22–23; 60:9–11; Hg 2:7; Zec 14:21).

Lesson 9

Proto-Isaiah 28–30: During the Crisis of Assyria's Attack

—— Isaiah 28:1–4 ——

This is a proclamation of woe to the drunkards of Ephraim that warns them of their impending doom. Ephraim was the tribe that dominated the central highlands in the northern kingdom of Israel, so this "woe" is addressed to them. Since the Assyrian king, Sargon, captured and destroyed the northern capital Samaria and deported the people in 722 BC, this passage must date before then, perhaps between 725 and 722, during the Assyrian siege of the city.

28:1

> **1 Woe to the proud crown of the drunkards of Ephraim, and to the fading flower of its glorious beauty, which is on the head of the rich valley of those overcome with wine!**

As usual, the word "woe" came from the funeral lament, and it is used as if to claim that the persons to whom it is addressed is already dead. The proud drunks of Ephraim apparently wore crowns of flowers during drinking bouts, but the flower was fading.

28:2–4

> **2 Behold, the Lord has one who is mighty and strong; like a storm of hail, a destroying tempest, like a storm of mighty, overflowing waters,**

he will cast down to the earth with violence. [3]The proud crown of the drunkards of Ephraim will be trodden under foot; [4]and the fading flower of its glorious beauty, which is on the head of the rich valley, will be like a first-ripe fig before the summer: when a man sees it, he eats it up as soon as it is in his hand.

The Lord is as strong as a destructive storm, and He will cast down the drunks violently, as the first sweet, soft fig of summer is eaten immediately. The Lord's storm was Sargon's army that destroyed the city in 722 BC and took its people captive, as the proclamation asserts.

—— Isaiah 28:5–6 ——

[5]In that day the LORD of hosts will be a crown of glory, and a diadem of beauty, to the remnant of his people; [6]and a spirit of justice to him who sits in judgment, and strength to those who turn back the battle at the gate.

This is a proclamation of salvation "on that day" for the remnant of survivors of Ephraim's survivors. While the flower crowns of the drunks faded, the Lord will become the glorious, beautiful crown for the remnant of "his people"—that is, the people faithful to Him. The Lord also promises to be a "spirit of justice" for judges and "strength" for warriors. This brings to mind Isaiah 11:2–5, where the Spirit of the Lord will bring the Messiah gifts of wisdom, knowledge, and counsel, and justice will gird Him.

Historically, a significant number of northerners escaped to Jerusalem and built such a large settlement to the northwest of the city that King Hezekiah built a wall that included them, sections of which can still be seen in the Jewish Quarter of Jerusalem today.

—— Isaiah 28:7–13 ——

A prophecy of warning against the drunk priests and prophets in Judah who should teach the people knowledge but fail so badly it is as if they were stuttering in a foreign language. The "woe" oracle in 28:1–4 may have been placed before this prophecy to connect the fate of drunks in Ephraim with those in Judah.

28:7–8

[7]These also reel with wine and stagger with strong drink; the priest and the prophet reel with strong drink, they are confused with wine, they stagger with strong drink; they err in vision, they stumble in giving judgment. [8]For all tables are full of vomit, no place is without filthiness.

The "strong drink" here does not refer to distilled spirits, since that had not yet been discovered (a medieval discovery), but rather a type of beer from fermented bread. (Brewing beer with hops was also a medieval invention of monks.) Priests were forbidden from drinking "wine or strong drink" when they enter the Temple because they had to make important decisions with a clear head and teach the people there (see Lv 10:8–11). By drunkenness, the prophets cannot see authentic visions and the priests make themselves incapable of good judgment. They become disgusting as well.

28:9–10

[9]"Whom will he teach knowledge, and to whom will he explain the message? Those who are weaned from the milk, those taken from the breast? [10]For it is precept upon precept, precept upon precept, line upon line, line upon line, here a little, there a little."

A rhetorical question about whom the Lord will teach knowledge and explain messages is answered mockingly: weaned children? (Weaning took place at about age three). They may be babies, but at least they are not drunk.

The translation of "precept" is very conjectural, since the word written is *saw*, which some take for *miswa* (precept), yet is quite different. "Line" is the correct translation of the Hebrew word *qaw*, but the line is more likely an imitation of words meant to mock someone who rattles on, as modern folks say, "Yada, yada, yada," to dismiss someone's words as nonsense. That is the likely meaning here.

28:11–13

[11]Nay, but by men of strange lips and with an alien tongue the LORD will speak to this people, [12]to whom he has said, "This is rest; give rest to the weary; and this is repose"; yet they would not hear. [13]Therefore

the word of the LORD will be to them precept upon precept, precept upon precept, line upon line, line upon line, here a little, there a little; that they may go, and fall backward, and be broken, and snared, and taken.

Here Isaiah says that the Lord will speak to the people through foreigners that He is offering them rest and repose, but the people do not want to listen. For them, the word of the Lord in verse 13 will be more of "yada, yada," as in verse 10, where the same words are repeated.

—— Isaiah 28:14–22 ——

A reproach and a warning to people who have made a covenant with death.

28:14–15

14Therefore hear the word of the LORD, you scoffers, who rule this people in Jerusalem! 15Because you have said, "We have made a covenant with death, and with Sheol we have an agreement; when the overwhelming scourge passes through it will not come to us; for we have made lies our refuge, and in falsehood we have taken shelter";

This is a prophecy ("hear the word of the Lord") where the Lord reproaches the ruling class of Jerusalem that scoff at the Lord's word. The Lord accuses them in verse 15 of having made a covenant with death and Sheol that will protect them from the "overwhelming scourge" of the Assyrian invasion directed by Sennacherib in 701 BC. They claim to make lies and falsehood their protection, perhaps assuming that they can lie to Sennacherib about their alliance with Egyptian Pharaoh Shebitku in his revolt against Assyria.

28:16–22

16therefore thus says the LORD God, "Behold, I am laying in Zion for a foundation a stone, a tested stone, a precious cornerstone, of a sure foundation: 'He who believes will not be in haste.' 17And I will make justice the line, and righteousness the plummet; and hail will sweep away the refuge of lies, and waters will overwhelm the shelter."
18Then your covenant with death will be annulled, and your agreement with Sheol will not stand; when the overwhelming scourge passes through you will be beaten down by it. 19As often as it passes

through it will take you; for morning by morning it will pass through, by day and by night; and it will be sheer terror to understand the message. [20]For the bed is too short to stretch oneself on it, and the covering too narrow to wrap oneself in it. [21]For the LORD will rise up as on Mount Perazim, he will rage as in the valley of Gibeon; to do his deed—strange is his deed! and to work his work—alien is his work! [22]Now therefore do not scoff, lest your bonds be made strong; for I have heard a decree of destruction from the LORD God of hosts upon the whole land.

This prophecy ("thus says the Lord") warns those who made the covenant with death.

16

The true precious foundational cornerstone will be in Zion, and people of faith will not be hasty to trust anyone outside Jerusalem. Jesus cites this verse after He finishes the parable about the people who rented the vineyard and killed the owner's servants and son (see Mt 21:42; Mk 12:10).

17–20

In building upon this foundation, the Lord will use justice and righteousness as the plummet and line that mark out true and straight walls, against which the storm cannot prevail. On the other hand, the "shelter of lies" will be swept away. Jesus uses similar imagery at the conclusion of the Sermon on the Mount when He speaks of those who listen to Him as "building on rock" while those who do not live His words are building on "sand" (Mt 7:24–27). The warning adds (vv. 18–19) that the covenant with death and Sheol will not help them and in fact these are the people who will be beaten down by the Assyrian storm whenever it happens. Jerusalem's defenses will be as inadequate as a bed or blanket that is too short for a person.

21–22

Instead of trusting in deceit and covenants with death, trust in the Lord, who is able to bring about victory against Sennacherib's massive Assyrian army, even as He did in the past. David defeated the Philistines at Mt. Perazim (see 2 Sm 5:17–21) but fully attributed the victory to the Lord:

"The Lord has broken through my enemies before me, like a bursting flood" (5:20). The Lord defeated the Canaanite kings at Gibeon by pelting them with hailstones and making the sun and moon to stand still so Joshua could chase them down (Jo 10:9–15). Learn from the past and do not scoff or else Isaiah will issue a decree from the Lord God of hosts for the destruction of the whole land.

—— Isaiah 28:23–29 ——

A wisdom poem about the farmer working in right order with the correct tools.

28:23

> **23Give ear, and hear my voice; hearken, and hear my speech.**

This verse is the introductory command to listen to the following wisdom.

28:24–26

> **24Does he who plows for sowing plow continually? does he continually open and harrow his ground? 25When he has leveled its surface, does he not scatter dill, sow cummin, and put in wheat in rows and barley in its proper place, and spelt as the border? 26For he is instructed aright; his God teaches him.**

Two rhetorical questions to which the answer is "No, no one plows continuously." The reader knows the farmer will eventually plant seed after plowing because God teaches him correctly.

28:27–28

> **27Dill is not threshed with a threshing sledge, nor is a cart wheel rolled over cummin; but dill is beaten out with a stick, and cummin with a rod. 28Does one crush bread grain? No, he does not thresh it for ever; when he drives his cart wheel over it with his horses, he does not crush it.**

A farmer also uses the proper tools in harvesting herbs such as dill and cummin seed or the grains used for bread.

28:29

[29]This also comes from the Lord of hosts; he is wonderful in counsel, and excellent in wisdom.

Such wisdom about proper tools is also a gift from God, whose counsel and wisdom are excellent for farmers. The point seems to be that if the Lord's wisdom is so excellent in farming, then one must trust in His wisdom in every aspect of life.

—— Isaiah 29:1–8 ——

A description that develops from a threatening warning to Jerusalem (vv. 1–3) to salvation that rises from a whisper to a tempest (vv. 4–6) to full salvation in the form of the defeat and disappearance of the nations who attack Jerusalem (vv. 7–8).

29:1–3

[1]Ho Ariel, Ariel, the city where David encamped! Add year to year; let the feasts run their round. [2]Yet I will distress Ariel, and there shall be moaning and lamentation, and she shall be to me like an Ariel. [3]And I will encamp against you round about, and will besiege you with towers and I will raise siege works against you.

The first stanza is a prophecy of warning that starts with "woe" ("Ho" is just the transliteration of the original Hebrew word, *Hoy*) directed against Jerusalem. The city is identified as "Ariel," which is frequently translated as "lion of God," since *ari* means "lion." However, in Ezekiel 43:16, the word "ariel" refers to the "hearth of the altar." The same word also appears in the Mesha Stele, a stone monument by King Mesha of Moab (840s BC, mentioned in 2 Kings 3:4), where in line 12 it refers to an "altar of David" that Mesha brought to Moab as booty. Here, Ariel is identified as "the city where David encamped"—that is, Jerusalem.

The message in this stanza is that the years and annual feasts may pass by, perhaps a reference to the last years of the Assyrian King Sargon, who died in 705 BC, but the Lord ("I") will distress Ariel with an enemy siege. The people will lament and the city will become "like an Ariel"—that is, like a hearth where burnt scraps remain.

29:4–6

[4]Then deep from the earth you shall speak, from low in the dust your words shall come; your voice shall come from the ground like the voice of a ghost, and your speech shall whisper out of the dust. [5]But the multitude of your foes shall be like small dust, and the multitude of the ruthless like passing chaff. And in an instant, suddenly, [6]you will be visited by the LORD of hosts with thunder and with earthquake and great noise, with whirlwind and tempest, and the flame of a devouring fire.

In this stanza, the prophet speaks to the city, whose voice will come from the earth and whisper like a ghost. In contrast (v. 5), a great multitude of enemies will appear, but all of a sudden the Lord of hosts will appear with thunder, earthquake (a common enough occurrence in the region), a great storm, and fire. The multitude of enemies, despite their huge numbers, will be merely as "dust" or "chaff" in the face of this wind, and therefore they will be completely blown away by the Lord's appearance (v. 6).

29:7–8

[7]And the multitude of all the nations that fight against Ariel, all that fight against her and her stronghold and distress her, shall be like a dream, a vision of the night. [8]As when a hungry man dreams he is eating and awakes with his hunger not satisfied, or as when a thirsty man dreams he is drinking and awakes faint, with his thirst not quenched, so shall the multitude of all the nations be that fight against Mount Zion.

The Lord's salvation is described by comparing the enemies to ephemeral things that disappear: they are like a dream, especially as when a hungry person dreams of food or a thirsty person dreams of drinking but finds he is still hungry and thirsty when he awakens. So also will the enemies disappear suddenly, without a trace.

—— Isaiah 29:9–12 ——

A prophecy of warning (vv. 9–10) with a commentary (vv. 11–12).

29:9–10

[9]Stupefy yourselves and be in a stupor, blind yourselves and be blind! Be drunk, but not with wine; stagger, but not with strong drink! [10]For

the LORD has poured out upon you a spirit of deep sleep, and has closed your eyes, the prophets, and covered your heads, the seers.

The prophecy warns that the Lord has poured a "deep sleep" upon the prophets, not for them to receive an encounter with God, as Abram did in his deep sleep (see Gn 15:12ff), but to stupefy and blind the people in order to prevent them from knowing the future.

29:11–12

11And the vision of all this has become to you like the words of a book that is sealed. When men give it to one who can read, saying, "Read this," he says, "I cannot, for it is sealed." 12And when they give the book to one who cannot read, saying, "Read this," he says, "I cannot read."

These verses give a further explanation of the preceding warning with the image of giving a book to an illiterate person and asking him to read it. Just as the illiterate are unable to read a book, so will the prophets and seers be unable to understand what is going to happen. Presumably only Isaiah remains faithful to the Lord and can present authentic prophecies.

—— Isaiah 29:13–14 ——

13And the LORD said: "Because this people draw near with their mouth and honor me with their lips, while their hearts are far from me, and their fear of me is a commandment of men learned by rote; 14therefore, behold, I will again do marvelous things with this people, wonderful and marvelous; and the wisdom of their wise men shall perish, and the discernment of their discerning men shall be hid."

The Lord reproaches the people for honoring Him with their lips when their hearts are far from Him (v. 13, cited by Jesus in Mt 15:8–9). This is followed by a prophecy of warning that the Lord's marvels and wonders will cause the people's wisdom and discernment of the present political situation to perish (v. 14). The so-called wise and discerning people were urging King Hezekiah to join the revolt initiated by Pharaoh Shebitku, whose son, Taharqa (Tirhakah in Is 37:9 and 1 Kgs 19:9) led the army, along with King Luli of Tyre and Sidon, and King Sidka of Ashkelon. Though that advice would perish when all of the rebels were defeated by King Sennacherib of Assyria, yet the Lord will do marvels in saving Jerusalem (see Is 37:36–38).

—— Isaiah 29:15–16 ——

15Woe to those who hide deep from the LORD their counsel, whose deeds are in the dark, and who say, "Who sees us? Who knows us?" 16You turn things upside down! Shall the potter be regarded as the clay; that the thing made should say of its maker, "He did not make me"; or the thing formed say of him who formed it, "He has no understanding"?

A cry of woe (v. 15) is directed to those people who try to hide their ideas from the Lord and say, "Who sees or knows" what we are doing. The woe that dooms them is applied because it is impossible to hide anything from the Lord God, and He will be fully aware of their plans, which contradict His own.

Verse 16 is a reproach to these people, who act as if the Lord their maker did not form them or understand them. The content of the threat remains ominously unstated.

—— Isaiah 29:17–24 ——

A description of salvation as a transformation of the world situation that will lead to authentic recognition of the Lord's glory.

29:17–21

17Is it not yet a very little while until Lebanon shall be turned into a fruitful field, and the fruitful field shall be regarded as a forest? 18In that day the deaf shall hear the words of a book, and out of their gloom and darkness the eyes of the blind shall see. 19The meek shall obtain fresh joy in the LORD, and the poor among men shall exult in the Holy One of Israel. 20For the ruthless shall come to nought and the scoffer cease, and all who watch to do evil shall be cut off, 21who by a word make a man out to be an offender, and lay a snare for him who reproves in the gate, and with an empty plea turn aside him who is in the right.

The salvation takes shape as a transformation of nature (v. 17) and of society (vv. 18–21).

17

The RSV reads "fruitful field," but the Hebrew text reads "Carmel," which means the "vineyard of God" (hence the RSV translation). However, it is better to keep Lebanon and Carmel, which refer to two mountain ranges, the former in Phoenicia, which had been defeated in the revolt against Sennacherib of Assyria, and the latter in Israel. These regions would have been under Assyria's control after the rebellion failed, but here the Lord promises that both mountains will be transformed into fruitful places, like new gardens of Eden.

18–19

The unlikely weak people will be transformed too: the deaf, blind, meek, and poor. This transformation of society will be accomplished by the Lord, and people will exult in the Holy One. Of course, one's thoughts run easily to the Beatitudes, particularly the blessedness of the poor (see Mt 5:3; Lk 6:20) and the meek (Mt 5:5).

20–21

The other side of salvation is the punishment of the ruthless, the scoffers, evil doers, slanderers (v. 21a), those who cannot take a criticism without entrapping the critic (v. 21b), and those who pervert justice for the innocent (v. 21c). Isaiah was well aware of such crimes and reproved the people who committed them.

29:22–24

> **22Therefore thus says the LORD, who redeemed Abraham, concerning the house of Jacob: "Jacob shall no more be ashamed, no more shall his face grow pale. 23For when he sees his children, the work of my hands, in his midst, they will sanctify my name; they will sanctify the Holy One of Jacob, and will stand in awe of the God of Israel. 24And those who err in spirit will come to understanding, and those who murmur will accept instruction."**

In this oracle ("Thus says the Lord"), He identifies Himself as the redeemer of Abraham who addresses the house of Jacob with a proclamation of salvation: no more will the people be ashamed. Jacob will see his children—that is, the descendants whom the Lord has bestowed—then they will sanctify the Lord's name and stand in awe in His presence. Consider this line in light of the way Jesus begins His prayer, "Our Father, who art in heaven, hallowed be thy name" (Mt 6:9; Lk 11:2). "Hallowed" is old English for "sanctified," and Jesus is teaching the need to sanctify the Father's name in prayer, and again in John 17.

This glorification of God will even help the people who err and murmur to understand the truth about God and accept His instruction. The ultimate goal is not their destruction but their conversion.

— Isaiah 30:1–5 —

A proclamation of woe for those who rebel against God by devising their own plans to trust in the power of Pharaoh Shebitku's rebellion against Sennacherib of Assyria.

30:1–3

> **1"Woe to the rebellious children," says the LORD, "who carry out a plan, but not mine; and who make a league, but not of my spirit, that they may add sin to sin; 2who set out to go down to Egypt, without asking for my counsel, to take refuge in the protection of Pharaoh, and to seek shelter in the shadow of Egypt! 3Therefore shall the protection of Pharaoh turn to your shame, and the shelter in the shadow of Egypt to your humiliation.**

Hezekiah joined Judah to Pharaoh's rebellion, which was doomed to fail, so Isaiah warned that those who joined him would be put to shame and humiliation, which indeed took place. Pharaoh Shebitku sent his son Tirhakah (Taharqa) with an army that was defeated in the open field, and so took refuge in Lachish, a Judahite city southwest of Jerusalem. Then Sennacherib attacked Lachish and destroyed it, bringing humiliation to those who trusted the Egyptians.

30:4–5

[4]For though his officials are at Zoan and his envoys reach Hanes, [5]every one comes to shame through a people that cannot profit them, that brings neither help nor profit, but shame and disgrace."

In 715, the same year when Hezekiah became king of Judah, Pharaoh Bakenrenef, the second and last king of the Twenty-Fourth Dynasty of Egypt, died. An Ethiopian Shabaka wiped out any contenders from the Twenty-Fourth Dynasty and went to Memphis to establish the Twenty-Fifth Dynasty. He extended his control over the western oases (Hanes) and the Nile Delta (Zoan, also known as Tanis). Despite the rapid growth of the Ethiopian Dynasty's power, they would be unable to bring profit and would only cause shame, as indeed was the case in 701 BC when the rebellion failed.

—— Isaiah 30:6–7 ——

[6]An oracle on the beasts of the Negeb. Through a land of trouble and anguish, from where come the lioness and the lion, the viper and the flying serpent, they carry their riches on the backs of asses, and their treasures on the humps of camels, to a people that cannot profit them.
[7]For Egypt's help is worthless and empty, therefore I have called her "Rahab who sits still."

The Lord speaks a prophecy of warning to reproach the people for trusting in Egypt. The people may want to do trade with Egypt, but that will not profit them. The journey across the Negeb (Negev) desert was safe from Assyrian attack, since they controlled the road along the Mediterranean Sea. However, the desert was full of other dangers from beasts of prey and poisonous serpents, so the plans remain futile. "Rahab" was an ancient name for the sea that had rebelled against God and was the place of chaos (Jb 9:3; 26:12; Ps 29:10). In the Bible, it came to symbolize Egypt. Here, Rahab is Egypt, not in an effective rebellion but actually sitting still, unable to accomplish anything. Therefore, trusting Egypt is futile.

—— Isaiah 30:8–17 ——

An overview of Isaiah's prophecies during the period of the rebellion against Sennacherib.

30:8

> **8And now, go, write it before them on a tablet, and inscribe it in a book, that it may be for the time to come as a witness for ever.**

First, the Lord commands Isaiah to write this message on a tablet or in a book so as to be a witness against the people.

30:9–11

> **9For they are a rebellious people, lying sons, sons who will not hear the instruction of the Lord; 10who say to the seers, "See not"; and to the prophets, "Prophesy not to us what is right; speak to us smooth things, prophesy illusions, 11leave the way, turn aside from the path, let us hear no more of the Holy One of Israel."**

The reason for the command to write is that the people are rebellious liars who refuse to hear the Lord's instruction. They tell prophets to speak "smooth" easy lessons that are illusions rather than the true path laid out by the Lord.

30:12–14

> **12Therefore thus says the Holy One of Israel, "Because you despise this word, and trust in oppression and perverseness, and rely on them; 13therefore this iniquity shall be to you like a break in a high wall, bulging out, and about to collapse, whose crash comes suddenly, in an instant; 14and its breaking is like that of a potter's vessel which is smashed so ruthlessly that among its fragments not a sherd is found with which to take fire from the hearth, or to dip up water out of the cistern."**

An oracle ("thus says") that prophesies a warning of disaster, like a bulging wall that suddenly collapses or a pottery vessel that shatters into small, unusable pieces. The reason for the disaster is the same as in verses 9–10: they despise God's word and trust in oppression and perversity. While the word of God would be based on His principles of right, people who reject God's word base their decisions on their own ideas. They must use oppression to enforce their ideas because their lack of objective principles makes it necessary to use the principle of "might makes right." Modern people can easily recognize that such is the history of dictatorships well into the present era.

30:15–17

[15]For thus said the LORD God, the Holy One of Israel, "In returning and rest you shall be saved; in quietness and in trust shall be your strength." And you would not, [16]but you said, "No! We will speed upon horses," therefore you shall speed away; and, "We will ride upon swift steeds," therefore your pursuers shall be swift. [17]A thousand shall flee at the threat of one, at the threat of five you shall flee, till you are left like a flagstaff on the top of a mountain, like a signal on a hill.

This oracle ("thus said the Lord") is another prophecy of warning. It begins in verse 15b by reminding the people of the Lord's message that they would be saved if they returned to Him and lived in quiet trust of the Lord. However, they refused to trust the Lord and preferred to trust in cavalry for their speed. The warning in verses 16b-17 is that they will need speed to run away because the victorious Assyrian pursuers will be swift too. It will take very few Assyrians to make the army run away, and the soldiers will be like a lonely flagstaff on a mountain that all can see as an abandoned signal of utter failure and defeat.

—— Isaiah 30:18 ——

[18]Therefore the LORD waits to be gracious to you; therefore he exalts himself to show mercy to you. For the LORD is a God of justice; blessed are all those who wait for him.

This is a distinct prophecy of salvation that ends with a beatitude for those who wait for the Lord. The obvious conclusion is to wait for the Lord in order to receive His gracious mercy.

—— Isaiah 30:19–26 ——

Perhaps in response to the preceding prophecy, the prophet here offers a description of the salvation that the Lord offers.

30:19

> **[19]Yea, O people in Zion who dwell at Jerusalem; you shall weep no more. He will surely be gracious to you at the sound of your cry; when he hears it, he will answer you.**

The prophet addresses the people of Jerusalem to assure them that they will cease weeping because the Lord will answer them.

30:20–21

> **[20]And though the LORD give you the bread of adversity and the water of affliction, yet your Teacher will not hide himself any more, but your eyes shall see your Teacher. [21]And your ears shall hear a word behind you, saying, "This is the way, walk in it," when you turn to the right or when you turn to the left.**

The preceding promise of the Lord's comfort is here followed by the realistic description that they may suffer "adversity" and "affliction" as their food and drink. Yet even if they do suffer, they are still to wait for the Lord their Teacher, whom they will see and hear. Later, Christians would understand this as fulfilled in Jesus Christ, the Lord they could see, hear, and touch (see 1 Jn 1:1–3), who was addressed as "Teacher" (see Mt 10:24–25; 19:16; 26:18; Mk 4:38; 9:38; 10:17, 20; 13:1; 14:14; Lk 6:40; 18:18; 21:7; 22:11; Jn 1:38; 3:2; 11:28; 13:13–14; 20:16—all of these are said by disciples or Jesus; many other uses are made by opponents). Further, Jesus identifies Himself as "the Way" (see Jn 14:6), so He has been understood as the fulfillment of this promise.

30:22

> **[22]Then you will defile your silver-covered graven images and your gold-plated molten images. You will scatter them as unclean things; you will say to them, "Begone!"**

When the people actually start to learn from the Lord, they will "defile"—that is, destroy—their idols, even if they are covered with precious silver and gold. The monetary value will fade in comparison to the good that the Lord will teach them.

30:23–25a

[23]And he will give rain for the seed with which you sow the ground, and grain, the produce of the ground, which will be rich and plenteous. In that day your cattle will graze in large pastures; [24]and the oxen and the asses that till the ground will eat salted provender, which has been winnowed with shovel and fork. [25a]And upon every lofty mountain and every high hill there will be brooks running with water.

The salvation will eventually take them from the "bread of adversity" and the "water of affliction" to a prosperity that comes from abundant rain on their crops and cattle grazing on rich pastures and so much provender that it is fed to them with shovels and pitchforks. While modern farmers are accustomed to fattening cattle on silage in feed lots, this was a luxury reserved only for the richest kings and landowners.

30:25b–26

[25b]In the day of the great slaughter, when the towers fall. [26]Moreover the light of the moon will be as the light of the sun, and the light of the sun will be sevenfold, as the light of seven days, in the day when the LORD binds up the hurt of his people, and heals the wounds inflicted by his blow.

The day of the great slaughter of the enemies and the falling towers of their cities will mark the beginning of the salvation. At that point, the lights of the heavens—sun, moon, and stars—will shine with tremendous brilliance as the Lord binds up His people's wounds. He may have been the one to punish them, but He will also heal them.

—— Isaiah 30:27–33 ——

Here is another description of the Lord's salvation.

30:27–28

[27]Behold, the name of the LORD comes from far, burning with his anger, and in thick rising smoke; his lips are full of indignation, and

his tongue is like a devouring fire; [28]his breath is like an overflowing stream that reaches up to the neck; to sift the nations with the sieve of destruction, and to place on the jaws of the peoples a bridle that leads astray.

The act of salvation begins when the Lord, who is the judge of the nations, comes with burning anger, indignation, and fire. He "sifts" the nations in a sieve in order to judge which are destroyed and which are left for redemption. He is so thoroughly in control that He will even place a bridle on the peoples, and He will lead them "astray—that is, cause them to wander aimlessly because they do not know the Lord.

30:29–30

[29]You shall have a song as in the night when a holy feast is kept; and gladness of heart, as when one sets out to the sound of the flute to go to the mountain of the LORD, to the Rock of Israel. [30]And the LORD will cause his majestic voice to be heard and the descending blow of his arm to be seen, in furious anger and a flame of devouring fire, with a cloudburst and tempest and hailstones.

The people of Israel will rejoice in song when the Lord does judgment. Their joyful singing will be joined by the Lord's majestic voice and His destroying arm in anger and flame. This, of course, refers to a tremendous storm with thunder and lightning that will destroy the enemies with hail and lightning.

30:31–33

[31]The Assyrians will be terror-stricken at the voice of the LORD, when he smites with his rod. [32]And every stroke of the staff of punishment which the LORD lays upon them will be to the sound of timbrels and lyres; battling with brandished arm he will fight with them. [33]For a burning place has long been prepared; yea, for the king it is made ready, its pyre made deep and wide, with fire and wood in abundance; the breath of the LORD, like a stream of brimstone, kindles it.

The final destruction of the Assyrian enemies comes when the Lord's voice in the storm "smites" them with His rod of punishment for attacking Jerusalem, the holy city. The sound of triumphal music, in timbrels and lyres, will accompany this victory, just as Israel's singing would (v. 32).

The final destruction will be in a burning place that will be deep and wide enough to accommodate all the enemies. The source of burning will be the Lord's breath, which pours out "like a stream of brimstone," burning the enemies thoroughly. This image will certainly have an influence on the idea of hell as a place of burning and brimstone, but that will develop later in the Bible (see Is 66:24 in Trito-Isaiah from the fifth century BC, and New Testament teaching about Gehenna).

Lesson 10

Isaiah 31–33

—— Isaiah 31:1–3 ——

This section combines a woe oracle that reproaches those who trust in Egypt and a prophecy of warning against evildoers who trust the Egyptians.

31:1

> **[1]Woe to those who go down to Egypt for help and rely on horses, who trust in chariots because they are many and in horsemen because they are very strong, but do not look to the Holy One of Israel or consult the Lord!**

Woe to those who trust in Egyptian cavalry rather than in the Lord.

31:2–3

> **[2]And yet he is wise and brings disaster, he does not call back his words, but will arise against the house of the evildoers, and against the helpers of those who work iniquity. [3]The Egyptians are men, and not God; and their horses are flesh, and not spirit. When the Lord stretches out his hand, the helper will stumble, and he who is helped will fall, and they will all perish together.**

A prophecy of warning that in fidelity to His word, the Lord will arise against the evildoers who trust in the Egyptians, mere men with horses of flesh. The Lord is God who causes the Egyptian helper to fall, along with the Israelites who trusted in them, such that both will perish.

— Isaiah 31:4–9 —

This section is an oracle ("thus the Lord said") of salvation.

31:4–5

> **4For thus the Lord said to me, As a lion or a young lion growls over his prey, and when a band of shepherds is called forth against him is not terrified by their shouting or daunted at their noise, so the Lord of hosts will come down to fight upon Mount Zion and upon its hill. 5Like birds hovering, so the Lord of hosts will protect Jerusalem; he will protect and deliver it, he will spare and rescue it.**

The oracle of salvation, in which the Lord is like a growling lion who does not fear a band of shepherds coming to attack Him. Therefore, He will not fear the large Assyrian army attacking Jerusalem in 701 BC. He will hover over Jerusalem to protect, deliver, spare, and rescue it.

31:6–7

> **6Turn to him from whom you have deeply revolted, O people of Israel. 7For in that day every one shall cast away his idols of silver and his idols of gold, which your hands have sinfully made for you.**

A summons for the rebellious people who have worshiped idols to turn to the Lord and cast away the idols of silver and gold they have made sinfully.

31:8–9

> **8"And the Assyrian shall fall by a sword, not of man; and a sword, not of man, shall devour him; and he shall flee from the sword, and his young men shall be put to forced labor. 9His rock shall pass away in terror, and his officers desert the standard in panic," says the Lord, whose fire is in Zion, and whose furnace is in Jerusalem.**

The promise of salvation for Israel means the destruction and death of the Assyrians. However, they will not die in battle against the Egyptians or the people of Judah but will die by a non-human sword. This refers to the plague that came upon them during the Assyrian siege of Jerusalem, as described in Isaiah 37:36 and 2 Kings 19:35.

Isaiah 32:1–8

Unlike the typical prophetic style of Isaiah, this passage is a wisdom poem. It lacks the usual oracles from the Lord or direct address to the sinners but acknowledges the good effects of virtue and then contrasts them with the evil effects of the wicked and foolish. Proverbs includes a number of sayings that link the king with justice and righteousness (see Prv 16:10, 13; 20:28). Proverbs 25 is described as "the proverbs of Solomon which the men of Hezekiah king of Judah copied" and contains a number of wisdom sayings about the role of the king. The wisdom about the kings, plus the contrast of good and evil, flow from the wisdom tradition, influencing the prophet Amos, and later Jeremiah and Ezekiel, who used proverbs and wisdom imagery in their ministry. Inclusion of wisdom motifs fit the sophisticated character of Isaiah, while remaining distinctive in this passage.

32:1–5

> **1Behold, a king will reign in righteousness, and princes will rule in**
> **justice. 2Each will be like a hiding place from the wind, a covert from**
> **the tempest, like streams of water in a dry place, like the shade of a**
> **great rock in a weary land. 3Then the eyes of those who see will not be**
> **closed, and the ears of those who hear will hearken. 4The mind of the**
> **rash will have good judgment, and the tongue of the stammerers will**
> **speak readily and distinctly. 5The fool will no more be called noble,**
> **nor the knave said to be honorable.**

This section describes the messianic king and his reign in righteousness and justice as the condition for a good society. The use of the future tense in these verses combines wisdom ideas about the effects of the righteous king with the prophetic hope for the future laid out in the preceding oracles and descriptions of salvation.

1–2

The hope for a future righteous king and just princes compares them to welcome relief in various difficult circumstances: a shelter from winds or storms; streams in the desert; shade in a hot weary land. The prophecy of the Messiah in Isaiah 11:1–5 brings out both the gifts of the Spirit of the Lord that lead to wisdom and understanding (11:2–3, also influenced by the wisdom tradition) and to judgment in righteousness that is not through mere externals (11:4–5). Such hopes arise whenever people change rulers, praying that the next one will be better than the previous. Since this process continues through the ages, the hope for a Messiah stays active in the hearts of the faithful.

3–5

Having a righteous king and just princes leads to an entire nation's moral improvement. Modern people understand that dictators and oppressors are the gatekeepers of information, using propaganda and deceit to sway their citizens, usually to act wickedly. The righteous king will let people see and hear true knowledge (v. 3), leading the rash to have good judgment and "stammerers"—that is, those who do not know what to say about various issues—to speak clearly. The truth about fools and knaves will be known, and once they are exposed, the people will reject them in favor of the king's righteousness (v. 5).

32:6–8

> **6For the fool speaks folly, and his mind plots iniquity: to practice ungodliness, to utter error concerning the LORD, to leave the craving of the hungry unsatisfied, and to deprive the thirsty of drink. 7The knaveries of the knave are evil; he devises wicked devices to ruin the poor with lying words, even when the plea of the needy is right. 8But he who is noble devises noble things, and by noble things he stands.**

As is seen throughout Proverbs, this section describes the fools and the wicked. Such descriptions are meant to motivate the wise observer to avoid folly and wickedness and choose wisdom and virtue. Notice the progression in verse 6 from speaking folly to plotting iniquity to practicing ungodliness, uttering theological errors about the Lord, and finally neglect of the poor. The fool does not start out to neglect the poor, but the progression from folly to wickedness and falsehood develops easily. Similarly, in verse 7, the knaves make evil plans to ruin the poor with lies in the courtroom, using the institution of justice to pervert justice. In contrast, the obvious conclusion is to seek righteousness, opening one's eyes to what is true so as to become one of the noble, dignified people who join the righteous king in doing right (v. 8). These factual statements are meant to evoke a decision to join the king.

— Isaiah 32:9–14 —

A prophecy of warning to the complacent women of Jerusalem, as was the case in an earlier prophecy in Isaiah 3:16ff.

32:9

> **9Rise up, you women who are at ease, hear my voice; you complacent daughters, give ear to my speech.**

A summons for the women and girls to listen to the prophet, using terms typical of wisdom literature where both wisdom and folly are personified as women.

32:10

> **10In little more than a year you will shudder, you complacent women; for the vintage will fail, the fruit harvest will not come.**

The warning that the grape and fruit harvest will fail within a year.

32:11–12

> **11Tremble, you women who are at ease, shudder, you complacent ones; strip, and make yourselves bare, and gird sackcloth upon your loins.**
> **12Beat upon your breasts for the pleasant fields, for the fruitful vine,**

Here the prophet commands the wealthy women at ease to show signs of grief for the loss of grapes and fruit. Such loss of food and danger of starvation transfer the women from ease and comfort to bodily actions that are signs of grief.

32:13–14

> **13for the soil of my people growing up in thorns and briers; yea, for all the joyous houses in the joyful city.**
> **14For the palace will be forsaken, the populous city deserted; the hill and the watchtower will become dens for ever, a joy of wild asses, a pasture of flocks;**

The reasons for the grieving will be the abandonment of the fields, which will become full of thorns and briars when they are no longer tended. This will result in a lack of wine for the "joyous houses" and the forsaking of the palace and city.

—— Isaiah 32:15–20 ——

This is a description of salvation that is meant to go along with 32:9–14 by looking beyond the present distress to the transformation of the land that the Spirit will accomplish.

32:15

> **15Until the Spirit is poured upon us from on high, and the wilderness becomes a fruitful field, and the fruitful field is deemed a forest.**

The Spirit of the Lord will be the necessary gift that precedes the return to abundant crops even in the wilderness. This gift of the Spirit that fills the Messiah (Is 11:1–5) led to a transformation of all the earth and its animals (11:6–9). So, too, here the Spirit will make the desert and forest into places of abundant crops.

32:16–18

> **16Then justice will dwell in the wilderness, and righteousness abide in the**
> **fruitful field. 17And the effect of righteousness will be peace, and the re-**
> **sult of righteousness, quietness and trust for ever. 18My people will abide**
> **in a peaceful habitation, in secure dwellings, and in quiet resting places.**

Beyond the increase of crops, the Spirit will effect justices and righteousness that bring about peace, quiet, and trust among the inhabitants of the land after the Assyrian army has departed (see v. 19).

32:19

> **19And the forest will utterly go down, and the city will be utterly laid low.**

The "forest" is a symbol of the enemy army, since they march with a "forest" of spears, bows, and other weapons. The "city" refers to the Assyrian capital, which will be destroyed.

32:20

[20]Happy are you who sow beside all waters, who let the feet of the ox and the ass range free.

The whole passage concludes with a beatitude for those who live near water and allow their oxen and asses to roam freely. No one will steal them, they will be strong after eating well, and they will be able to work the wilderness and forests to make them as fruitful as verse 15 promises.

—— Isaiah 33:1–24 ——

This passage is rather complicated, but it seems to be a lament that is answered by an oracle of salvation. As in many distressful situations, people experience a variety of sometimes contradicting moods and feelings. So too, here are the different aspects of reaction to danger that get expressed as each segment is defined.

33:1

[1]Woe to you, destroyer, who yourself have not been destroyed; you treacherous one, with whom none has dealt treacherously! When you have ceased to destroy, you will be destroyed; and when you have made an end of dealing treacherously, you will be dealt with treacherously.

This is a proclamation of woe to a treacherous destroyer whom no one else has destroyed or dealt treacherously. This "treacherous destroyer" is not identified more fully anywhere in this chapter, but one may assume that it refers to the Assyrian enemy. The content of the woe is that now he will be destroyed and dealt with treacherously, presumably by the Lord. This woe introduces the psalm with an objective overview about what is happening from the Lord's perspective.

33:2

[2]O LORD, be gracious to us; we wait for thee. Be our arm every morning, our salvation in the time of trouble.

The human experience of the distress begins here with petitions "in the time of trouble" that give the quality of lament to the prayer. The Lord is directly addressed to be gracious because the troubled people are waiting for Him. They want Him as their "arm"—their strength and salvation—since they recognize their own weakness.

33:3–4

> **[3]At the thunderous noise peoples flee, at the lifting up of yourself nations are scattered; [4]and spoil is gathered as the caterpillar gathers; as locusts leap, men leap upon it.**

They express confidence in the power of the Lord's thunder and lifting Himself up. The Lord is clearly fighting for them, so the enemy nations scatter and leave behind spoils, which Israel then gathers like caterpillars or locusts swarming a field. This refers to Isaiah 37:36 and 2 Kings 19:35, which attribute the departure of the Assyrian army from Jerusalem to the Lord's angel slaying them, apparently by a plague. Presumably, after the Assyrian survivors left, the people despoiled them.

33:5–6

> **[5]The LORD is exalted, for he dwells on high; he will fill Zion with justice and righteousness; [6]and he will be the stability of your times, abundance of salvation, wisdom, and knowledge; the fear of the LORD is his treasure.**

The Lord's victory is followed by a hymn, which recognizes that the exalted Lord dwells "on high" in heaven and at the same time is present on earth to fill Zion with justice and righteousness, the qualities that the wisdom poem above ascribed to the king (Is 32:1). His presence on earth will bring "stability," "abundance of salvation, wisdom, knowledge and fear of the Lord." These are precisely what the Lord's Spirit would bring the Davidic Messiah (Is 11:2–5) but now will fill all of Jerusalem.

33:7–9

> **[7]Behold, the valiant ones cry without; the envoys of peace weep bitterly. [8]The highways lie waste, the wayfaring man ceases. Covenants are broken, witnesses are despised, there is no regard for man. [9]The land mourns and languishes; Lebanon is confounded and withers away; Sharon is like a desert; and Bashan and Carmel shake off their leaves.**

The response to the promise of salvation and the hymn (33:3–6) is a return to the present realities, which are quite unpleasant.

7

The word for "valiant ones" (*erellam*) is very obscure and may be related to "Ariel" (Is 29:1, 2), as the "residents of Ariel," though others assume the word means "lion," hence "valiant ones." In either definition, these locals are "crying"—that is, "screaming" outside—while the envoys of peace weep bitterly. This certainly recalls the encounter between the Assyrian Rabshakeh and Hezekiah's ambassadors (Is 36, especially vv. 21–22, where they are silent to the abshakeh but rend their clothes in grief).

8

The catastrophe causes human commerce to cease, since the Assyrians control the roads and no one can fulfill promises and covenants with each other.

9

Finally, the land itself grieves throughout the districts. Lebanon's King Luli had joined the Egyptian rebellion against Assyria and was the first country to fall to Sennacherib's forces. Sharon, the usually green coastal area is like a desert, Bashan, a fertile plateau in modern central Jordan, and Mt. Carmel on Israel's west coast are losing the leaves off their trees. The land feels the catastrophe of the Assyrian invasion.

33:10–13

> **10"Now I will arise," says the LORD, "now I will lift myself up; now**
> **I will be exalted. 11You conceive chaff, you bring forth stubble; your**
> **breath is a fire that will consume you. 12And the peoples will be as**
> **if burned to lime, like thorns cut down, that are burned in the fire."**
> **13Hear, you who are far off, what I have done; and you who are near,**
> **acknowledge my might.**

The Lord responds to these troubles with an oracle of salvation, promising to arise to help Israel against the enemies first (v. 10). First, the enemy is like chaff or stubble that breathes out the fire of its own quick self-destruction (v. 11). They will be burned, like lime, which is burned before being used to enrich soil, or like thorns burned in a sudden blaze of a fire (v. 12). Yes, the Lord's might is far superior than the greatest of armies. This is the good news for all people.

33:14–16

14The sinners in Zion are afraid; trembling has seized the godless: "Who among us can dwell with the devouring fire? Who among us can dwell with everlasting burnings?" 15He who walks righteously and speaks uprightly, who despises the gain of oppressions, who shakes his hands, lest they hold a bribe, who stops his ears from hearing of bloodshed and shuts his eyes from looking upon evil, 16he will dwell on the heights; his place of defense will be the fortresses of rocks; his bread will be given him, his water will be sure.

At the same time, when the Lord arises (v. 10), not only are the foreign invaders in fear, but so are the sinners in Zion as their rhetorical question about dwelling with God's everlasting fire seeks an answer. However, in Psalms 15 and 24, guardians at the Temple gate ask, "Who can enter the Temple?" and give answers based on authentic morality. Here the answers are similar: walking righteously, speaking uprightly, despising oppression, bribes, bloodshed, and evil (v. 15). As in Psalms 15 and 24, those who can answer correctly will dwell in safety, with enough bread and water, even when the Lord's devouring fire blazes against the wicked.

33:17–19

17Your eyes will see the king in his beauty; they will behold a land that stretches afar. 18Your mind will muse on the terror: "Where is he who counted, where is he who weighed the tribute? Where is he who counted the towers?" 19You will see no more the insolent people, the people of an obscure speech which you cannot comprehend, stammering in a tongue which you cannot understand.

A description of two sides of the Lord's salvation.

17

The people will see the king in his beauty, referring to his royal garments instead of the sackcloth he wore during the siege (see Is 37:1; 2 Kgs 19:1).

Also, the people will be able to view their land stretching off into the distance, without enemies blocking the view or hunting them down.

18–19

The other side of salvation is that the people will only have to look back on the Assyrians, musing with questions about the mighty army, "Where are they now?" The insolent foreigners will no more be seen in the land.

33:20–22

> **[20]Look upon Zion, the city of our appointed feasts! Your eyes will see Jerusalem, a quiet habitation, an immovable tent, whose stakes will never be plucked up, nor will any of its cords be broken. [21]But there the Lord in majesty will be for us a place of broad rivers and streams, where no galley with oars can go, nor stately ship can pass. [22]For the Lord is our judge, the Lord is our ruler, the Lord is our king; he will save us.**

In response, the people together express their confidence that Zion Jerusalem, the place of feasts to the Lord, will be immovable (v. 20). However, the true source of strength is the Lord in His majesty. Broad rivers and streams, such as the Nile, Tigris, and Euphrates, along which the great empires had been built, were used for protection, for navies, and trade. The Lord's majesty will be like such a river, but not a physical river that can actually be navigated. His presence is Jerusalem's protection, and that is enough (v. 21). His role as judge, ruler, and king will be the source of salvation in which the people can be confident (v. 22).

33:23–24

> **[23]Your tackle hangs loose; it cannot hold the mast firm in its place, or keep the sail spread out. Then prey and spoil in abundance will be divided; even the lame will take the prey. [24]And no inhabitant will say, "I am sick"; the people who dwell there will be forgiven their iniquity.**

Finally, two other aspects of salvation are described here. First, the enemy ships will fail, so their goods will be taken as spoils by the people of Jerusalem (v. 23). After the siege of Jerusalem, many people would be weak with hunger and susceptible to disease, especially dysentery from bad water and food. Second, sickness will cease and the sinners will be forgiven (v. 24). Both physical and spiritual disorder will be repaired by the Lord, who saves thoroughly from enemies, sin, and disease.

Lesson 11

Isaiah 36–39: Historical Narratives

Isaiah did not compose these four chapters; rather, they center on episodes with King Hezekiah that concern Isaiah. The history of Israel found in Joshua, Judges, Samuel, and Kings is a long work known as the "Deuteronomistic History." These books contain very old materials from a number of sources (which are frequently mentioned throughout the books, including the royal chronicles, the "Wars of the Lord," and others). These historical books are guided by the principles laid down in Deuteronomy, and they use a fairly consistent style of Hebrew writing, especially in the editorialized sections. The Deuteronomistic style is quite different from the writing style of Isaiah, so these chapters were clearly imported into the book at a later stage of its final editing.

Isaiah 36–39 come directly from 2 Kings 18:13, 17–20:19 and 2 Chronicles 32:1, 9–26. Since 2 Kings concludes the whole Deuteronomistic history with the release of King Jehoiachin from a Babylonian prison in 561 BC (an event also recorded by the Babylonians, see Pritchard ANET 308 for the full clay tablet text), it therefore follows that Kings was not finished until after that final event. This means that these passages from 2 Kings found in Isaiah 36–39 were written down at least 170 years after Isaiah's lifetime, though they describe a number of events that concern Isaiah's contacts with King Hezekiah, who ruled from 715 to 687 BC. Isaiah 36–39 treat three events: the invasion of Judah by King Sennacherib of Assyria in 701 BC (36–37), Hezekiah's deadly sickness and healing (38), and the visit of Babylonian ambassadors (39), each of which we will examine here.

Note, however, that Isaiah 28–33 belong to this period between 705 and 700, when Isaiah excoriates Judah for relying on political alliances with Egypt to fight Assyria. In place of such alliances, Isaiah calls the people to repent of injustice and rely on the Lord.

— Isaiah 36–37 —

The episode begins in Hezekiah's fourteenth year as king, which was 701 BC. Tirhakah (Egyptian "Taharqa"), the son of Egyptian Pharaoh Shebitku, had led an army against the Assyrians, while King Luli of Tyre and Sidon and King Sidka of Ashkelon joined the revolt against Assyria. Sennacherib reconquered Phoenicia first, replacing Luli with Ethbaal as king of Tyre and Sidon. Next, he reconquered the Philistine cities and defeated Tirhakah (Taharqa), who retreated to the Judahite city of Lachish, which the Assyrians attacked, forcing Taharqa to retreat to Egypt (Is 36:1–2 summarizes this attack). Sennacherib then attacked other cities in Judah. A room in Sennacherib's palace was decorated with stone panels of bas reliefs depicting the siege and conquest of Lachish—now located in the British Museum in London. After his success at Lachish, Sennacherib sent "Rabshakeh," which means "chief cupbearer," who was an important official. Hezekiah sent three of his officials to receive his message. Note that it begins, "Thus says the great king" (v. 3), which shows that this was a standard opening of messages, hence the name "messenger formula" applied to oracles from the Lord, who is the great king. The message (36:3–10) warns Hezekiah that he cannot trust in words as a strategy, nor in Egypt, nor in the Lord, since Hezekiah had destroyed the high places (i.e., shrines.) The Rabshakeh thinks these were the Lord's sanctuaries. However, they were dedicated to Baal, and Hezekiah destroyed them as part of his fidelity to the Lord. (See 2 Kgs 18:3–7 for a report on the Lord's pleasure in Hezekiah's purification of the land of the high places.) In fact, the Rabshakeh claims that the Lord told Assyria to destroy Judah, as was said by Isaiah in Isaiah 10:5–7.

— Isaiah 36:11–20 —

The Judahite officials try to get the Rabshakeh to speak Aramaic, which was the international language of diplomacy, to prevent the soldiers from understanding the Rabshakeh's threats. However, the Rabshakeh insists on using Hebrew and speaks loudly to the soldiers to make sure they understand the threat of impending Assyrian doom that awaits them. He tells the soldiers to trust neither Hezekiah nor the Lord but rather trust Sennacherib who promises land and prosperity to any traitors in the city (vv. 16–17). He warns them that the gods of the nations could not save them, and neither can the Lord save Jerusalem (vv. 18–20). The irony is that by saying the Lord is as weak as the other gods, the Rabshakeh is undermining his case with the Lord. In the face of these threats and promises, the people are silent and the Judahite diplomats are afraid (vv. 21–22).

— Isaiah 37:1–4 —

These verses relate Hezekiah's fear at the threats, but his response is to go pray in the Temple and send both government officials and priests to Isaiah to ask for his prayers. Since the Rabshakeh had insulted the Lord, maybe the Lord will punish the Assyrians instead of the Judahites.

— Isaiah 37:6–7 —

> **6Isaiah said to them, "Say to your master, 'Thus says the Lord: Do not be afraid because of the words that you have heard, with which the servants of the king of Assyria have reviled me. 7Behold, I will put a spirit in him, so that he shall hear a rumor, and return to his own land; and I will make him fall by the sword in his own land.'"**

When Hezekiah sends messengers to Isaiah, he relates an oracle of assurance, beginning with the messenger formula ("Thus says the Lord") that the Rabshakeh had used, though from his king. The assurance begins with a command, "do not be afraid," typical for those who are in the Lord's presence. Since the Assyrian officials had reviled the Lord in the process of making their arrogant threats, the Lord will put “a spirit” in Sennacherib that makes him follow a rumor to return to Assyria, where he will die.

—— Isaiah 37:8–13 ——

Rabshakeh returns after Sennacherib’s victory at Lachish with a second message, which entails the disconcerting news that Tirhakah (Taharqa) was attacking. This may refer to another revolt in 690 when Prince Tirhakah again revolted against Sennacherib and convinced Hezekiah to join him in the revolt. While this revolt occurred, Pharaoh Shebitku died and Tirhakah became the third and last king of the Twenty-Fifth Dynasty from Kush (Ethiopia). The emphasis in Isaiah 37:10–13 is on the message rather than the details of the historical background. The Rabshakeh again tells Hezekiah not to rely on God’s promise to protect Jerusalem from Sennacherib because God is no stronger than the gods of the other nations that Sennacherib has conquered.

—— Isaiah 37:14–20 ——

Hezekiah responds to the threat by praying to the Lord of hosts, God of Israel, “enthroned above the cherubim,” the only God of the earth’s kingdoms, who “made heaven and earth” (37:16). He asks the Lord to see and hear Sennacherib’s words that “mock the living God” (37:17). Hezekiah admits that the Assyrians have conquered the nations and destroyed their gods, but “they were no gods, but the work of men’s hands, wood and stone” (37:18–19). He concludes by asking the Lord to save them since He “alone” is the Lord (37:20). Hezekiah’s faith in the Lord as the only God was the strength he sought against Sennacherib’s arrogance.

—— Isaiah 37:21–35 ——

In response to the prayer, Isaiah delivered a message with four parts. First, the oracle that the Lord has heard Hezekiah’s prayer: “Thus says the Lord, the God of Israel,” who will save Jerusalem because of the prayer of faith.

Second, the Lord heard that Sennacherib had mocked Jerusalem (37:22) but poses to him rhetorical questions, "Whom have you mocked and reviled? Against whom have you raised your voice and haughtily lifted your eyes?" He sees "the Holy One of Israel" as the real object of Assyrian mockery (37:23). A list of Assyrian boasts about their conquests (37:24–27) is answered by the Lord, against whom Sennacherib has "raged" with "arrogance." Therefore, the Lord decrees, "I will put my hook in your nose and my bit in your mouth, and I will turn you back on the way by which you came" (37:28–29). Third, the Lord promises Jerusalem and Judah that they will eat produce that grows spontaneously for two years and then be able to plant their farms (37:30). A remnant of survivors will be saved in Jerusalem by the zeal of the Lord (37:31–32). Fourth, the Lord decrees that Sennacherib will not attack nor conquer Jerusalem but will return home because the Lord "will defend this city to save it, for my own sake and for the sake of my servant David" (37:33–35).

Isaiah 37:36–38

The aftermath was that Sennacherib attacked Judah, taking forty-six cities and forts, capturing 200,150 prisoners, and increasing Judah's tribute (2 Kgs 18:14–16 says that Hezekiah paid three hundred talents of silver and thirty talents of gold, which were stripped from the Temple's silver and gold leaf ornamentation). However, Jerusalem was not captured, and Hezekiah kept his throne, which was not the case with other kings conquered by Sennacherib in Phoenicia and Philistia. Both Isaiah 37:36 and 2 Kings 19:35 credit the departure of the Assyrian army from Jerusalem to the Lord's angel slaying them, apparently by a plague, as in the tenth plague in Egypt (see Ex 11:4–6; 12:12–13, 23, 29–30).

Sennacherib returned to Assyria, and in 681, he was assassinated by his two older sons (Is 37:37–38; see also 2 Kgs 19:36–37; 2 Chr 32:21). The Assyrian records are silent on this point, except for some hints that his older sons were envious of the appointment of their younger brother, Esarhaddon, as the heir apparent. However, the Babylonian Chronicles and the Nabonidus Inscription confirm the Bible's story of Sennacherib's assassination.

— Isaiah 38 —

Isaiah 38 treats an occasion when Hezekiah became sick to "the point of death" and Isaiah told him to prepare for death (38:1). Still, Hezekiah prayed, asking the Lord to "remember now . . . how I have walked before thee in faithfulness and with a whole heart, and have done what is good in thy sight" (38:2–3). Again, the Lord responded through Isaiah to Hezekiah's prayer and promised to add fifteen years to his life as well as deliver him and the city from the Assyrians (see 38:4–6). He even added a sign that He would fulfill the promise: the sun will turn back ten degrees on a sundial, which the text reports as having happened (see 37:7–8)

38:9 says that Hezekiah wrote a prayer after his recovery, which is an individual song of thanksgiving (37:10–20).

38:10–15

> **10I said, In the noontide of my days I must depart; I am consigned to the gates of Sheol for the rest of my years. 11I said, I shall not see the LORD in the land of the living; I shall look upon man no more among the inhabitants of the world. 12My dwelling is plucked up and removed from me like a shepherd's tent; like a weaver I have rolled up my life; he cuts me off from the loom; from day to night thou dost bring me to an end; 13I cry for help until morning; like a lion he breaks all my bones; from day to night thou dost bring me to an end. 14Like a swallow or a crane I clamor, I moan like a dove. My eyes are weary with looking upward. O LORD, I am oppressed; be thou my security! 15But what can I say? For he has spoken to me, and he himself has done it. All my sleep has fled because of the bitterness of my soul.**

This section looks back to the suffering with the phrases, "I said" (vv. 10, 11) and describes the profound pain he felt.

10–12

These verses describe various ways of accepting the nearness of death: "consigned to Sheol" (the place to which the shades of the dead went);

seeing neither the Lord nor man in the world; plucking up his tent; rolling up life; cutting the thread. This is a sad recitation of different ways of describing death.

13–14

As would be typical of laments, the painful crying out to the Lord ends with a plea, "be my security."

15

However, he recognizes that the Lord is the one who brought him close to death, which implies, the question: So what is the use of praying? All he knows at this point is bitterness.

38:16–20

> **[16]O LORD, by these things men live, and in all these is the life of my**
> **spirit. Oh, restore me to health and make me live! [17]Lo, it was for my**
> **welfare that I had great bitterness; but thou hast held back my life**
> **from the pit of destruction, for thou hast cast all my sins behind thy**
> **back. [18]For Sheol cannot thank thee, death cannot praise thee; those**
> **who go down to the pit cannot hope for thy faithfulness. [19]The living,**
> **the living, he thanks thee, as I do this day; the father makes known**
> **to the children thy faithfulness. [20]The LORD will save me, and we will**
> **sing to stringed instruments all the days of our life, at the house of**
> **the LORD.**

A petition and a description of the Lord's deliverance.

16

Despite the tremendous pain and seeming uselessness of prayer, since the Lord had brought the sickness about, he prays anyway: "Restore me to health and make me live!"

17

This gives a retrospect on the sickness, recognizing that it was for his own good, apparently because it led him to repent of his sins. The Lord did not let him die and kept him from "the pit of destruction."

18–19

He now gives the reasons why the Lord saved him: people cannot thank and praise the Lord in Sheol; only the living can thank God. Therefore, it was good to keep him alive so he could offer praise, as seen in this psalm of thanksgiving.

20

A proclamation that the Lord will save him and that he will sing hymns in the Temple for the rest of his life.

38:21–22

The aftermath, according to which Isaiah orders a poultice of dried figs which was applied to Hezekiah's boil (v. 21). Oddly, Hezekiah asks for a sign that he will recover and return to worshiping in the Temple (v. 22), while the sign was already described above in 38:4–6.

— Isaiah 39 —
The Babylonian Embassy

The historical background to this episode is the complex relationship between Babylon and Assyria. In 729, the Assyrian king Tiglath-Pileser invaded and captured Babylon, killed King Nabu-ukin-zer, and called himself the "king of Babylon," out of Assyrian respect for Babylon as the source of Assyrian culture. In 721, Merodach-Baladan II, a Chaldean, became the king of Babylon and revolted successfully against Assyria. However, in 711, the Assyrian king, Sargon, conquered Babylon from the Chaldeans and returned it to the native Babylonians. Then in 703, a Chaldean named Marduk-zakir-shum II, took Babylon from King Sennacherib of Assyria and reigned as its king for a month, followed by Merodach-Baladan II, who ruled for nine months. King Sennacherib of Assyria defeated him on the plains of Kish and forced him to flee into the swamps to save his life. In 700, King Bel-Ibni rebelled against Sennacherib but died, so in 699, Sennacherib appointed his son, Ashur-nadin-shumi as the king of Babylon. In 694, in another rebellion against the Assyrians, the Babylonians killed King Ashur-nadinshumi, Sennacherib's son. The next year, 693, Nergal-ushezib, a Chaldean, became the king of Babylon for a year, followed in 692 by Mushezib-Marduk, another Chaldean, who badly beat Sennacherib in battle in 691. Finally, in 689, Sennacherib put down the revolt and sacked the city of Babylon. From this point on, Sennacherib ruled Babylon, as did his son, Esarhaddon. This context of revolt in Babylon, Egypt, and Judah might explain how there could be a defeat of Judah and yet a retreat by the Assyrians from capitalizing on their victory. After Judah and Egypt were reconquered, Sennacherib had to leave for Mesopotamia to finish dealing with the Babylonians. For this reason, he accepted Judah's tribute at Nineveh. This would also allow for Hezekiah to have won some sort of victory, or at least a stalemate, in the attack on Jerusalem in 701.

39:1–8

Hezekiah welcomed envoys from Merodach-baladan, who was king of Babylon between 721 and 711. Hezekiah displayed his wealth to the envoys in order to show off and to indicate interest in an alliance against the Assyrians who ruled both nations (39:1–2).

Isaiah learned from Hezekiah that they were Babylonians who had seen everything he owned (39:3–4). In response, Isaiah spoke an oracle from the Lord that everything Hezekiah owns and his family will all be taken away to Babylon (39:5–7). Hezekiah gives one of the most cynical responses possible when he tells Isaiah, "The word of the LORD which you have spoken is good." For he thought, "There will be peace and security in my days" (39:8).

This episode points to the destruction of Jerusalem and the whole kingdom by the Babylonians in 587. As such, it forms a very good link to Deutero-Isaiah (40–55), which belongs to a later period when the exile in Babylon has taken place and is about to come to an end in the 540s BC.

Lesson 12

Deutero-Isaiah 40–41

As stated in the introduction, chapters 40 through 55 are identified as Deutero-Isaiah, which means "second Isaiah." These chapters belong to the period of the Babylonian exile, particularly the late 540s BC when Cyrus the king of Persia was about to complete his conquest of the Babylonian Empire. We will abbreviate Deutero-Isaiah (D-I) here. The intent of the commentary is to help make sense of the texts by connecting them to the historical background.

—— Isaiah 40:1–11 ——
The Summons to Be a Prophet to the Exiles

In chapter 6 we saw an account of Isaiah's call to be a prophet, or at least, a reassurance of the call. Jeremiah 1 and Ezekiel 1–2 also describe such prophetic calls. This section is also such a call, without indicating the prophet's name, since the purpose is to present the message and not the life of the messenger. This unit has four parts to it.

40:1–2

> **1Comfort, comfort my people, says your God. 2Speak tenderly to Jerusalem, and cry to her that her warfare is ended, that her iniquity is pardoned, that she has received from the Lord's hand double for all her sins.**

The verbs of the first section are all plural imperatives, by which God orders a group of people to comfort the people and speak tenderly to Jerusalem that the double punishment she has received is at an end. This is the core of D-I's message: the exile occurred because Judah had sinned and God punished the sin by removing the people from the land, as Moses had threatened would happen if the people broke the covenant. However, at this point, the punishment is completed and the message of comfort is to be proclaimed to the exiles in Babylon as well as to any of the survivors in the ruins of Jerusalem. The real this comfort is that iniquity is now pardoned, and God has forgiven the people.

40:3–5

3A voice cries: "In the wilderness prepare the way of the LORD, make straight in the desert a highway for our God. 4Every valley shall be lifted up, and every mountain and hill be made low; the uneven ground shall become level, and the rough places a plain. 5And the glory of the LORD shall be revealed, and all flesh shall see it together, for the mouth of the LORD has spoken."

The anonymous voice of the prophet cries out plural imperatives to a group, "prepare the way" and "make straight" the highway that will lead the people out of exile and back to the promised land. Here D-I introduces one of his most important themes—the Exodus from Egypt is the prototype of all salvation. Therefore, the Lord will save Israel from Babylonian exile the way He saved the people from Egypt. This salvation will manifest the glory of the Lord to all flesh, and its occurrence is certain because the Lord has proclaimed it. Later, in the first centuries BC and AD, the Dead Sea Scrolls will use 40:3 more often than any other text, and the four Gospels will mention it in reference to John the Baptist's ministry in the desert to indicate his preparation for Christ.

40:6–8

6A voice says, "Cry!" And I said, "What shall I cry?" All flesh is grass, and all its beauty is like the flower of the field. 7The grass withers, the flower fades, when the breath of the LORD blows upon it; surely the people is grass. 8The grass withers, the flower fades; but the word of our God will stand for ever.

The prophet hears a voice telling him to announce the futility of all humanity in the face of the eternal word of God. At the time, Babylon seemed to be a mighty human power and tiny Israel appeared to be in a hopeless situation because of its obvious defeat and smallness. However, the Lord assures the prophet that all human beings fade like grass and that God's word determines history. A scan of history indicates that every great empire has been destroyed and has faded into obscurity. Until nineteenth-century explorers and archaeologists from Christian lands learned to read ancient languages, the literature of these great civilizations was lost. However, the Word of God was proclaimed throughout them and continues its spread, and will do so long after modern philosophers have become footnotes to history.

40:9–11

> **[9]Get you up to a high mountain, O Zion, herald of good tidings; lift up your voice with strength, O Jerusalem, herald of good tidings, lift it up, fear not; say to the cities of Judah, "Behold your God!" [10]Behold, the LORD God comes with might, and his arm rules for him; behold, his reward is with him, and his recompense before him. [11]He will feed his flock like a shepherd, he will gather the lambs in his arms, he will carry them in his bosom, and gently lead those that are with young.**

The imperatives ("get up," "lift up," "fear not," "say") are all feminine singular, and the word "herald" is a feminine form, since "Zion," "Jerusalem," is the one who will do the proclaiming. Cities and nations are feminine in Hebrew because they are the mother of the people who inhabit them. Later, D-I will describe Jerusalem as a widow whom the Lord marries so she can bring forth many children (see Is 54). Here, Zion's message is: "Behold your God" who is strong and powerful, a shepherd who will feed his flock and return them to their true pasture in the promised land.

—— 40:12–31 ——
The Lord's Disputation with Israel

The opening proclamation of salvation and release from exile is apparently not well-received. The people do not believe the Lord can accomplish this new exodus, so the prophet speaks the Lord's response in the form of a disputation with them. Each of the four sections in this unit begins with rhetorical questions that let the Lord make assertions that contradict the assumptions held by the Jewish exiles in Babylon in regard to their plight there.

40:12–17

> **[12]Who has measured the waters in the hollow of his hand and marked off the heavens with a span, enclosed the dust of the earth in a measure and weighed the mountains in scales and the hills in a balance? [13]Who has directed the Spirit of the LORD, or as his counselor has instructed him? [14]Whom did he consult for his enlightenment, and who taught him the path of justice, and taught him knowledge, and showed him the way of understanding? [15]Behold, the nations are like a drop from a bucket, and are accounted as the dust on the scales; behold, he takes up the isles like fine dust. [16]Lebanon would not suffice for fuel, nor are its beasts enough for a burnt offering. [17]All the nations are as nothing before him, they are accounted by him as less than nothing and emptiness.**

Three rhetorical questions about the Lord's power and wisdom begin the unit. Presumably the exiles had come to believe that the Lord allowed them to go into exile because He was in fact powerless to prevent the catastrophe. The questions about His Spirit and wisdom assume that the exiles believed their exile to be foolish or without logical purpose.

In answer to these questions, the Lord asserts that the nations who defeated Judah and brought the people into captivity are tiny and insignificant, "less than nothing and emptiness." Therefore the exile of Judah to Babylon is not the result of the Lord's weakness but is caused by something else. The answer is not stated here, but later it will be clear that Judah went into exile as a punishment for its sins.

40:18–24

> **[18]To whom then will you liken God, or what likeness compare with him? [19]The idol! a workman casts it, and a goldsmith overlays it with gold, and casts for it silver chains. [20]He who is impoverished chooses for an offering wood that will not rot; he seeks out a skilful craftsman to set up an image that will not move. [21]Have you not known? Have you not heard? Has it not been told you from the beginning? Have you not understood from the foundations of the earth? [22]It is he who sits above the circle of the earth, and its inhabitants are like grasshoppers;**

who stretches out the heavens like a curtain, and spreads them like a tent to dwell in; [23]who brings princes to nought, and makes the rulers of the earth as nothing. [24]Scarcely are they planted, scarcely sown, scarcely has their stem taken root in the earth, when he blows upon them, and they wither, and the tempest carries them off like stubble.

The opening question asks the people if they have something that can compare with God (v. 18). His answer is "the idol." A common belief among ancient people is that if a nation is defeated by another nation, then the gods of the loser were defeated in a fight by the gods of the winner. Read the *Iliad* by Homer to see an example of this mentality. Since the Babylonians defeated Israel, their god Marduk must be stronger than the Lord. Therefore, the Jewish exiles were tempted to worship Marduk instead of the Lord.

However, the Lord then mocks the idols as the works of human craft that cannot even move from place to place. In contrast, the Jews should know that the Lord sits above earth; it is small to Him. He stretches out the heavens and brings the world's rulers to nothing. Therefore, the exiles should conclude that the Lord was not defeated by Babylon or Marduk. Judah lost its war with Babylon for some other reason—its own sin and disobedience.

40:25–26

[25]To whom then will you compare me, that I should be like him? says the Holy One. [26]Lift up your eyes on high and see: who created these? He who brings out their host by number, calling them all by name; by the greatness of his might, and because he is strong in power not one is missing.

This section begins more personally, with the Lord asking whether anything in creation can be compared to Him. He answers His own question by asking them to look at the stars of heaven and asking who created them. Of course, it is the Lord, who continues to call them out by name. It is important to remember that the Babylonians worshiped gods who were forces of nature, and the stars controlled the destinies of "gods and men," according to their creation myth, the *Enuma Elish*. Furthermore, God "created" the stars, a verb for which only God is ever the subject, while the Babylonians believed that the father god, Apsu, and mother god, Tiamat, procreated the other deities and were then each killed by their grandchildren gods.

40:27–31

> **[27]Why do you say, O Jacob, and speak, O Israel, "My way is hid from the LORD, and my right is disregarded by my God"? [28]Have you not known? Have you not heard? The LORD is the everlasting God, the Creator of the ends of the earth. He does not faint or grow weary, his understanding is unsearchable. [29]He gives power to the faint, and to him who has no might he increases strength. [30]Even youths shall faint and be weary, and young men shall fall exhausted; [31]but they who wait for the LORD shall renew their strength, they shall mount up with wings like eagles, they shall run and not be weary, they shall walk and not faint.**

The introductory rhetorical question is not concerned with cosmic issues but with the exiles' assumption that God does not see nor care about the suffering in Babylonian captivity. In answer, the Lord asserts that He is "everlasting God," (unlike the Babylonian first deities Apsu and Tiamat, who can die) and the creator of all, who cannot become weak and whose own mind is unsearchable. While it seems that the people are forgotten by God, the reality is that their punishment fits into His plan and will become part of their salvation. Therefore, the Lord is the one who most assuredly empowers weak and faint human beings. However, they must wait for the Lord, whose plan is inscrutable, to give a strength that far exceeds human limitations.

—— Isaiah 41:1–29 ——
A Series of Trial Speeches

In these oracles, the Lord puts the nations and their gods on trial to determine who is the true deity: the Lord or the pagan gods. This was very appropriate where the worship of the god Marduk, king of the gods, was the center of life. Every New Year festival, the creation myth, *Enuma Elish,* was read in public to describe Marduk's ascent to leadership and his claim to power over all gods and human beings.

41:1–5

[1]Listen to me in silence, O coastlands; let the peoples renew their strength; let them approach, then let them speak; let us together draw near for judgment. [2]Who stirred up one from the east whom victory meets at every step? He gives up nations before him, so that he tramples kings under foot; he makes them like dust with his sword, like driven stubble with his bow. [3]He pursues them and passes on safely, by paths his feet have not trod. [4]Who has performed and done this, calling the generations from the beginning? I, the LORD, the first, and with the last; I am He. [5]The coastlands have seen and are afraid, the ends of the earth tremble; they have drawn near and come.

1

The summons of the coastlands—that is, the farthest reaches of the empire—to trial.

2–4

The Lord pleads His case, claiming to be the one who really has power to stir up Cyrus, the Persian king who came from the east and was about to conquer the Babylonian Empire.

5

Cyrus had conquered Lydia and the islands off the coast of Asia Minor (modern Turkey). These islands are therefore witnesses that the Lord has summoned Cyrus to conquer Babylon and the Babylonian gods and people can do nothing to stop it.

41:6–7

[6]Every one helps his neighbor, and says to his brother, "Take courage!" [7]The craftsman encourages the goldsmith, and he who smooths with the hammer him who strikes the anvil, saying of the soldering, "It is good"; and they fasten it with nails so that it cannot be moved.

These verses, along with 40:19–20, form fragments that describe steps in the process of fashioning idols. 44:9–20 is a much longer description of the same, and other examples can be found in Wisdom 13:10–19; 14:1, 7–8, 11, 12–31; 15:7–17. Fashioning an idol requires help from a number of craftsmen and needs their approval as they fix it in one place with nails, since it cannot even stand on its own power. Why, then, would anyone prefer these idols to the living God?

41:8–13

> **8But you, Israel, my servant, Jacob, whom I have chosen, the offspring**
> **of Abraham, my friend; 9you whom I took from the ends of the earth,**
> **and called from its farthest corners, saying to you, "You are my servant,**
> **I have chosen you and not cast you off"; 10fear not, for I am with you,**
> **be not dismayed, for I am your God; I will strengthen you, I will help**
> **you, I will uphold you with my victorious right hand. 11Behold, all**
> **who are incensed against you shall be put to shame and confounded;**
> **those who strive against you shall be as nothing and shall perish. 12You**
> **shall seek those who contend with you, but you shall not find them;**
> **those who war against you shall be as nothing at all. 13For I, the LORD**
> **your God, hold your right hand; it is I who say to you, "Fear not, I**
> **will help you."**

The Lord assures Israel of salvation and summons the exiles not to fear.

The form of speech here is called the assurance of salvation, which is central to D-I's message. The background for this form is seen in the psalms, whose place in life was the Temple. One form of psalm is the lament of the individual, in which a person prays by describing the painfully difficult circumstances of his life. That part of the psalm was then answered by an assurance that the Lord would hear the prayer, a statement usually made by a priest in the Temple who is performing a sacrifice for the person. D-I uses this form as a response to the exiles' laments about their misery in Babylon. Perhaps D-I took this priestly role because he, like Jeremiah and Ezekiel, was a priest, or at least belonged to priestly circles of influence.

8–9

This is an address to Israel that begins with addressing Israel-Jacob as "my servant" and reviews past dealings with the people from their beginning with Abraham. Twice, the Lord mentions that He has chosen the people, and therefore He will not cast off His servant. This serves to point out that the following statement of assurance in the present is based on a whole history of past choice and care for His servant nation, Israel.

10

The statement of assurance is begun with a double command not to fear or be dismayed. "Fear not" is commonly said by God or His angels when present to save people (Gn 15:1 to Abram; Jo 1:9; before wars in Dt 20:1, 31:6–8 and 2 Chr 20:17; Lk 1:13, 30; 2:10–11). The word "dismay" is from a root meaning "gaze," but the form here indicates gazing about nervously or in fear. Instead of fear of the hard circumstances, the Lord assures Israel of His strength, help, and being upheld with His victorious right hand.

11–12

This is a proclamation that Israel's enemies will be thoroughly defeated through shame, confusion, and eventually death.

13

This verse repeats the assurance that the Lord God will support Israel and identifies Him as the one who assures them with a promise of help and the words, "Fear not."

41:14–16:
Oracle of Salvation

> **[14]Fear not, you worm Jacob, you men of Israel! I will help you, says the LORD; your Redeemer is the Holy One of Israel. [15]Behold, I will make of you a threshing sledge, new, sharp, and having teeth; you shall thresh the mountains and crush them, and you shall make the hills like chaff; [16a]You shall winnow them and the wind shall carry them away, and the tempest shall scatter them. [16b]And you shall rejoice in the LORD; in the Holy One of Israel you shall glory.**

This oracle supplements 41:8–13, which focuses on the Lord's words to Israel's enemies. Verses 14–16 address Jacob-Israel, the exiles who are in Babylon, with a promise of God's help to transform the nation into a strength far beyond its capacities.

14

The oracle begins with the Lord's command, "fear not," in order to dispel their fear. Quite likely, the Israelite exiles felt the same fear as the rest of Babylon's population as Cyrus's army moved south through Mesopotamia. The command is backed up by the Lord's promise of help and His self-identification as both the Redeemer and Holy One. The reference to suffering Israel as a "worm" probably comes from Psalms 22:6, "I am a worm and no man."

15–16a

The Lord promises Israel a new future of total transformation. While the Lord addresses the exiles as a "worm," which is very soft and vulnerable, now He promises to make them into a threshing sledge with sharp iron teeth. Such a sledge was made of heavy blocks of wood joined together, with a row of iron teeth on the bottom. A draft animal would pull it in circles over pile of grain so as to thresh the grain from the chaff. Then Israel will winnow the hills and mountains so as to let the wind carry them away as something light and insignificant.

16b

The end of the oracle is a prophecy that the people will praise the Lord Holy One, an element of this form which is derived from vow to praise God in the Psalms of lament. In these psalms, the person describes the suffering, petitions God's help, and then make a vow to praise God, often with accompanying sacrifices (see Ps 71:14–15).

41:17–20: Proclamation of Salvation

17When the poor and needy seek water, and there is none, and their tongue is parched with thirst, 17bI the LORD will answer them, I the God of Israel will not forsake them. 18I will open rivers on the bare heights, and fountains in the midst of the valleys; I will make the wilderness a pool of water, and the dry land springs of water. 19I will put in the wilderness the cedar, the acacia, the myrtle, and the olive; I will set in the desert the cypress, the plane and the pine together; 20that men may see and know, may consider and understand together,

that the hand of the LORD has done this, the Holy One of Israel has created it.

17a

The section begins with an allusion to a lament made by the exiles—they are thirsty and parched because of their poverty during the exile in Babylon.

17b–19

The proclamation of salvation proper is laid out here, beginning with God's turning toward Israel to answer the poor (v. 17b) and His promise to accomplish a variety of saving acts for the journey home to Israel across the dreadfully waterless desert. He will even plant trees that will provide much needed shade so that the journey home will be more like a walk in a park rather than an arduous trip through the desolate desert.

20

According to the prophet, salvation's purpose is to prove to other peoples that the Lord is God with all power to save.

41:21–29:
The Lord Puts the Babylonian Gods on Trial

**21Set forth your case, says the LORD; bring your proofs, says the King of
Jacob. 22Let them bring them, and tell us what is to happen. Tell us the
former things, what they are, that we may consider them, that we may
know their outcome; or declare to us the things to come. 23Tell us what
is to come hereafter, that we may know that you are gods; do good, or do
harm, that we may be dismayed and terrified. 24Behold, you are nothing,
and your work is nought; an abomination is he who chooses you. 25I
stirred up one from the north, and he has come, from the rising of the
sun, and he shall call on my name; he shall trample on rulers as on mortar, as the potter treads clay. 26Who declared it from the beginning, that
we might know, and beforetime, that we might say, "He is right"? There
was none who declared it, none who proclaimed, none who heard your
words. 27I first have declared it to Zion, and I give to Jerusalem a herald
of good tidings. 28But when I look there is no one; among these there is
no counselor who, when I ask, gives an answer. 29Behold, they are all a
delusion; their works are nothing; their molten images are empty wind.**

The king of Babylon had ordered his soldiers to capture idols from throughout the empire and set up these deities in Babylon. He believed that at least one of them, if not the whole collection, would be able to protect the city from the advancing army of Cyrus the Persian. The prophet here puts these gods on trial, speaking for the Lord God.

21

Summons to trial by the king of Jacob—that is, by the Lord. The bad thing for the gods is that the Lord God of Jacob-Israel is also the judge. One possible reason to use the name "Jacob" is that the Lord was the one who changed his name to Israel after wrestling with the angel of the Lord at Penuel (see Gn 32:24–28). Prior to that, he had lived with his uncle Laban, who still worshiped various deities (see Gn 31:19, 31–35), and later Jacob ordered his family to get rid of their idols (see Gn 35:2–4).

22–23

The Lord's demand for proof of divine power is to ask for the power to foretell the future through the prophets of the gods, or actually accomplish some good or harm for either the worshipers or their enemies.

24

The Lord's verdict that the gods are nothing and whoever chooses these gods is an abomination. This last judgment is related to Deuteronomy 18:9–11; 7:26; 27:15, where making or worshiping idols turns the worshiper into an abomination.

25–28

The Lord presents His evidence for His divinity: He has stirred up Cyrus from Persia, which is east of Babylon ("from the rising of the sun"), who comes "from the north" because He first conquered Asia Minor, which is north (v. 25). The second proof is that the Lord had predicted both Israel's captivity and the coming of Cyrus, while none of the Babylonian deities had done so. He had made this prediction known to "Zion . . . Jerusalem—that is, Israel—first, since that is His people.

29

The verdict is that the gods are a "delusion," "nothing," and an "empty wind," and therefore, the exiles need pay no attention to them or the Babylonian claims against them.

Lesson 13

DEUTERO-ISAIAH 42–43

—— Isaiah 42:1–4 ——
The First Servant of the Lord Song

The Lord is speaking to an unnamed audience, presumably the exiles, and introduces someone He calls "my servant." This follows a pattern in various vocation texts, such as when the Lord designates Gideon to deliver Israel from oppression by Moab (see Jgs 6), or Saul as the first king (see 1 Sm 9:15–17), or David as a new king (see 1 Sm 16). However, this particular passage will be quoted by God the Father at Jesus's baptism by John: "Behold, a voice from heaven, saying, 'This is my beloved Son, with whom I am well pleased'" (Mt 3:17; Mk 1:11; Lk 3:22). The hovering of the Holy Spirit over Jesus (Mt 3:16; Mk 1:10; Lk 3:22; Jn 1:32) also shows that Jesus is designated as the servant of the Lord. This passage is also manifested when the Father speaks at the transfiguration (see Mt 17:5; Mk 9:7; Lk 9:35), just as Jesus begins His journey toward His suffering and death in Jerusalem, where He will fulfill the role of the suffering servant described in Isaiah 50:4–9 and 52:13–53:12.

42:1

> **1 Behold my servant, whom I uphold, my chosen, in whom my soul delights; I have put my Spirit upon him, he will bring forth justice to the nations.**

Verse 1 speaks primarily of the Lord's relationship with the servant: the Lord upholds him and has put His Spirit upon him. He is chosen and the

Lord's "soul" delights in him. Only the last phrase mentions His ministry of bringing justice. Note that this is not a ministry just to Israel but to the nations of the world.

42:2–3

> **[2]He will not cry or lift up his voice, or make it heard in the street; [3]a bruised reed he will not break, and a dimly burning wick he will not quench; he will faithfully bring forth justice.**

A description of the quality of His ministry is given here: He will "faithfully bring forth justice," indicating complete dedication to His mission. This will be done in gentleness, without loud speech to the public. He will not bring destruction to the "bruised reed" or the "smoldering wick." When people are wounded, He will not destroy them but heal what life is actually present within them by bringing justice to them. These verses were cited by Saint Matthew to make sense of Jesus's commands to the people He healed that they should not make their healing known publicly (see Mt 12:16–20). While the Father designated Jesus as the servant of the Lord at the Baptism and Transfiguration, the evangelist could see this further lived out in Jesus's ministry.

42:4

> **[4]He will not fail or be discouraged till he has established justice in the earth; and the coastlands wait for his law.**

The Lord's designation of the servant concludes with a statement of assurance that He will not fail until justice is established on all the earth. Unlike most of D-I's oracles that focus on Israel's deliverance from Babylon, this servant song goes back to the tradition of Israel's mission to the whole world, rooted in Abram's call in Genesis 12:1–3.

—— Isaiah 42:5–9 ——

This oracle of vocation is distinct from the call of the servant in 42:1–4. The text does not say who is being called, with the obvious possibility being the servant, as seen by the connections with the call of the servant in Isaiah 49:1–9, but also Israel.

42:5

[5]Thus says God, the LORD, who created the heavens and stretched them out, who spread forth the earth and what comes from it, who gives breath to the people upon it and spirit to those who walk in it:

This is the messenger formula ("thus says") followed by an identification of God the Lord as the creator. Calling the God the Lord "creator" (see D-I 40:26, 28; 41:20; 43:1, 7, 15; 45:7, 8, 12, 18; 48:7; 54:16) is a very important concept in D-I, who employs the Hebrew root *bara'* more than any book of the Bible. Consistently in the Bible, only God is the creator since the term never refers to anyone else. The next two ideas seem related to Psalms 102, showing God the Lord as stretching out the heavens (also in D-I 40:22; 44:24; 45:12; 48:13), which may reflect Psalms 102:2. Proclaiming that God the Lord gives breath and spirit to people may reflect Psalms 104:29–30.

42:6–7

[6a]"I am the LORD, I have called you in righteousness, I have taken you by the hand and kept you; [6b]I have given you as a covenant to the people, a light to the nations, [7]to open the eyes that are blind, to bring out the prisoners from the dungeon, from the prison those who sit in darkness.

This section describes the call and mission.

6a

The person has been called "in righteousness," probably a description of that person's moral characteristic. The Lord takes him in a very personal way, leading him by the hand, as he does Israel in 41:13, keeping guard over him.

6b–7

The mission is to be a "covenant to the people" of Israel, as is true of the servant in 49:8 and a "light to the nations," as is true of the servant in 49:6. The mission to open the eyes of the blind first appeared in Proto-Isaiah 29:18, and then in 35:5 and 42:16. The New Testament understands Jesus's ministry of healing the blind in light of these texts (see Mt 11:4–5). The mission to liberate prisoners is very applicable to the exiles in Babylon, and the theme appears in 42:22 and in the call of the servant in 49:9.

42:8–9

> **[8]I am the LORD, that is my name; my glory I give to no other, nor my praise to graven images. [9]Behold, the former things have come to pass, and new things I now declare; before they spring forth I tell you of them."**

This is a concluding statement that identifies the Lord as the only God and therefore is capable of making such a call.

8

The Lord gave His name in Exodus 3:14–16, and it remains the same in the exile. 42:8 reminds the listeners of the first commandment (see Ex 20:3–5), which demands that Israel "shall have no other gods before me" (Ex 20:3), prohibiting graven images and their worship by bowing down or serving them because "I the Lord your God am a jealous God" (Ex 20:4–5).

9

The Lord's ability to make these claims is confirmed by the fact that He has declared earlier prophecies that came true, particularly the Babylonian captivity and exile. Therefore, when He makes new claims, He informs the people before they come to pass as even more proof that He is the only God who exists.

—— Isaiah 42:10–13 ——

This is a hymn of praise, such as conclude a number of sections of D-I: 44:23; 45:8; 49:13; 51:3; 52:7–10. Like hymns in the psalter, D-I uses the command to praise, which is often extended by the jussive form of the verbs ("let" a third person subject "roar," "lift up voices," "sing," "give glory"). However, while the psalms move from praise to a description of what the Lord has already done, D-I's hymns describe what the Lord is about to do. They are to begin praising God before they see Him take action, thereby affirming faith. This is a very important point in the spiritual life. Many people complain that God does not hear their prayers, or they waste time complaining about their sufferings. It is usually better to praise God in the midst of difficulties before the difficulties are over and make that an act of faith that He can and will act.

42:10–12

> **[10]Sing to the LORD a new song, his praise from the end of the earth! Let the sea roar and all that fills it, the coastlands and their inhabitants. [11]Let the desert and its cities lift up their voice, the villages that Kedar inhabits; let the inhabitants of Sela sing for joy, let them shout from the top of the mountains. [12]Let them give glory to the LORD, and declare his praise in the coastlands.**

These verses form the summons to praise the Lord. The command to "sing a new song" is also found in Psalms 96:1 and 98:1, which are also hymns. The Lord creator ought to receive His praise from the ends of the earth, since he created it all (Ps 96:1–3; 98:1–4). The jussive summons of the sea to roar in praise is found in Psalms 96:11 and 98:7, and the dry land (Kedar is in northern Arabia, while Sela means "rock," and may refer to the desert city of Petra in Jordan, which also means "rock"). The coastlands refer to western Asia Minor, thereby describing the ends of the earth in terms of the geographical regions D-I knew.

42:13

> **[13]The LORD goes forth like a mighty man, like a man of war he stirs up his fury; he cries out, he shouts aloud, he shows himself mighty against his foes.**

This description of the Lord being praised shows Him as a mighty warrior who shouts a great battle cry against His enemies and will ultimately defeat them (see Ps 18:6–16; 114). This passage thus refers to Babylon and its deities' defeat.

—— Isaiah 42:14–17 ——

This section is a proclamation of salvation in response to an implied lament of the people who say that God has been silent and has not shouted out in victory, as the preceding hymn claims.

42:14

> **[14]For a long time I have held my peace, I have kept still and restrained myself; now I will cry out like a woman in travail, I will gasp and pant.**

This is God's admission that He has been silent for a while—there had not been a prophet since Ezekiel in the 570s BC, and D-I is speaking in the late 540s. However, now there is a changed situation and the Lord will cry out "like a woman in travail" during childbirth (see a similar allusion to a lament and the Lord's change of attitude in the first proclamation of salvation in 41:17).

42:15–16

> **15I will lay waste mountains and hills, and dry up all their herbage; I will turn the rivers into islands, and dry up the pools. 16And I will lead the blind in a way that they know not, in paths that they have not known I will guide them. I will turn the darkness before them into light, the rough places into level ground. These are the things I will do, and I will not forsake them.**

As in the proclamation of salvation in 41:18–20, here, too, the Lord will change mountains, hills, and rivers in a way that allows Him to lead the blind on paths of light back to their homeland in Israel.

42:17

> **17They shall be turned back and utterly put to shame, who trust in graven images, who say to molten images, "You are our gods."**

However, part of the salvation of the exiles includes the punishment of those who worship idols. This may refer not only to the pagan Babylonians but also to those exiles who had turned away from the Lord in order to worship the Babylonians gods. Such people may have thought that those deities were victorious over the Lord, and therefore He should be abandoned in their favor. The Lord will prove all such idolatry to be false when He punishes them.

—— Isaiah 42:18–25 ——

The use of various questions to the deaf and blind people addressed in this section indicates that it is a disputation.

42:18

[18]Hear, you deaf; and look, you blind, that you may see!

This section begins with a summons to the deaf and blind to look and see the truths that the Lord is trying to tell them. He will make the truth so obvious that they will be able to "see" His evidence.

42:19–22

[19]Who is blind but my servant, or deaf as my messenger whom I send? Who is blind as my dedicated one, or blind as the servant of the LORD? [20]He sees many things, but does not observe them; his ears are open, but he does not hear. [21]The LORD was pleased, for his righteousness' sake, to magnify his law and make it glorious. [22]But this is a people robbed and plundered, they are all of them trapped in holes and hidden in prisons; they have become a prey with none to rescue, a spoil with none to say, "Restore!"

These verses are the first questions and the Lord's answers.

19–20

The first questions are rhetorical, with an ironical twist that is asking whether the servant, who in this dispute appears to be Israel, is blind and deaf. In this interpretation, Israel sees but does not observe and has open ears that do not hear, much like the accusation against the people in Proto-Isaiah 6:9–10: "Go, and say to this people: 'Hear and hear, but do not understand; see and see, but do not perceive.' Make the heart of this people fat, and their ears heavy, and shut their eyes; lest they see with their eyes, and hear with their ears, and understand with their hearts, and turn and be healed." Similarly the exiles do not really see, understand, nor listen to the Lord.

21–22

This section explains that the Lord had made His law clear and glorious, but the people did not "see" nor "hear" what it meant. As a result of disobeying God, they were punished with being robbed, plundered, and imprisoned. The Lord had told them this would happen, especially through Jeremiah and Ezekiel, but they would not listen.

42:23–25

> **[23]Who among you will give ear to this, will attend and listen for the time to come? [24]Who gave up Jacob to the spoiler, and Israel to the robbers? Was it not the LORD, against whom we have sinned, in whose ways they would not walk, and whose law they would not obey? [25]So he poured upon him the heat of his anger and the might of battle; it set him on fire round about, but he did not understand; it burned him, but he did not take it to heart.**

This second set of questions addresses the exiles so they can better understand their situation. In verse 23, the Lord asks the exiles if they will listen even now. Verse 24 then asks them who punished Jacob/Israel. He answers rhetorically with another question, since it is so obvious that the Lord gave them up to plunder and spoils because they had sinned. Verse 25 describes the Lord's wrath but still Israel does not understand and take it to heart.

— Isaiah 43:1–7 —

As in 41:8–13, this is an oracle of salvation that comes in response to the preceding disputation of 42:18–25.

43:1–4

> **[1]But now thus says the LORD, he who created you, O Jacob, he who formed you, O Israel: "Fear not, for I have redeemed you; I have called you by name, you are mine. [2]When you pass through the waters I will be with you; and through the rivers, they shall not overwhelm you; when you walk through fire you shall not be burned, and the flame shall not consume you. [3]For I am the LORD your God, the Holy One of Israel, your Savior. [3b]I give Egypt as your ransom, Ethiopia and Seba in exchange for you. [4]Because you are precious in my eyes, and honored, and I love you, I give men in return for you, peoples in exchange for your life.**

This is the first of two oracles of salvation in this section.

1

This verse introduces the Lord God who "created" and "formed" Jacob/Israel, applying the idea of the Lord as creator as applied to the people and their salvation. This introductory description of the Lord is followed by the assurance of salvation, “Fear not,” and its substantiation in three phrases, “I have redeemed you, I have called you, you are mine.”

2

Here the Lord proclaims salvation to the people, whether they walk through water or fire, which are two opposite kinds of danger that are mentioned in order to cover any and all forms of danger. The people will be able to pass through all types of danger because the Lord will accompany them; they are not the source of their own safety.

3a

The substantiation of this promise is that the Lord is God, the Holy One of Israel, and their Savior.

3b

Another proclamation of salvation means that other, much greater nations of Egypt and Ethiopia will be given in exchange for small Israel.

4

This verse substantiates the promise by pointing out that the Lord loves Israel as a precious and honored people, more valued to Him than the other nations.

43:5–7

> **5Fear not, for I am with you; 5bI will bring your offspring from the east,**
> **and from the west I will gather you; 6I will say to the north, Give up,**
> **and to the south, Do not withhold; bring my sons from afar and my**
> **daughters from the end of the earth, 7every one who is called by my**
> **name, whom I created for my glory, whom I formed and made.”**

This section is another oracle of salvation following the same structure as verses 1–4.

5a

Assurance of salvation, “Fear not,” backed up by the Lord substantiating this assurance by stating He is present with the people: “I am with you.”

5b–6

The proclamation of salvation takes the form of the promise to bring the exiles' children back home to Israel from the east, west, and south to which they had been exiled.

7

The substantiation of this salvation is that the Lord has created His chosen people for His own glory. He will be faithful to His glory, and therefore the salvation is certain.

—— Isaiah 43:8–15 ——

Trial speech between the Lord and the nations and their gods (recall the earlier trial speeches in 41:1–5 and 41:21–29).

43:8

> **8Bring forth the people who are blind, yet have eyes, who are deaf, yet have ears!**

The Israelites are summoned to be witnesses for the Lord's case. This is ironic since they were portrayed as blind and deaf both here and in Isaiah 42:18–21. Despite their blindness and deafness they are to witness to the Lord.

43:9a

> **9Let all the nations gather together, and let the peoples assemble.**

This verse summons all the nations and peoples, who will have to decide whether their gods are real or whether the Lord is the only God.

43:9b–c

> **9bWho among them can declare this, and show us the former things? Let them bring their witnesses to justify them, and let them hear and say, It is true.**

The Lord asks the gods to defend themselves by showing that they can make prophetic statements about history. Verse 9c even asks the gods to produce their own witnesses to "justify" them, which is a Hebrew idiom meaning to declare them innocent in court.

43:10a

> **[10a]"You are my witnesses," says the LORD, "and my servant whom I have chosen, that you may know and believe me and understand that I am He.**

The Lord acknowledges blind and deaf Israel, His "servant," as His witnesses to knowledge and faith in Him. In fact, the reason Israel is His servant is to make known this faith.

43:10b–13

> **[10b]Before me no god was formed, nor shall there be any after me. [11]I, I am the LORD, and besides me there is no savior. [12]I declared and saved and proclaimed, when there was no strange god among you; and you are my witnesses," says the LORD. [13]"I am God, and also henceforth I am He; there is none who can deliver from my hand; I work and who can hinder it?"**

The Lord declares the verdict: He alone is God and there is no other. These verses assert His divine nature and the actions by which He demonstrates it: He is the savior (v. 11b), He declared and saved (v. 12a), no one can deliver from His hand or hinder His work (v. 13b).

43:14–15

> **[14]Thus says the LORD, your Redeemer, the Holy One of Israel: "For your sake I will send to Babylon and break down all the bars, and the shouting of the Chaldeans will be turned to lamentations. [15]I am the LORD, your Holy One, the Creator of Israel, your King."**

The trial concludes with a final oracle by the Lord, who defines Himself as the Redeemer and Holy One of Israel at the beginning and at the end as the Holy One, Creator of Israel, and King. Again, as is common in D-I, the Lord unites the ideas of redemption and creation in Himself. Between these triumphant statements concerning the Lord's identity, He vows to defeat Babylon and its Chaldean people for the sake of Israel. Therefore, these statements focus not only on His creative act but also on His redemptive work. This also brings out the importance of recognizing the outcome of this trial—namely, that the Lord alone is God.

—— Isaiah 43:16–21 ——

Proclamation of salvation, (previous proclamations of salvation are 41:17–20 and 42:14–17), which is usually a response to an expression of lament in a psalm. The priest or a prophet would proclaim salvation after someone prays through their sorrow or pain. Here, the proclamation comes after a trial speech in which Israel is blind and deaf, but the Lord is nonetheless declared the only God who will defeat the Chaldeans of Babylon and now promises to save Israel in a new exodus.

43:16–17

> **16Thus says the LORD, who makes a way in the sea, a path in the mighty waters, 17who brings forth chariot and horse, army and warrior; they lie down, they cannot rise, they are extinguished, quenched like a wick:**

The messenger formula ("Thus says the Lord") is expanded by descriptions of the Lord's past saving actions at the Red Sea, which He opened for Israel but which became the means of destroying Pharaoh's army. This look at the past salvation from slavery in Egypt becomes a model of the deliverance of the people from a different foreign exile in Babylon.

43:18–21

> **18"Remember not the former things, nor consider the things of old. 19Behold, I am doing a new thing; now it springs forth, do you not perceive it? 19bI will make a way in the wilderness and rivers in the desert. 20The wild beasts will honor me, the jackals and the ostriches; for I give water in the wilderness, rivers in the desert, to give drink to my chosen people, 21the people whom I formed for myself that they might declare my praise.**

The actual oracle proclaiming salvation.

18–19a

After the Lord identified Himself as the one who worked wonders at the Red Sea, the oracle begins by telling the exiles to forget about that former act of salvation because a new and greater one is about to take place. The question, "do you not perceive it?" implies that the conquest of the Babylonian Empire by Cyrus the Persian will be an element of this saving act.

19b–21

The newness is seen in that the Lord Himself will lead the people, whereas in the Exodus, an angel had done so (Ex 23:23: "When my angel goes before you, and brings you" into the promised land). Another aspect of the newness is that the desert will be transformed as even the animals praise God and the desert will become watered. This transformation of the desert brings out the link frequently made in D-I that the Lord who is the Redeemer is also the Creator, and He combines these two aspects in one salvific act. Also note in verse 21 that the chosen people is defined as the people God formed to declare His praise. This indicates the important point that worshiping God is Israel's highest purpose; this applies to every Christian and, indeed, every human being and creature (such as the jackals and ostriches).

—— Isaiah 43:22–28 ——

This is a disputation and trial speech between the Lord and Israel, based on the charge made by the people that the Lord had "delivered" Jacob/ Israel to destruction and reviling (v. 28). Here the Lord answers the charge. Another trial between Israel and the Lord is found in 50:1–3 (see Lesson 16).

43:22–25

> **22"Yet you did not call upon me, O Jacob; but you have been weary of me, O Israel! 23You have not brought me your sheep for burnt offerings, or honored me with your sacrifices. I have not burdened you with offerings, or wearied you with frankincense. 24You have not bought me sweet cane with money, or satisfied me with the fat of your sacrifices. 24bBut you have burdened me with your sins, you have wearied me with your iniquities. 25"I, I am He who blots out your transgressions for my own sake, and I will not remember your sins.**

These verses form a disputation. The Lord argues against Israel's complaints that they have been abandoned and reviled during their Babylonian exile.

22

The Lord's first argument is that the people had turned away from Him, not praying for His help and becoming tired of having God in their lives.

23–24a

The second argument is that Israel has not brought the Lord the sacrifices that are His due. In *The Spirit of the Liturgy*, Joseph Cardinal Ratzinger (Benedict XVI) pointed out that the purpose of Israel's liberation from Egypt and occupation of the Promised Land was that the people might offer God worship in the ways He set forth; here Our Lord reminds them that they did not do so.

24b

Ratzinger also pointed out that worship was not acceptable if it was offered apart from moral integrity. The giving of laws and commandments that guide the moral life take up less space than the liturgical laws in the Torah, but they are an absolute requirement for the worship to be acceptable to the Lord. Therefore, the Lord concludes His arguments by declaring that Israel's sins "burdened" and "wearied" Him because they were incessant.

25

Having presented this series of arguments in the face of Israel's complaints, based on the facts of Israel's sins and failures as recorded by the pre-exilic prophets, the Lord ends the disputation with a surprising claim; He forgives their sins. He does not forgive them because they deserve it, but for His own sake.

43:26–28

> **26 Put me in remembrance, let us argue together; set forth your case, that you may be proved right. 27 Your first father sinned, and your mediators transgressed against me. 28 Therefore I profaned the princes of the sanctuary, I delivered Jacob to utter destruction and Israel to reviling.**

This forms the trial speech properly speaking, as seen in verse 26: "let us argue together" (Hebrew verb *shafat*, meaning to "judge," and therefore come to judgment or trial). Of course, the unspoken problem is that the Lord, who is judge of all, is inviting Israel to put Him on trial. It seems imprudent to accept this challenge, especially after the Lord's preceding disputation.

26

Summons to trial and a request that Israel state its case proving that the Lord was wrong in abandoning them.

27

The Lord states His case: sin permeates the people's history, from their first father and throughout the lives of their mediators and heroes. While this easily refers to Adam's sin, this charge also applies to Abraham, who lied twice out of cowardice before two different kings that Sarah was his sister instead of his wife. Sin is found throughout Israel's sacred history, even among its heroes. For example, Moses killed a man and later disobeyed God's command to speak to the rock for water; Aaron fashioned the golden calf; David committed adultery and murder.

28

The Lord gives His verdict: I profaned the sanctuary and destroyed you because of your sins. Therefore you deserved the punishment. Case closed.

Lesson 14

Deutero-Isaiah 44–46

—— Isaiah 44:1–5 ——

These verses contain an oracle to assure future salvation to the exiles.

44:1–2a

> **1"But now hear, O Jacob my servant, Israel whom I have chosen!**
> **2Thus says the Lord who made you, who formed you from the womb**
> **and will help you:**

The introduction to the oracle.

1

First, the Lord summons Jacob/Israel, His chosen servant, to listen to His word.

2a

The prophetic messenger formula in which the Lord defines Himself as the maker who formed Israel in the womb and as a promised helper during their difficult Babylonian exile.

44:2b

> **2bFear not, O Jacob my servant, Jeshurun whom I have chosen.**

The statement of salvation takes the usual form in D-I, "Fear not," with a repetition of identifying Jacob/Jeshurun as the Lord's "chosen." Jeshurun is a name for Israel found elsewhere only in poetic texts in Deuteronomy (32:15; 33:5, 26). The root may be *jashar*, meaning to be "upright."

44:3–5

[3]For I will pour water on the thirsty land, and streams on the dry ground; I will pour my Spirit upon your descendants, and my blessing on your offspring. [4]They shall spring up like grass amid waters, like willows by flowing streams. [5]This one will say, 'I am the LORD's,' another will call himself by the name of Jacob, and another will write on his hand, 'The LORD's,' and surname himself by the name of Israel."

The Lord promises to transform both the land and the people, promising salvation in the future.

3

While the dry land will be transformed by the outpouring of water, Israel's descendants will be transformed by the outpouring of the Lord's Spirit.

4–5

The Lord's intervention will result in growth like that of grass and willow trees beside running streams. A similar idea is promised in Psalms 1:3, though the wicked will be like dried chaff (Ps 1:4). During the period leading up to the destruction of Jerusalem, the prophet Jeremiah had also said the one who trusts in the Lord "is like a tree planted by water, that sends out its roots by the stream, and does not fear when heat comes" (Jer 17:8). The people's prosperity will also lead them to profess the identity as Jacob and Israel, which comes from the Lord, and their identity as belonging to the Lord. Verse 5 may stand in contrast to those exiles in Babylon who may have become ashamed of their identity as God's people, but the Lord's salvation will make them profess it boldly.

— Isaiah 44:6–23 —

This unit is composed of three distinct subunits, each having its own proper formal structure. Together, they form a strong critique of the pagan idols.

44:6–8

[6a]Thus says the LORD, the King of Israel and his Redeemer, the LORD of hosts: [6b]"I am the first and I am the last; besides me there is no god. [7a]Who is like me? Let him proclaim it, let him declare and set it forth

> **before me. [7b]Who has announced from of old the things to come? Let them tell us what is yet to be. [8]Fear not, nor be afraid; have I not told you from of old and declared it? And you are my witnesses! Is there a God besides me? There is no Rock; I know not any."**

This short trial speech is against the gods and nations.

6a

This is the messenger formula by the Lord under three titles: King of Israel, Redeemer, and Lord of hosts. While king and redeemer emphasize His role in salvation, the Lord of hosts, which include all the heavenly beings, refers to His creative power.

6b

The Lord makes His claim to be the first and the last and therefore the only God. This will influence the book of Revelation, where God speaks this claim (Rv 1:8) and so does Jesus Christ (Rv 1:17; 2:8; 22:13), indicating that He is also the one God, since He and the Father are one (Jn 10:30; 1:1; 5:17–18; 14:9; 17:21).

7a

The summons for the gods to come and dispute the Lord's claims with a rhetorical question, "Who is like me?" which assumes that the answer is "Nobody." However, if someone has a different answer, let him stand up and prove in the Lord's presence that there is another god.

7b

In this trial with the gods, this criteria of evidence is laid out. Which deity is able to predict the future and make it happen? Again, the assumed answer is "the Lord."

8

This is a direct address to the various witnesses to speak up and answer the Lord's claims without fear of reprisal or contradiction from the pagan gods. The Lord is, in fact, the one who has the authority and power to tell them to "Fear not," since He had decreed both the exile through the earlier prophets and the salvation from exile by D-I. The Lord alone is the rock of salvation.

44:9–20

> [9]All who make idols are nothing, and the things they delight in do not profit; their witnesses neither see nor know, that they may be put to shame. [10]Who fashions a god or casts an image, that is profitable for nothing? [11a]Behold, all his fellows shall be put to shame, and the craftsmen are but men; [11b]let them all assemble, let them stand forth, they shall be terrified, they shall be put to shame together. [12]The iron smith fashions it and works it over the coals; he shapes it with hammers, and forges it with his strong arm; he becomes hungry and his strength fails, he drinks no water and is faint. [13]The carpenter stretches a line, he marks it out with a pencil; he fashions it with planes, and marks it with a compass; he shapes it into the figure of a man, with the beauty of a man, to dwell in a house. [14]He cuts down cedars; or he chooses a holm tree or an oak and lets it grow strong among the trees of the forest; he plants a cedar and the rain nourishes it. [15]Then it becomes fuel for a man; he takes a part of it and warms himself, he kindles a fire and bakes bread; also he makes a god and worships it, he makes it a graven image and falls down before it. [16]Half of it he burns in the fire; over the half he eats flesh, he roasts meat and is satisfied; also he warms himself and says, "Aha, I am warm, I have seen the fire!" [17]And the rest of it he makes into a god, his idol; and falls down to it and worships it; he prays to it and says, "Deliver me, for thou art my god!" [18]They know not, nor do they discern; for he has shut their eyes, so that they cannot see, and their minds, so that they cannot understand. [19]No one considers, nor is there knowledge or discernment to say, "Half of it I burned in the fire, I also baked bread on its coals, I roasted flesh and have eaten; and shall I make the residue of it an abomination? Shall I fall down before a block of wood?" [20]He feeds on ashes; a deluded mind has led him astray, and he cannot deliver himself or say, "Is there not a lie in my right hand?"

This satire on making idols is meant to taunt the people who do such foolishness. Of course, in Israel, the making of idols was forbidden in the first commandment (see Ex 20:4–6), and those who do so "hate" the Lord and will be punished for three or four generations, since they reject the one God who is the source of all being. This satire on the folly of making idols is especially relevant in 539 BC, when Babylon's King Nabonidus brought idols from the surrounding towns and cities, somewhat as hostages, to protect themselves and therefore the city from Cyrus.

9–12

These verses form a general verdict that idol makers will be put to shame. In modern Western culture, shame has become less of a concern, as has honor, due to general acceptance of immodesty and a decline of family virtues. However, in the Middle East and many other cultures, the two ends of the moral spectrum are shame, which must be avoided at all costs, and honor, which is to be sought for oneself and for the groups to which one belongs. For that reason, this taunt threatens idolatry makers with shame.

9–11a

The taunt begins with a statement of the basic principle that all idol makers are "nothing," in Hebrew, *tohu.* This word means "void" in Genesis 1:2 as a description of the cosmos before God began to speak creation into existence in 1:3, "Let there be light." The Babylonian creation myth, *Enuma Elish,* also began with the chaos of the father god, Apsu (fresh water), and mother god, Tiamat (salt water chaos), but their giving birth to the gods of the sun, wind, storm, et cetera led to order. This taunt song proclaims that the gods are still nothing and chaos, which their "witnesses"—that is, their worshipers—cannot understand, and that brings shame on the witnesses and their associates.

11b–12

Perhaps with Nabonidus's desperate attempt to win the gods' protection, the song portrays the idol makers assembling in their own weakness. They are terrified, put to shame, hungry, and faint with thirst. If those who make the idols are so weak, how can the idols have any strength? The assumption behind this taunt is that the idols made by weak men are also weak and shameful.

13–20

This longer section of the taunt elaborates the processes of making the idols into four actions, with accompanying work, followed by a wisdom reflection (vv. 18–19) and a repetition of the verdict that idolatry brings one shame.

13

The design of the idol is sketched out here.

14–16

These verses indicate the choice of a tree and cutting it down. However, he does not use the whole tree for his mighty idol in whom he trusts for deliverance (v. 17). He uses part of the wood for fuel, which proves that the idol is already as prone to become nothing as the wood from which it was made. Furthermore, eating the food cooked over the wood actually gives more strength to the idol maker than does the idol which he will worship.

17

He makes the idol, worships it, and prays to it for deliverance.

18–19

These verses ponder the idol makers' lack of wisdom and thought. Though Israel had been accused by God of shutting its eyes and ears to prevent understanding when they sinned through idolatry (Is 6:9–10), here the assertion applies to the idol makers. Verse 19 explains this folly by their lack of reflection on the obvious issue that they burn the wood for fuel and then worship the left-over part of it. Such makes no sense.

20

The idol makers have gone astray by putting their faith in gods who cannot deliver them (v. 20). The phrase "feeds on ashes," may refer to sheep in a pasture, or it can also mean "herds ashes," as one who sweeps away the ashes after making an idol is herding these useless remains.

44:21–22

21Remember these things, O Jacob, and Israel, for you are my servant; I formed you, you are my servant; O Israel, you will not be forgotten by me. 22I have swept away your transgressions like a cloud, and your sins like mist; return to me, for I have redeemed you.

After the preceding descriptive taunt song against the folly of idolatry, the Lord speaks directly to Jacob/Israel, His servant whom He has formed, with three messages. First, the Lord commands Israel to remember this lesson on the folly of idolatry. That was the sin against the first commandment in the Decalogue (see Ex 20:3–6) that caused them to be abandoned into exile in the first place. Second, the Lord will not forget them, a message He will repeat in 49:15–16. Third, the Lord has forgiven their transgressions in a way similar to a wind sweeping away a cloud or mist; therefore, return to the Lord who has redeemed them. The Lord addresses the people directly so that each person will take it to heart.

44:23

> **[23]Sing, O heavens, for the LORD has done it; shout, O depths of the earth; break forth into singing, O mountains, O forest, and every tree in it! For the LORD has redeemed Jacob, and will be glorified in Israel.**

Hymns conclude a number of sections of D-I (42:10–13; 45:8; 49:13; 51:3; 52:7–10), including here, perhaps imitating the Temple worship. Since the preceding section criticizes the gods and puts them on trial, this hymn seems like a victory song, recounting the Lord's successful defeat of the pagan gods. Appropriately, the heavens, earth, mountains, and forests are summoned to sing this hymn to their creator and, by implication, not to the false gods. The reason for creation to offer this hymn is that the Lord has redeemed Jacob and will be glorified in them. This hymn unites the themes of the Lord as creator and redeemer, as is common in D-I. The promise that the Lord will be glorified in Israel also means that they will join the worship and adoration that is due Him once they return to their homeland.

— Isaiah 44:24–45:7 —
Oracle Concerning Cyrus the Persian

The historical background on this oracle concerning Cyrus began twenty years before the Jews' liberation from exile. Cyrus II, son of King Cambyses of Persia and Princess Mandane, daughter of King Astyages of Media, became the king of Persia in 559 BC. Persia was subject to the Medes, so in 550 BC, Cyrus attacked his suzerain and grandfather, Astyages, King of the Medes. Since King Nabonidus of Babylon feared the Mede empire, he supported Cyrus. Astyages's own troops revolted against him and handed him over to Cyrus in fetters. Cyrus then conquered Ecbatana, the Mede capital, with help from the Mede general, Harpagus, whom Astyages had wronged.[1] In 549, King Croesus of Lydia (in western Asia Minor) declared war against Cyrus, with Egypt, Babylon, and Sparta as his allies.[2]

Cyrus attacked Croesus in 546 at Pteria, forcing Croesus to return to his capital, Sardis, to wait for help from his Egyptian, Babylonian, and Spartan allies. Cyrus besieged Sardis and defeated Croesus's famous cavalry with a camel cavalry, since horses turn away from camels.[3] Cyrus captured Sardis but spared Croesus's life[4] and appointed a Lydian, Pactyes, as governor of Sardis. He marched back to Ecbatana with Croesus as an honored prisoner and at times a counselor.[5] General Harpagus enlisted the Ionians and Aeolians to help conquer the Carians, Caunians, Cnidians, Pedasians, and Lycians of southern Asia Minor,[6] adding these regions to the Persian Empire. However, not long afterward, Pactyes, the Lydian governor of Sardis, revolted. At Croesus's advice, Cyrus sent an army to capture Pactyes but spare the people of Sardis. Pactyes fled Sardis but was captured.[7] General Harpagus continued the conquest of Asia Minor by taking Phocaea,[8] and the Ionian cities in 545, inducing the Ionians on the coastal islands to surrender willingly.[9] These may be the many distant islands and coastlands to which Isaiah and Ezekiel refer (Is 24:15; 40:15; 41:1,5; 42:4,10,12; 49:1; 51:5; 59:18; 60:9; 66:19; Ez 26:15; 27:3, 15, 35; Jer 31:10).

After 545, the Persians focus on Mesopotamia with a view to taking Babylon, a feat which occurred in October 539 BC. This oracle on Cyrus

---

1 Herodotus, *The History*, 107–130.
2 Herodotus, 1.71.
3 Herodotus, 1.76–81.
4 Herodotus, 1.84–91.
5 Herodotus, 1.152–153.
6 Herodotus, 1.171–177.
7 Herodotus, 1.154–161.
8 Herodotus, 1.162–164.
9 Herodotus, 1.169.

happened between 545 and 539, with the above mentioned history providing background details.

This is a royal oracle, a form similar to Psalms 2, in which the Lord recognizes the king as His anointed one (messiah) and makes promises to him. It is not used elsewhere in D-I. The text has two parts, the introduction in 44:24–28 and the oracle proper in 45:1–7.

44:24–28:
Introduction, with Messenger Formula and Address to Israel

> **[24a]Thus says the LORD, your Redeemer, who formed you from the womb: [24b]"I am the LORD, who made all things, who stretched out the heavens alone, who spread out the earth – Who was with me? – [25]who frustrates the omens of liars, and makes fools of diviners; who turns wise men back, and makes their knowledge foolish; [26a]who confirms the word of his servant, and performs the counsel of his messengers; [26b]who says of Jerusalem, 'She shall be inhabited,' and of the cities of Judah, 'They shall be built, and I will raise up their ruins'; [27]who says to the deep, 'Be dry, I will dry up your rivers'; [28]who says of Cyrus, 'He is my shepherd, and he shall fulfil all my purpose'; saying of Jerusalem, 'She shall be built,' and of the temple, 'Your foundation shall be laid.'"**

24a
The oracle begins with the messenger formula as the Lord addresses Israel by defining Himself as the Redeemer who formed Israel from the womb. The Hebrew word for "redeemer" is a term used particularly for the members of a family who had the responsibility to protect family land from being sold outside the clan, or to redeem family members who have been enslaved, or to avenge the murder of a family member. Whenever the Lord calls Himself Redeemer, He is taking a family role, hence the connection with forming Israel in the womb.

24b–28
These introductory verses are self-descriptions of the Lord meant to evoke praise from the exiles as they listen.

24b

The Lord is the maker of all things, unlike the pagan deities who personified various forces of nature, such as the wind or storm. He stretched out the heavens alone, in contrast to Babylonian gods who formed an army to attack their saltwater grandmother, Tiamat, kill her, and cut her torso lengthwise in two, from which they made the heavens with the top and the earth from the bottom half. Contrast that with Genesis 1, and answer the Lord's question by realizing that no other gods were with the Lord.

25

The Babylonians were well-known for the use of omens and divination (see Dn 2 for lists of different kinds of wise men, diviners, and magicians, each term referring to a special form of magic). Just as Daniel repeatedly showed himself the Lord's servant who was superior to the Babylonian magicians, so, too, here, the Lord asserts that His superiority makes them into liars and fools because their gods do not exist and therefore cannot know the future.

26a

In contrast, the Lord confirms the words of His servant, the prophet who writes this book of Deutero-Isaiah, along with His other prophets.

26b

The word of salvation that the Lord gives through His servant is that Jerusalem will be inhabited.

27

Since the Lord controls all waters, drying up whole seas and rivers, He can easily direct the history of His people Israel by "drying up" the Babylonian Empire.

28

Then comes the shocking and amazing announcement that He will use a Gentile, Cyrus, to fulfill His purpose of setting His people free to rebuild Jerusalem and the Temple. In the earlier history of Israel, the Lord used Israelites—Moses, Saul, David, and others—to save the people against all odds. Now he will use a Persian to save them. The exiles would have been quite taken aback by this announcement.

45:1–7:
The Oracle to Cyrus

**1Thus says the LORD to his anointed, to Cyrus, whose right hand I
have grasped, to subdue nations before him and ungird the loins of
kings, to open doors before him that gates may not be closed: 2“I
will go before you and level the mountains, I will break in pieces the
doors of bronze and cut asunder the bars of iron, 3aI will give you the
treasures of darkness and the hoards in secret places, 3bthat you may
know that it is I, the LORD, the God of Israel, who call you by your
name. 4For the sake of my servant Jacob, and Israel my chosen, I call
you by your name, I surname you, though you do not know me. 5I
am the LORD, and there is no other, besides me there is no God; I
gird you, though you do not know me, 6that men may know, from
the rising of the sun and from the west, that there is none besides
me; I am the LORD, and there is no other. 7I form light and create
darkness, I make weal and create woe, I am the LORD, who do all
these things.**

1

The messenger formula is repeated, but now it is addressed to Cyrus. Cyrus is called the Lord's "anointed," a term usually applied to the kings of Israel (Saul in 1 Sm 10:1; David in 1 Sm 16:13; Solomon 1 Kgs 1:39, etc.) but here applied to a Gentile king. The verse also describes the various things the Lord does for Cyrus. Grasping his right hand is an expression of giving him power so that he can subdue nations, their kings, and open the gates of their cities. The power to "ungird the loins of kings" means that he can dethrone them, as he already had done to Croesus of Lydia and was about to do the Nabonidus of Babylon.

2–4

These verses are the message of the oracle.

2–3a

The Lord promises to give Cyrus victories by breaking down and entering the well-fortified city gates so He can open the treasuries of the nations to him.

3b–4

The oracle statement has a twofold purpose. First, Cyrus is to know that the Lord God of Israel has called him by name to fulfill this mission. It is interesting to read the "Cyrus Cylinder," a clay barrel on which is written the Persian's version of his conquests, and see that Cyrus attributed his victories not to his own gods but to Marduk of Babylon. This Akkadian text was meant as propaganda to win the favor of the Babylonians.

Second, the Lord's purpose is for Jacob/Israel, the Lord's servant, to free them from Babylon and return them home to Jerusalem. In fact, Cyrus did that in the spring of 538 BC, just a few months after his conquest of Babylon in October of 539.

5

The Lord asserts that no other gods exist and He is the only God. Many ancient peoples, including the Israelites, believed that their deity was the chief among other gods. D-I gives one of the clearest Bible statements that the other gods do not exist. Later, Daniel will think of the other deities as angels or demonic forces (see Dn 10:13, 20–21; 12:1; Michael is the prince or guardian angel of Israel).

6

A further purpose in using Cyrus is to let all peoples know that the Lord is the only God and there is no other.

7

As in Genesis 1:3–4, the Lord forms light and dark, and therefore has charge of all things. The logical conclusion is that He is in charge of all creation and of all history. The creator and redeemer is the same Lord God, besides whom there is no other.

—— Isaiah 45:8 ——

8"Shower, O heavens, from above, and let the skies rain down righteousness; let the earth open, that salvation may sprout forth, and let it cause righteousness to spring up also; I the LORD have created it.

A hymn of praise to the Lord who controls creation, as seen in the skies, rain, and earth, as well as the salvation that springs up with righteousness (Hebrew *tzedeq*). Being righteous means vindication in a court case (see Ex 23:6–8), from which comes the sense of being correct and true (see Lv 19:35–36; Dt 25:13–16, where it describes honest weights and measures; Dt 16:19–20, to define correct and honest judicial procedure). This hymn follows the Cyrus oracle by summoning the listeners to praise the Lord as Creator and Redeemer for promising to save Israel through Cyrus. The virtue of righteousness (*tzedeq*) will fall from heaven as a gift from God, and this gift will cause righteousness (Hebrew *tzedaqah*) to spring up from earth, not only as the moral virtue of being right and correct, but also in the sense of victory in battle as a vindication of the rightness of the Lord's cause.

—— Isaiah 45:9–13 ——
The Lord's Disputation with Israel

This section is the Lord's response in a disputation with those exiles who object to 45:1–7, where the Lord designates Cyrus as his "messiah" ("anointed one" in 45:1) and therefore the means of working out salvation for Israel. In essence, the people do not have the right to tell the Lord how to run the world or work out their salvation.

45:9–10

> **9"Woe to him who strives with his Maker, an earthen vessel with the potter! Does the clay say to him who fashions it, 'What are you making'? or 'Your work has no handles'? 10Woe to him who says to a father, 'What are you begetting?' or to a woman, 'With what are you suffering labor pains?'"**

Woes addressed to Israel regarding creatures who rebel against their creator. The clay vessel has no right to object to the way it is made, and no one has the right to complain to parents about the children to whom they give birth. Israel should therefore conclude that they have no right to tell God how to run His world or work out their salvation. That would especially be true since they were the ones who got themselves into exile through their sins.

45:11–12

> **[11]Thus says the LORD, the Holy One of Israel, and his Maker: "Will you question me about my children, or command me concerning the work of my hands? [12]I made the earth, and created man upon it; it was my hands that stretched out the heavens, and I commanded all their host.**

Oracle to the nations about Israel. While the Lord may speak harshly to the people for doubting His salvific plan, the Lord will be equally clear that He, the Holy One of Israel and their Maker, will save them. Therefore, the gentiles have no grounds for telling Him how to save Israel or run the universe.

45:13

> **[13]I have aroused him in righteousness, and I will make straight all his ways; he shall build my city and set my exiles free, not for price or reward," says the LORD of hosts.**

The Lord defends His choice of Cyrus as the instrument to set Israel free. The Lord recognizes Cyrus's righteousness (*tzedeq*) as a moral quality of being correct, honest, and good (see 45:8 above).

—— Isaiah 45:14–17 ——

An oracle to Cyrus followed by one statement of faith that accepts the Lord's decision to use Cyrus to save Israel and one that rejects idolatry.

45:14

> **[14]Thus says the LORD: "The wealth of Egypt and the merchandise of Ethiopia, and the Sabeans, men of stature, shall come over to you and be yours, they shall follow you; they shall come over in chains and bow down to you. They will make supplication to you, saying: 'God is with you only, and there is no other, no god besides him.'"**

The oracle begins with the usual messenger formula and then promises Cyrus that he will rule not only Babylon but Egypt, Ethiopia, and the Sabaeans in Africa. These nations' submission will be complete by recognizing that the Lord is the one and only God. And He is the one who directed and empowered Cyrus, thereby spreading and evoking faith among these foreigners.

45:15

[15]Truly, thou art a God who hidest thyself, O God of Israel, the Savior.

This declaration is a profession of faith by an exile, perhaps by D-I himself. This person accepts God's choice to act in hidden ways by using Cyrus as the means of saving Israel from exile. Its purpose is to evoke the same act of faith among all the exiles.

45:16–17

[16]All of them are put to shame and confounded, the makers of idols go in confusion together. [17]But Israel is saved by the LORD with everlasting salvation; you shall not be put to shame or confounded to all eternity.

These verses are another profession of faith, but it contrasts with the preceding verse in the God of Israel as a Savior with those who make idols, a regular theme in D-I (see 44:9, 20). The purpose is to induce any exiles tempted to worship the pagan gods to forsake this source of shame and confusion in order to accept the everlasting salvation promised by the Lord.

—— Isaiah 45:18–46:13 ——

This long section comes as the Lord's victory statement following Cyrus's defeat of Babylon. The chief clue to its unity involves the following: the first part (45:18–19) reads as an introductory oracle to the next two parts, with 45:18 introducing 45:20–25 and 45:19 introducing 46:1–13.

45:18–19

[18]For thus says the LORD, who created the heavens (he is God!), who formed the earth and made it (he established it; he did not create it a chaos, he formed it to be inhabited!): "I am the LORD, and there is no other." [19]"I did not speak in secret, in a land of darkness; I did not say to the offspring of Jacob, 'Seek me in chaos.' I the LORD speak the truth, I declare what is right."

An oracle that forms the introduction of the next two sections (45:20–25 and 46:1–13).

18

This oracle forms the introduction to the trial speech against the nations and their gods in 45:20–25, where the Lord informs them that He is the only God who expects faith and even offers them His salvation. Remember that the Babylonian creation myth, the *Enuma Elish,* professed that the earth was created when the god Marduk killed his grandmother Tiamat and cut her body in two to form the sky and earth from her corpse. The Lord, the sole God, claims to be the creator of all and desires not chaos but human beings who will inhabit the earth, as He says in the first commandment: "Be fruitful and multiply, and fill the earth" (Gn 1:28). He did not create the world and its inhabitants to live in chaos (Hebrew *tohu*), the very term used in Genesis 1:2, when it says "the world was formless and void." The nations and gods will have the meaning of this explained to them in 45:20–25.

19

This verse introduces the message of salvation addressed to Israel in 46:1–13. The oracle assumes that some of the exiles had been claiming that the Lord had spoken in the secret of darkness. He denies that here and professes that his word is right and true. The impact will be laid out in 46:1–13.

45:20–25

20"Assemble yourselves and come, draw near together, you survivors of the nations! They have no knowledge who carry about their wooden idols, and keep on praying to a god that cannot save. 21aDeclare and present your case; let them take counsel together! 21bWho told this long ago? Who declared it of old? Was it not I, the LORD? And there is no other god besides me, a righteous God and a Savior; there is none besides me. 22"Turn to me and be saved, all the ends of the earth! For I am God, and there is no other. 23By myself I have sworn, from my mouth has gone forth in righteousness a word that shall not return: 'To me every knee shall bow, every tongue shall swear.' 24"Only in the LORD, it shall be said of me, are righteousness and strength; to him

> **shall come and be ashamed, all who were incensed against him. [25]In the LORD all the offspring of Israel shall triumph and glory."**

A trial speech with the nations and their gods after Cyrus defeated Babylon.

20–21a

A summons to trial for those who survived the Persians' capture of Babylon. It describes the people as foolishly carrying around and praying to the idols that were just defeated, not so much by Cyrus but by the Lord.

21b

The Lord poses rhetorical questions to these people and gods and answers them by saying it is the Lord who foretold Cyrus's conquest. Therefore, the trial's verdict is that only the Lord is God and there is no other righteous savior God besides Him.

22

After the Lord receives the favorable verdict proclaiming that He is God, He then invites all the nations, not only the exiles of Israel, to turn to Him and be saved. Such a call to universal salvation will be a theme in Isaiah 56:1–8, which opens Trito-Isaiah. The earlier prophets gave many oracles condemning Israel. Following the people's punishment, oracles of comfort and the promise of renewal (see Jer 30–33; Ez 34, 36–48) typically took place. This formula of condemnation and hope was a pattern in the earlier prophets' preaching. Here, the defeated Babylonians and other nations to the "ends of the earth" are offered salvation. The basis for this promise is that the Lord is the only God that exists, and as D-I had said many times already, the other gods are false. Therefore, as the only God who exists, the Lord offers to save everyone who turns to Him in faith.

23–25

The Lord concludes the trial speech with a solemn oath concerning the ramifications for those who turn to Him, the only God, and be saved.

In the context of this trial, the Lord swears righteously and irrevocably that every knee shall bow to Him, a sign of worship, and every tongue swear faith. In the face of this statement, everyone has a choice to bow and swear willingly and be saved, or unwillingly and suffer subjugation as God's enemy.

This act of faith will be either a willing proclamation that righteousness and strength come from Him or shame for those who continue to worship the pagan gods, as was stated in the taunt song in 44:9–20, especially verses 9 and 11. Of course, any exiles who are tempted to follow the foreign gods also experience shame, which, again, was a horrible threat in a culture that craved honor.

Finally, the Lord's "offspring" (Hebrew "seed"), Israel, will experience victory (Hebrew root *tzadaq*) and glory as they share in the Lord's victory over the nations and foreign deities who are in fact non-deities.

46:1–13

> **[1]Bel bows down, Nebo stoops, their idols are on beasts and cattle; these things you carry are loaded as burdens on weary beasts. [2]They stoop, they bow down together, they cannot save the burden, but themselves go into captivity. [3]"Hearken to me, O house of Jacob, all the remnant of the house of Israel, who have been borne by me from your birth, carried from the womb; [4]even to your old age I am He, and to gray hairs I will carry you. I have made, and I will bear; I will carry and will save. [5]"To whom will you liken me and make me equal, and compare me, that we may be alike? [6]Those who lavish gold from the purse, and weigh out silver in the scales, hire a goldsmith, and he makes it into a god; then they fall down and worship! [7]They lift it upon their shoulders, they carry it, they set it in its place, and it stands there; it cannot move from its place. If one cries to it, it does not answer or save him from his trouble. [8]"Remember this and consider, recall it to mind, you transgressors, [9]remember the former things of old; for I am God, and there is no other; I am God, and there is none like me, [10]declaring the end from the beginning and from ancient times things not yet done, saying, 'My counsel shall stand, and I will accomplish all my purpose,' [11]calling a bird of prey from the east, the man of my counsel from a far country. I have spoken, and I will bring it to pass; I have purposed, and I will do it. [12]"Hearken to me, you stubborn of heart, you who are far from deliverance: [13]I bring near my deliverance, it is not far off, and my salvation will not tarry; I will put salvation in Zion, for Israel my glory."**

This message of salvation for Israel corresponds to the introduction in 45:19, and here has two aspects: the defeat of the Babylonian gods and salvation for Israel's exiles.

46:1–4

This announces the defeat of Babylon's two chief gods and contrasts the Lord with those inherently weak gods.

1–2

These verses are a victory song in short staccato lines (in Hebrew) that show the defeat of the gods Bel and Nebo. Throughout the exile, the Israelites would have witnessed the greatest feast of the Babylonian calendar, New Year, when a barge brought the statue of Nebo, the chief god of the Chaldeans and the son of Marduk, from his home temple in Borsippus, about fifteen miles southwest of Babylon. The Chaldean tribes had conquered Babylon, whose chief god was Marduk, and introduced their own god Nebo. As was typical of such changes of deity, a myth was developed that made the new god the son of the former god (e.g., Canaanite Baal was the son of the older creator god, Il; Zeus was the son of the older Greek god Chronos, or "Father Time"). The procession by barge from the Chaldean city of Borsippus symbolized this transfer of deities, without removing either one from the pantheon. Nebo's statue was carried through the streets of Babylon to the temple of Marduk Bel (Bel means "master," just as Baal in Hebrew and Canaanite). However, instead of triumphal processions with great crowds, Bel and Nebo are now defeated and are carried away on beasts of burden, powerless to save Babylon from Cyrus or even to save themselves.

3–4

The Lord now addresses the exiles as the "remnant," much as He had addressed the nations as "survivors" in 45:20, the beginning of the preceding section of this long poem. The Lord carries Israel from birth to old age—a stark contrast with Bel and Nebo, who must be carried by their children, the survivors of Babylon. The point that the Lord makes is that He carries Israel to save them, unlike Bel and

Nebo who must be carried by their people in order to be saved from destruction themselves.

5–8

Here is another trial speech against those who make and worship idols.

5

The Lord opens with a question to the nations about which god is equal to Him, similar to 40:18 within the first trial speech against the gods.

6–7

As in the taunt song against manufacturing idols in 44:9–20, or the trial in 40:19–20, humans using their own property, gold, and silver, for a made to order deity, is portrayed as an absurd response to the Lord's question in verse 5. Bowing down to one's own handiwork in adoration and then having to carry it around because it is too powerless to move is proof that the Lord is greater. Prayer will not be answered, either.

8

The verdict is that no one can compare to the Lord God, the only God. Therefore, the transgressors among the exiles need to learn from this and call it to mind repeatedly lest they fall into other idolatrous temptations and get punished again.

9–13

9–10

The Lord opens His address by commanding them to remember Israel's past history. The first conclusion is that there is no other God than the Lord, since He predicts what will happen and makes it come about. This has been the history from Abraham to the present. The Lord's plans are effective, and they can therefore trust that He is about to save the exiles from Babylon.

11

The "bird of prey from the east" refers to Cyrus, who came from Persia, which is east of Mesopotamia. This is the Lord's plan and it will happen just as He promised.

12–13

The Lord again tells Israel to listen, calling them stubborn and far from deliverance. While that description may define them at the moment, the Lord announces this lengthy poem's main point: He will bring His deliverance and salvation close to them in time and space. They will celebrate salvation in Jerusalem, to which He will return them. All of this will be not on their account but to give Himself the glory that is His due, a message present also in Trito-Isaiah 60:21; 61:3.

Lesson 15

Deutero-Isaiah 47–48

—— Isaiah 47:1–15 ——

An elegy on the overthrow of Babylon, similar to Isaiah 13–14 and Jeremiah 50–51.

47:1–4

The command to Babylon to be humiliated.

> **[1]Come down and sit in the dust, O virgin daughter of Babylon; sit on the ground without a throne, O daughter of the Chaldeans! For you shall no more be called tender and delicate. [2]Take the millstones and grind meal, put off your veil, strip off your robe, uncover your legs, pass through the rivers. [3]Your nakedness shall be uncovered, and your shame shall be seen. I will take vengeance, and I will spare no man. [4]Our Redeemer—the Lord of hosts is his name—is the Holy One of Israel.**

1–2

Commands to be humiliated and brought low.

3–4

The reason to expose Babylon's shame is that the Lord will take vengeance on any and all people, since He, the Redeemer, is the Holy One of Israel who cannot tolerate anything unholy.

47:5–7

> **[5]Sit in silence, and go into darkness, O daughter of the Chaldeans; for you shall no more be called the mistress of kingdoms. [6]I was angry**

with my people, I profaned my heritage; I gave them into your hand, you showed them no mercy; on the aged you made your yoke exceedingly heavy. [7]You said, "I shall be mistress for ever," so that you did not lay these things to heart or remember their end.

The Lord decrees silence and darkness along with deposing Babylon from possessing her empire because she has been ruthless to Israel. Clearly, the Lord had punished them, as they deserved for their sins. However, the Babylonian's absence of mercy, particularly on the aged, plus Babylon's arrogant claim to rule ("be mistress") an empire forever invoke the Lord's wrath.

47:8–9

[8]Now therefore hear this, you lover of pleasures, who sit securely, who say in your heart, "I am, and there is no one besides me; I shall not sit as a widow or know the loss of children": [9]These two things shall come to you in a moment, in one day; the loss of children and widowhood shall come upon you in full measure, in spite of your many sorceries and the great power of your enchantments.

The Lord accuses Babylon of two sins and threatens her with double punishment.

8

This verse lists Babylon's two sins: loving pleasure and making divine claims, such as "I am," which is the Lord's name in Exodus 3:14, and there is no one besides her. The Lord had made it clear that there is no one besides Him, which He proved in many trial speeches. Therefore, Babylon's claims are false.

9

The double punishment is loss of her children—that is, her inhabitants—and widowhood, meaning the loss of her god, Marduk Bel.

47:10–12

[10]You felt secure in your wickedness, you said, "No one sees me"; your wisdom and your knowledge led you astray, and you said in your heart, "I am, and there is no one besides me." [11]But evil shall come upon

you, for which you cannot atone; disaster shall fall upon you, which you will not be able to expiate; and ruin shall come on you suddenly, of which you know nothing.
12Stand fast in your enchantments and your many sorceries, with which you have labored from your youth; perhaps you may be able to succeed, perhaps you may inspire terror.

The Lord tells Babylon that her wisdom and knowledge led her astray into the arrogant belief that there is no one besides Babylon. However, Babylon's wisdom and knowledge did not prevent her destruction and ruin, a future which, in fact, she was not able to know. However, God knew and foretold it through D-I. In verse 12, he taunts Babylon to continue in its wisdom, which, as Daniel 2 indicates, included a diverse array of magical practices. The "perhaps" is mocking Babylon to continue down its self-destructive path.

47:13–15

13You are wearied with your many counsels; let them stand forth and save you, those who divide the heavens, who gaze at the stars, who at the new moons predict what shall befall you.
14Behold, they are like stubble, the fire consumes them; they cannot deliver themselves from the power of the flame. No coal for warming oneself is this, no fire to sit before!
15Such to you are those with whom you have labored, who have trafficked with you from your youth; they wander about each in his own direction; there is no one to save you.

The Lord describes the wise counselors and magicians, especially astrologers who "gazed" at the stars and planets and "divided the heavens" into constellations to foretell the destiny of the kingdom. In fact, in the *Enuma Elish,* Marduk creates the stars and constellations to control the "destinies of gods and men." However, here the Lord predicts a coming fire, not for their use in warming themselves but for their utter destruction. See Deuteronomy 18:9–11 for a strong condemnation of occult practices.

—— Isaiah 48:1–11 ——

The Lord summons Jacob/Israel to know that He who had predicted both the old prophecies about their punishment and the new prophecies of their redemption was now about to bring redemption, not for Israel's sake, but for His own.

48:1–2

> **[1]Hear this, O house of Jacob, who are called by the name of Israel, and who came forth from the loins of Judah; who swear by the name of the LORD, and confess the God of Israel, but not in truth or right. [2]For they call themselves after the holy city, and stay themselves on the God of Israel; the LORD of hosts is his name.**

The Lord summons Jacob/Israel to listen to Him. The summons has seven clauses which describe Jacob: they are called Israel, the particular people He summons are from the tribe of Judah; they swear by the Lord; they profess faith in the Lord, but not in truth or righteousness; they identify themselves by Jerusalem; and depend on the God of Israel, the Lord of hosts.

48:3–11

The Lord's utterance to Jacob.

> **[3]"The former things I declared of old, they went forth from my mouth and I made them known; then suddenly I did them and they came to pass. [4]Because I know that you are obstinate, and your neck is an iron sinew and your forehead brass, [5]I declared them to you from of old, before they came to pass I announced them to you, lest you should say, 'My idol did them, my graven image and my molten image commanded them.' [6a]"You have heard; now see all this; and will you not declare it? [6b]From this time forth I make you hear new things, hidden things which you have not known. [7]They are created now, not long ago; before today you have never heard of them, lest you should say, 'Behold, I knew them.' [8]You have never heard, you have never known, from of old your ear has not been opened. [8b]For I knew that you would deal very treacherously, and that from birth you were called a rebel. [9]For my name's sake I defer my anger, for the sake of my praise I restrain it for you, that I may not cut you off. [10]Behold, I have refined you, but not like silver; I have tried you in the furnace of affliction. [11]For my own sake, for my own sake, I do it, for how should my name be profaned? My glory I will not give to another.**

3–6a

The Lord had announced things in the past and they came about. The spiritual danger was that in their stubbornness and obstinacy, they might easily have attributed the various events to the pagan gods and idols. Therefore, the Lord announced them through His prophets to make sure that they knew it all came from Him. Such reasoning explains the frequent use of the trial speeches earlier in D-I.

6b–11

Now the Lord announces new events which were unknown to Israel.

6b–8a

The Lord announces that the new things are hidden and completely unknown to Israel.

8b

The Lord explains the reason for the secret; namely, Israel was a treacherous and rebellious nation. Therefore, Israel could not be trusted with the information any more than the people could be trusted with the covenant, law, and prophecies they had received before the exile. The Lord did not want to act toward them in anger constantly, so He restrained His anger to prevent completely destroying the people.

10

In light of God's restraint, He now explains that the time of exile was one of purification, a refining such as happens with silver. The image of refining people like silver would be familiar to the people, since it appears in texts such as Proverbs 17:3—"The crucible is for silver, and the furnace is for gold, and the Lord tries hearts"—and Psalms 66:10—"For you, O God, have tested us; you have tried us as silver is tried." However, here it is used to explain their experience in the exile, in contrast to those opinions which considered the exile a failure by the Lord and a victory for the Babylonian gods, such as is assumed in the earlier trial speeches in D-I.

11

The Lord does this not for the sake of Israel's pride or self-image but for His own glory. Because Israel's sins had profaned the Lord's name, they needed a time of punishment and purification from their national sins of idolatry, injustice to the poor, and the general acceptance of sin, such as described by Proto-Isaiah, Jeremiah, and Ezekiel. By explaining the exile here, God shows that His anger is rooted in His complete unwillingness to let the people attribute historical events to other deities or to offer them praise. From the first commandment of the Decalogue that prohibits other gods, the Lord states, "I am a jealous God" (Ex 20:5; 34:14; Dt 4:24; 6:15; 32:21). Therefore, no compromise to worship or give credit to any other deity is tolerable.

—— Isaiah 48:12–17 ——

This is a trial speech with Israel, who is summoned to listen (v. 12) to the Lord's arraignment of the false gods (vv. 14–15), drawing Israel closer to the Lord in trust (v. 16). God is truly the beginning and end who knows the best way for them to follow (v. 17).

48:12–13

> **[12]"Hearken to me, O Jacob, and Israel, whom I called! I am He, I am the first, and I am the last. [13]My hand laid the foundation of the earth, and my right hand spread out the heavens; when I call to them, they stand forth together.**

The Lord summons Jacob/Israel to listen to Him, particularly to His identity as the creator of the earth and heavens (also elsewhere in D-I). God fashioned the earth and heavens by His hand and, very importantly, called out in order to create. Bringing creation into existence by God's word is the basis of Genesis 1, seen in the repetition of "God said, let there be . . ." (Gn 1:3, 6, 9, 11, 14–15, 20, 22, 24, 26). Creating by a word stands in direct contrast to the Babylonian deities, who created each other through sexual union and created the universe through a violent war, including the killing of the grandmother goddess, Tiamat, in combat and shaping the universe with her corpse *(Enuma Elish)*. By asserting His power as creator, the Lord gives a basis for claiming that He is the Lord of history and salvation in verses 14–15.

The Lord also identifies Himself as the "first and last" (also in D-I, 41:4; 44:6). All of existence begins in God and its fulfillment will be in Him. This self-definition reinforces the oracle's conclusion (v. 17), which defines the Lord as the one who leads others for their own good and profit. God can make this claim because as the "first," He knows each person's origin, and as the "last," He knows each person's end. This notion of being the first and last is very important in Revelation, which treats the end of the world and God's control over the final purpose of all creation (Rv 1:8, 21:6: the Lord God is the Alpha and Omega—i.e., first and last letters of Greek alphabet; 1:17, 2:8, 22:13: Christ is the first and the last, passages which clearly equate God and Christ thereby claiming Jesus's divinity).

48:14–15

> **14"Assemble, all of you, and hear! Who among them has declared these things? The LORD loves him; he shall perform his purpose on Babylon, and his arm shall be against the Chaldeans. 15I, even I, have spoken and called him, I have brought him, and he will prosper in his way.**

The Lord assembles the gods to testify regarding His question concerning the things He was doing, especially with Cyrus. The answer is obviously the Lord, who loves, calls, and prospers Cyrus so that he can accomplish the Lord's purposes in history, including in Babylon, the chief city of Marduk Bel.

48:16

> **16Draw near to me, hear this: from the beginning I have not spoken in secret, from the time it came to be I have been there." And now the LORD God has sent me and his Spirit.**

The Lord speaks to Israel, telling them to draw near so as to understand that His words govern salvation history, even as His word calls creation into existence (v. 13). He is present in this history, whether to punish as He had decreed through Jeremiah and Ezekiel or in the promise of salvation spoken through His prophets. And His presence continues through D-I, whom He has sent and who has received His Spirit in order to be able to prophesy.

48:17

> **[17]Thus says the LORD, your Redeemer, the Holy One of Israel: "I am the LORD your God, who teaches you to profit, who leads you in the way you should go.**

This is an oracle from the Redeemer who is the Holy One of Israel. This oracle informs the exiles that as the Lord their God, He leads them for their own good—that is, for their profit. If they accept His leadership, they will prosper, so the oracle implies an imperative to follow the Lord's lead.

—— Isaiah 48:18–19 ——

> **[18]O that you had hearkened to my commandments! Then your peace would have been like a river, and your righteousness like the waves of the sea; [19]your offspring would have been like the sand, and your descendants like its grains; their name would never be cut off or destroyed from before me."**

The Lord desires that Israel had kept His commandments so that He would not have had to punish them but would have been able to bless and reward them. This serves well as a proper reaction from the Lord to the preceding trial speech about being the creator and redeemer who knows how to lead Israel because He knows best where they are going.

—— Isaiah 48:20–22 ——

Here the Lord commands Israel to leave Babylon. His words refer specifically to the trial with Israel in 12–17 that proved His ability to know where they should go. This order to leave Babylon will be for their "profit" (v. 17), but wicked people who doubt God will find no peace (v. 22).

48:20a

> **[20a]Go forth from Babylon, flee from Chaldea,**

The straightforward command to leave Babylon, which was ruled by the Chaldeans.

48:20b

> **[20b]declare this with a shout of joy, proclaim it, send it forth to the end of the earth; say, "The LORD has redeemed his servant Jacob!"**

The Lord commands Israel to leave with a shout of victory just like the psalms of praise (e.g., Ps 100).

48:21

> **[21]They thirsted not when he led them through the deserts; he made water flow for them from the rock; he cleft the rock and the water gushed out.**

This reflective passage on Exodus centers on the Lord's providence in the Israelites' past desert wanderings. The exiles know they will have to cross a desert, so recalling the provision of water in the Sinai will be important for them before setting out on their own journey.

48:22

> **[22]"There is no peace," says the LORD, "for the wicked."**

The Lord lays down a warning for those who, because of their wickedness, refuse to go back home to Jerusalem. They may think that staying in Babylon is better, but they will not find peace there. Such people may be "wicked" because they have not accepted the verdicts of the various trials that proved that God is the only God, the creator and redeemer. They may even still have some trust in the Babylonian deities. The Lord's warning also challenges those who reject His identity as the one who knows where Israel is supposed to go as well as those who are seeking peace.

Lesson 16

Deutero-Isaiah 49:1–52:3

—— Isaiah 49:1–7 ——

This unit is the second servant song: the call of the servant of the Lord.

In this song, the servant is the speaker, though he also reports the words which the Lord spoke to Him in verses 3, 6, and 7.

49:1

> **[1]Listen to me, O coastlands, and hearken, you peoples from afar. The Lord called me from the womb, from the body of my mother he named my name.**

The servant announces to the far distant coastlands that the Lord has called Him. These "coastlands" probably refer to the western coast and islands of Asia Minor (modern Turkey) which Cyrus had conquered as the western limit of his empire. King Croesus of Lydia (in western Asia Minor) had declared war against Cyrus in 549 BC. Cyrus defeated Croesus in 546, and by 545, his army had subjected all of Asia Minor, thereby making this the western edge of his empire. The servant's call from the Lord is apparently important even to these distant regions. Asia Minor would be one of the areas evangelized by Saints Paul, Peter, Philip, and other Christians 580 years later, and it would remain an important center of Christianity until the Turkish conquests in the fifteenth century.

The servant also wants these distant people, as well as his nearby listeners, to know that the Lord called him from his mother's womb. This resonates with the call of Jeremiah from his mother's womb (see Jer 1:4–5) and is implied in the promise of sons to Abraham, Isaac, and others who have important roles to play in the history of Israel. Later, the Church will read this in light of both John the Baptist and Jesus Christ, whose conceptions were announced by the Angel Gabriel with descriptions of their missions from God.

49:2

> **[2]He made my mouth like a sharp sword, in the shadow of his hand he hid me; he made me a polished arrow, in his quiver he hid me away.**

Making his mouth like a two-edged sword or polished arrow is clearly a reference to his mission to proclaim God's word, which is identified as a two-edged sword by the Ehud in Judges 3:16, 20–22 (see Is 11:4; Heb 4:12; Eph 6:17; Rv 1:16 makes direct reference to this verse). The image of the sword indicates close combat, and therefore a more intimate spread of the Word; the polished arrow is used for distance combat, indicating that his ministry of the Word will be wide reaching.

49:3

> **[3]And he said to me, "You are my servant, Israel, in whom I will be glorified."**

The servant's announcement about his call is followed by an oracle from the Lord that identifies him as servant Israel, in whom the Lord will be glorified. This verse leads many commentators to identify the servant as the whole people of Israel rather than as an individual. However, later in this passage we will see that the servant has a mission to Israel and Jacob, which indicates he is distinct from the nation as a whole. That will make more sense of the majority of passages about the servant of the Lord in succeeding chapters.

The oracle is filled with promise that his mission of spreading God's word will glorify the Lord.

49:4

> **[4]But I said, "I have labored in vain, I have spent my strength for nothing and vanity; yet surely my right is with the LORD, and my recompense with my God."**

Even with God's confident promise in the previous verse, the servant still responds with discouragement. His mission appears like a failure. At the same time, the servant affirms God's justice and reward is with Him, even despite any appearances to the contrary. Such was the confidence of Jesus Christ throughout His passion and of the martyrs in their sufferings and persecutions.

49:5–6

> **5And now the LORD says, who formed me from the womb to be his servant, to bring Jacob back to him, and that Israel might be gathered to him, for I am honored in the eyes of the LORD, and my God has become my strength—6he says: "It is too light a thing that you should be my servant to raise up the tribes of Jacob and to restore the preserved of Israel; I will give you as a light to the nations, that my salvation may reach to the end of the earth."**

Here the servant presents another oracle (in quotation marks) with a long introduction by which the servant recognizes and accepts the Lord's call from the womb to bring Jacob Israel—that is, the whole nation—back to the Lord. He also professes faith that the Lord has honored him and given him strength. The oracle of verse 6 is a response to the servant's faith and trust in God. The Lord announces that restoring Israel is too small a task, so His mission will be to the nations so that salvation might go to all people. This oracle is brought up in Luke 2:42, when Simeon identifies the infant Jesus as the "light for the revelation to the nations." Later, in Acts 1:8, Jesus promises the apostles the Holy Spirit so that they can take the Gospel to Jerusalem, Judea, Samaria, and the ends of the world, since His mission as Servant of the Lord is universal.

49:7

> **7Thus says the LORD, the Redeemer of Israel and his Holy One, to one deeply despised, abhorred by the nations, the servant of rulers: "Kings shall see and arise; princes, and they shall prostrate themselves; because of the LORD, who is faithful, the Holy One of Israel, who has chosen you."**

In this oracle, the Lord uses two titles for Himself: the Redeemer of Israel and His Holy One. As Redeemer, the Lord comes close to the one who is despised and abhorred; as the Holy One, He is set apart and beyond human control or ability to reduce Him to a human level. The Hebrew root for "holy" (*qadosh*) has two ancient meanings: to be on fire and to be set apart. Both notions are present in the burning bush of Exodus 3, since the fire appears and Moses is ordered to remove his shoes because he walks on holy ground. This title repeats at the end of the verse, revealing that the faithful and holy Lord will subdue the foreign kings and princes

Throughout this verse, the Lord speaks to the "servant of rulers" as an individual, indicated by the second person "you" singular as the one who is chosen. Though He is deeply despised and abhorred by the nations as a servant, the Lord will reverse this and cause the rulers to prostrate themselves before the servant whom the Lord, the Holy One has chosen.

The Hebrew word for "prostrate" is typically used of worship. The Greek word used here in the Septuagint (*proskuneo*) is commonly used in the New Testament for worshiping God (see Mt 4:10; Lk 4:8; Rv 14:7; 15:4; 19:10). Yet it also is used when the man with a legion of demons approaches Jesus (see Mk 5:6) and when the soldiers crowned Him with thorns (see Mk 15:19), showing the Lord's opponents in worship of Him, even if in fear or mockery at those points. Particularly important is when the disciples in the boat call Him the Son of God and worshiped Him (see Mt 14:3) and the proclamation that the angels worship Him (see Heb 1:6). The Lord's triumph for His Servant Jesus Christ occurs as His enemies, His disciples, and the angels worship Him.

—— Isaiah 49:8–13 ——

This oracle is a proclamation of salvation addressed to "you" singular, perhaps meaning the servant, whose salvific message is for everyone.

49:8a–b

> **[8]Thus says the LORD: "In a time of favor I have answered you, in a day of salvation I have helped you; I have kept you and given you as a covenant to the people,**

The Lord God announces that He has turned to answer the servant, who described himself as having labored in vain. His prayers are not stated here but are assumed when the Lord says He has answered them "in a time of favor," "on a day of salvation." In fact, the servant is a "covenant" to the people, a line that helps us understand Christ's words at the institution of the Eucharist, "This is my blood of the covenant" (Mt 26:28; Mk 14:24; Lk 22:20; 1 Cor 11:25). Clearly, Jesus sees Himself as fulfilling the servant of the Lord's role by becoming the covenant to the people.

49:8c

> **8c to establish the land, to apportion the desolate heritages;**

The purpose or goal of the day of salvation is stated in infinitive sentences about the reestablishment of the abandoned land of Israel. The Babylonians had twice removed people from the land—10,000 political leaders, soldiers, and artisans in 598 BC, and the rest of the population, except for the very poor, in 587. A depopulated land reverts back to wilderness fairly quickly.

49:9–11

> **9 saying to the prisoners, 'Come forth,' to those who are in darkness,**
> **'Appear.' They shall feed along the ways, on all bare heights shall be**
> **their pasture; 10 they shall not hunger or thirst, neither scorching wind**
> **nor sun shall smite them, for he who has pity on them will lead them,**
> **and by springs of water will guide them. 11 And I will make all my**
> **mountains a way, and my highways shall be raised up.**

A description of the journey the exiles will soon make from Babylon to Israel.

9

The prisoners and people in darkness are the most powerless in the community, yet even they are addressed with the Lord's command to come forth from the exile in Babylon.

10–11

The Israelites' journey is described as a new Exodus, including the promise that they will not hunger or thirst, despite the fact that they will travel through a desert. The Lord had provided food and water in the Sinai for Moses and the Israelites, so will He do for the exiles returning from Babylon. Also, similar to the Exodus, where a cloud protected them from the sun by day, neither the sun nor the wind will hurt them in the deserts between Mesopotamia and Israel.

49:12

> **[12]Lo, these shall come from afar, and lo, these from the north and from the west, and these from the land of Syene."**

The pledge of an exodus to the Promised Land includes the Babylonian exiles along with those who went to the north and west and the far south in Syene, now known as Aswan, Egypt, at the first cataracts of the Nile River.

49:13

> **[13]Sing for joy, O heavens, and exult, O earth; break forth, O mountains, into singing! For the LORD has comforted his people, and will have compassion on his afflicted.**

Hymns conclude a number of sections of D-I (42:10–13; 44:23; 45:8; 51:3; and 52:7–10), perhaps imitating the Temple worship. This verse is also a hymn in which the heavens, earth, and mountains rejoice because the Lord has comforted His people, as had been ordered in Isaiah 40:1: "Comfort ye, comfort ye my people." Now the Lord Himself has done so. The reason that the heavens, earth, and mountains are commanded to sing this hymn is that in traditional ancient covenant making ceremonies, dating to the Late Bronze Age, these were called to witness covenants. Also, humans have a shorter life span compared to the cosmic realities, the latter providing lasting witnesses (see Dt 32:1; Mi 6:1–2; Is 1:2).

— Isaiah 49:14–26 —

This is a unit with three parts (14–20, 21–23, 24–26), each begins with Israel making an assertion in the form of a lament that disputes the Lord's promise. The Lord responds to each lament by disputing the exiles' doubts and by proclaiming salvation.

49:14–20

[14]But Zion said, "The LORD has forsaken me, my LORD has forgotten
me." [15]"Can a woman forget her sucking child, that she should have
no compassion on the son of her womb? Even these may forget, yet I
will not forget you. [16]Behold, I have graven you on the palms of my
hands; your walls are continually before me. [17]Your builders outstrip
your destroyers, and those who laid you waste go forth from you. [18]Lift
up your eyes round about and see; they all gather, they come to you.
As I live, says the LORD, you shall put them all on as an ornament,
you shall bind them on as a bride does. [19]"Surely your waste and your
desolate places and your devastated land—surely now you will be too
narrow for your inhabitants, and those who swallowed you up will be
far away. [20]The children born in the time of your bereavement will yet
say in your ears: 'The place is too narrow for me; make room for me
to dwell in.'

14

The exiles, identified as Zion, their homeland of origin and destination after they are freed from Babylon, respond with a lack of faith flowing from despondency. The people think that God has abandoned and forgotten them in Babylon, an idea that D-I has been speaking against throughout the opening chapters of his prophecies.

15

The Lord responds with an analogy from human life: mothers never forget their children nor withhold compassion from them. God's love is even greater than that and He promises that He will never forget them. Later, reflecting on God's infinite nature from a philosophical standpoint, He will point out that it is metaphysically impossible for the all-knowing and eternal God ever to forget anything. But that is a reflection that would come centuries after this point in time when Israel is moving gradually to less primitive and more sophisticated understandings of God.

16

Instead of having forsaken Israel, the Lord asserts that Israel is permanently before Him, like a carving on the palms of someone's hand. He has never forsaken Israel and never will. Some Christians represent this image with a popular carving of a child in a hand.

17–20

Proclamation of salvation in two different ways, corresponding to the Lord's promises to Abram: land and descendants (Gn 12:1–2; 15:5–7, 18–21). The Lord had called Abram from Mesopotamia to receive the land and descendants, and now that the nation is back in Mesopotamia (Babylon), the double promise is repeated, though in terms of the return from the exile.

17–18

The homeland will be rebuilt faster than enemies can destroy it. The exiles are told to look around and see this. Of course, if they did look around, they would still see that they are in Babylon. However, D-I wants the people to catch his vision and imagine a wonderful restoration.

18–19

The depopulated land may have become desolate and waste, but the population will rebound and the empty land will be too small to hold them.

49:21–23

21Then you will say in your heart: 'Who has borne me these? I was bereaved and barren, exiled and put away, but who has brought up these? Behold, I was left alone; whence then have these come?'" 22Thus says the Lord God: "Behold, I will lift up my hand to the nations, and raise my signal to the peoples; and they shall bring your sons in their bosom, and your daughters shall be carried on their shoulders. 23Kings shall be your foster fathers, and their queens your nursing mothers. With their faces to the ground they shall bow down to you, and lick the dust of your feet. 23bThen you will know that I am the Lord; those who wait for me shall not be put to shame."

21

A first-person lament by the exiled people as a barren woman who, to her great surprise, suddenly realizes that she has many children. Lamentations, another book composed early in the exile, also expressed great concern about the nation's childlessness (Lam 1:5, 20; 5:3). Here, apparently, D-I is speaking this to his fellow exiles, posing the lament in the form of rhetorical questions. These questions help the exiles realize that their captivity was not a complete catastrophe, as the existence of the young children proves.

22–23a

The Lord responds with an unexpected proclamation of salvation. The nations and their kings and queens, who once oppressed Israel to death and caused her to be bereft of children, will bring forth her children. This salvation will entail the humbling of the former oppressors, as in 49:7.

23b

The result of this salvation is that the doubters who raised questions about posterity and the future of the nation will learn that the Lord is truly God. For those who trust in Him will not be put to shame (see also Ps 25:3; 69:6; Rom 9:33; 10:1; 1 Pt 2:6).

49:24–26

> **24Can the prey be taken from the mighty, or the captives of a tyrant be**
> **rescued? 25Surely, thus says the LORD: "Even the captives of the mighty shall be taken, and the prey of the tyrant be rescued, for I will contend with those who contend with you, and I will save your children. 26I**
> **will make your oppressors eat their own flesh, and they shall be drunk with their own blood as with wine. Then all flesh shall know that I am the LORD your Savior, and your Redeemer, the Mighty One of Jacob."**

Lament in a question form and a proclamation of salvation as an answer.

24

This lament concerns enemies, from whom captives cannot be taken. The exiles assume that they are the prey, and the Babylonians will not give them up.

25–26

The proclamation of salvation assures the captives that they can be set free from the mighty tyrants, since the Lord is obviously much stronger than Israel's foes. In verse 25b, the Lord moves from the general possibility of helping Israel to contending for her and saving her children. The oppressors will consume themselves instead of their captives. At that point, everyone will know that the Lord is the Savior and Redeemer of Jacob.

—— Isaiah 50:1–3 ——

This section is a trial speech between Israel and the Lord. (As in 43:22–8, see the lesson in which He has to defend why it was justifiable to send them into exile. The implication is that some people complained about being in the exile when they did not do anything wrong).

50:1a

> **[1a]Thus says the LORD: "Where is your mother's bill of divorce, with which I put her away? Or which of my creditors is it to whom I have sold you?**

The people's complaint is implied and unstated. This opens with the Lord speaking, apparently citing their charge that He has divorced Israel His bride and sold her children to creditors, as if God owed anything to the Babylonian captors.

50:1b

> **[1b]Behold, for your iniquities you were sold, and for your transgressions your mother was put away.**

The Lord answers their charge by saying that He had sent them into exile because of their iniquities and transgressions. Therefore, it is not the Lord who is the guilty party in this trial; Israel is.

50:2a

> **[2a]Why, when I came, was there no man? When I called, was there no one to answer?**

The next step is the Lord's rhetorical questions about no one giving Him an answer. The people are silenced by His answer to the charges and they accept that they are the guilty party.

50:2b–3

> **[2b]Is my hand shortened, that it cannot redeem? Or have I no power to deliver? Behold, by my rebuke I dry up the sea, I make the rivers a desert; their fish stink for lack of water, and die of thirst. [3]I clothe the heavens with blackness, and make sackcloth their covering."**

Still, though Israel is guilty and deserved their temporary exile, the Lord will bring them back. Since He has the power over nature to dry up seas and make rivers in deserts, so does He have the power to redeem Israel from exile. Today, geologists are well aware of the number of inland seas that have dried up throughout the world. The ancients were also aware of this, since fossils of sea creatures can still be found in the limestone of Israel, which was under the sea for about five million years. The ancients did not know how to date such things, but they understood the impression of fish in the limestone they quarried to be evidence of Israel having been under the sea.

—— Isaiah 50:4–9 ——
Third Servant Song as a Psalm of Confidence

This particular song emphasizes the servant's call from God, a call to speak words which the Lord had given him. However, his fidelity to speaking God's word became the cause of his suffering and difficulties, much as had been the case of Jeremiah just before the exile.

50:4–5a

> **[4]The LORD God has given me the tongue of those who are taught, that I may know how to sustain with a word him that is weary. Morning by morning he wakens, he wakens my ear to hear as those who are taught. [5]The LORD God has opened my ear.**

The servant describes how the Lord commissioned him for the ministry of the word (see Jer 20:8). The intended audience of the Lord's word is the "weary," presumably the exiles. Perhaps D-I is describing himself as the servant in this song. Also, the servant has an ongoing mission since the Lord wakens his ears "morning by morning" to be taught an ongoing message.

This passage can also be applied to Christ, who speaks the word that His Father taught Him:

- John 7:16: So Jesus answered them, "My teaching is not mine, but his who sent me."
- John 8:28: "I do nothing on my own authority but speak thus as the Father taught me."
- John 12:49–50: "For I have not spoken on my own authority; the Father who sent me has himself given me commandment what to say and what to speak. And I know that his commandment is eternal life. What I say, therefore, I say as the Father has bidden me."
- John 14:24: "The word which you hear is not mine but the Father's who sent me."
- John 17:8: "I have given them the words which you gave me."
- John 17:14: "I have given them thy word."

Jesus understands Himself to be a servant who receives God's Word rather than passing on His own ideas.

50:5b–6

5b And I was not rebellious, I turned not backward. 6 I gave my back to the smiters, and my cheeks to those who pulled out the beard; I hid not my face from shame and spitting.

However, the servant is attacked with violence, much like Jeremiah (see Jer 11:19, 21; 18:18; 20:10). Later, Christians will understand that Jesus fulfills this word during His passion, especially when He is being abused by the soldiers at Caiaphas's house (see Mt 26:67–68; Mk 14:65; Lk 22:63–65) and during the scourging (see Mt 27:26–30; Mk 15:19).

50:7–9

7 For the LORD God helps me; therefore I have not been confounded; therefore I have set my face like a flint, and I know that I shall not be

put to shame; [8]he who vindicates me is near. Who will contend with me? Let us stand up together. Who is my adversary? Let him come near to me. [9]Behold, the LORD God helps me; who will declare me guilty? Behold, all of them will wear out like a garment; the moth will eat them up.

The servant expresses his confidence in the Lord and His assurance that he will not be put to shame. Rather, he asks to face his attackers squarely, since he knows he will be vindicated by God and they will be ashamed.

7

The Middle East, like other cultures, puts a high value on gaining honor and avoiding shame. For that reason, the psalms frequently offer prayers against being shamed (see Ps 25:2–3, 20; 31:1, 17; 37:18–19).

8–9

This section begins with a statement of confidence that the Lord will vindicate this suffering servant soon (8a), followed by rhetorical questions that dare his opponents to come near and challenge him, since the Lord is already near (8b). Another act of confidence in God as his helper (9a) is followed by a rhetorical question about who will declare the servant guilty (9b). The song concludes with a statement of certainty that Israel's enemies will be destroyed, not the servant. Again, it is obvious to apply this confidence in God's vindication to Jesus Christ, whose resurrection vindicates Him after His trials, condemnations, torment and abuse, and death on the cross.

—— Isaiah 50:10–11 ——

[10]Who among you fears the LORD and obeys the voice of his servant, who walks in darkness and has no light, yet trusts in the name of the LORD and relies upon his God? [11]Behold, all you who kindle a fire, who set brands alight! Walk by the light of your fire, and by the brands which you have kindled! This shall you have from my hand: you shall lie down in torment.

These verses make a change from the preceding song, spoken by the servant in the first person, to an address to a previously unidentified group. The group is challenged by a rhetorical question to fear the Lord and obey His servant. Since the servant trusts the Lord completely, this group—again, presumably the exiles—ought to rely on God and the servant so they can walk in light rather than darkness. Verse 11b is difficult, but it seems to imply that if they do not follow the servant, then the Lord will cause them to experience torment.

—— Isaiah 51:1–8 ——

This section has three parts, each of which begins with the command to "hearken" or hear me. Note that the command to "listen" is addressed to three different groups.

51:1–3

**[1]"Hearken to me, you who pursue deliverance, you who seek the
LORD; look to the rock from which you were hewn, and to the quarry
from which you were digged. [2]Look to Abraham your father and to
Sarah who bore you; for when he was but one I called him, and I bless-
ed him and made him many. [3]For the LORD will comfort Zion; he will
comfort all her waste places, and will make her wilderness like Eden,
her desert like the garden of the LORD; joy and gladness will be found
in her, thanksgiving and the voice of song.**

First, those who pursue deliverance are told to return to their origins in Abraham and Sarah. Just as the Lord called him (from Mesopotamia, in fact) as individuals, the Lord was able to make them a multitude, despite the odds being against such an elderly couple. 51:3 motivates this trust by promising the Lord will comfort Zion, in fulfillment of the opening command of Isaiah 40:1 to "comfort" the exiles." This comfort will come in the form of a transformation of Zion's deserted wilderness land into a new garden of Eden filled with joy, gladness, and thanksgiving that has liturgical overtones for the restoration of the Temple.

51:4–6

**[4]"Listen to me, my people, and give ear to me, my nation; for a law
will go forth from me, and my justice for a light to the peoples. [5]My
deliverance draws near speedily, my salvation has gone forth, and my**

arms will rule the peoples; the coastlands wait for me, and for my arm they hope. [6]Lift up your eyes to the heavens, and look at the earth beneath; for the heavens will vanish like smoke, the earth will wear out like a garment, and they who dwell in it will die like gnats; but my salvation will be for ever, and my deliverance will never be ended.

The second command to listen is to "my people . . . my nation." The Lord's promise is that a law and justice will be a light to the "peoples"—that is, the Gentiles who do not know the law (v. 4). Then "salvation" and "deliverance" will cause the Lord to rule the peoples, not as a foreign imposition, but as a hope they have for their own future (v. 5). Finally, a cosmic transformation will end the heavens and earth, killing their inhabitants. Nonetheless, the Lord's promised salvation and deliverance will be eternal.

51:7–8

[7]"Hearken to me, you who know righteousness, the people in whose heart is my law; fear not the reproach of men, and be not dismayed at their revilings. [8]For the moth will eat them up like a garment, and the worm will eat them like wool; but my deliverance will be for ever, and my salvation to all generations."

The third group ordered to "hearken" are those who "know" righteousness, have God's law in their hearts, and have no fear of rejection. Because of their docility, this group will witness the destruction of the enemies while still enjoying the Lord's eternal salvation and deliverance.

—— Isaiah 51:9–52:3 ——

This long unit also has three subsections that begin with imperatives to awaken, addressed to the Lord ("Awake, awake, . . . O arm of the Lord awake"), to Jerusalem ("Rouse yourself, rouse yourself"), and to Zion ("Awake, awake, put on your strength, . . . put on your beautiful garments, . . . Shake yourself, . . . arise, . . . loose the bonds"). This use of imperatives to begin units is common in D-I, as in Isaiah 40:1 imperatives, "Comfort, comfort," and the imperatives at the start of each section of the preceding 51:1–8.

51:9–16

> **9Awake, awake, put on strength, O arm of the Lord; awake, as in**
> **days of old, the generations of long ago. Was it not thou that didst**
> **cut Rahab in pieces, that didst pierce the dragon? 10Was it not thou**
> **that didst dry up the sea, the waters of the great deep; that didst make**
> **the depths of the sea a way for the redeemed to pass over? 11And the**
> **ransomed of the Lord shall return, and come to Zion with singing;**
> **everlasting joy shall be upon their heads; they shall obtain joy and**
> **gladness, and sorrow and sighing shall flee away. 12"I, I am he that**
> **comforts you; who are you that you are afraid of man who dies, of**
> **the son of man who is made like grass, 13and have forgotten the Lord,**
> **your Maker, who stretched out the heavens and laid the foundations**
> **of the earth, and fear continually all the day because of the fury of**
> **the oppressor, when he sets himself to destroy? And where is the fury**
> **of the oppressor? 14He who is bowed down shall speedily be released;**
> **he shall not die and go down to the Pit, neither shall his bread fail.**
> **15For I am the Lord your God, who stirs up the sea so that its waves**
> **roar—the Lord of hosts is his name. 16And I have put my words in**
> **your mouth, and hid you in the shadow of my hand, stretching out the**
> **heavens and laying the foundations of the earth, and saying to Zion,**
> **'You are my people.'"**

This first subsection is a call for the Lord's arm to awake as in past acts of salvation.

9–10

The call for the Lord to awaken His arm is followed by the people questioning His past redemptive acts in Egypt. The people's lament suggests that God is not acting in their present situation in Babylon.

Particularly in the Exodus, the Lord promised that His "outstretched arm" would save Israel (Ex 6:6), and later, Israel celebrated that He had in fact done so (see Dt 4:34; 5:15; 7:19; 9:29; 11:2; 26:8; 2 Kgs 17:36; Ps 36:12; Jer 32:21). D-I especially recalls the Exodus with this image, as he refers to Rahab and the dragon (see the link between Rahab and the dragon or serpent in Job 26:12–13). Rahab is the name of a monster at the beginning of creation whom God took control of the seas and calmed its waves (see Ps 89:9–10). Frequently, Rahab is used to identify Egypt (see Ps 87:4; Is 30:7). Here D-I links the defeat of the monster at creation with the defeat of Egypt as a model of the defeat of Babylon, whose mother goddess was Tiamat, the salt water, who created a monster named Kingu, both of whom were defeated by the god Marduk. D-I claims that the Lord God defeats the forces of chaos in the past, present, and future by His mighty arm. Therefore, he calls for the Lord to awaken that arm to end Babylon's power. Note that Ezekiel, another prophet exiled to Babylon, also said that the Lord's outstretched arm would save the exiles (see Ez 20:33–34).

11

A promise of salvation, taken from Isaiah 35:10 as a response to the questions raised in verses 9b–10: the ransomed will indeed return from exile to Zion in joy and gladness.

12–15

The Lord Himself answers the people's questions in the lament of verses 9b–10. He is the one who comforts them (note again D-I's usage of comfort). This promise is followed by the Lord's own questions about Israel, as if He were lamenting their lack of faith. Who is Israel to fear mortal men while forgetting the Creator? These questions are followed by a promise to release the bowed down prisoners in exile, a promise supported by the Lord, who stirs up the sea and is therefore in charge of everything that appears to be chaos. This is in stark contrast to the *Enuma Elish,* wherein the father god of fresh water, Apsu, and the mother god of salt water, Tiamat, oppose each other and are later slain by the god of the wind and his son the storm god, Marduk. Now Babylon will be defeated, and the forces of nature deified by the Babylonians will be seen merely as forces of nature over which the Lord God has control.

16

The Lord addresses the prophet in words similar to the description of the servant in 50:4 and in 49:16. The Lord assures the prophet that the one who places His words in His mouth is the same one who created the earth and chose the people of Zion as His people. The Creator is the same as the Redeemer, and He therefore has the authority to give prophetic words that are effective in history.

51:17–23:

Jerusalem Is Ordered to Rouse Herself

**[17]Rouse yourself, rouse yourself, stand up, O Jerusalem, you who have
drunk at the hand of the LORD the cup of his wrath, who have drunk
to the dregs the bowl of staggering. [18]There is none to guide her among
all the sons she has borne; there is none to take her by the hand among
all the sons she has brought up. [19]These two things have befallen you—
who will condole with you?—devastation and destruction, famine and
sword; who will comfort you? [20]Your sons have fainted, they lie at
the head of every street like an antelope in a net; they are full of the
wrath of the LORD, the rebuke of your God. [21]Therefore hear this, you
who are afflicted, who are drunk, but not with wine: [22]Thus says your
LORD, the LORD, your God who pleads the cause of his people: "Be-
hold, I have taken from your hand the cup of staggering; the bowl of
my wrath you shall drink no more; [23]and I will put it into the hand of
your tormentors, who have said to you, 'Bow down, that we may pass
over'; and you have made your back like the ground and like the street
for them to pass over."**

17–20

The command for Jerusalem to rouse herself starts another lament over the destruction, famine, and sword that have overtaken her. Jerusalem is here identified as the one who drank the cup of the Lord's wrath. This image of the cup of wrath is common in the Old Testament (see Job 21:20; Ps 11:6; 60:3; 75:8; Jer 25:15–17, 27; Ez 23:31–34; Zech 12:2) and will be used by Jesus (see Mt 20:22–23; Mk 10:38–39), in Gethsemane (see Mt 26:39; Mk 14:36; Lk 22:42; Jn 18:11), and in Revelation (see Rv 14:10; 18:6). Jerusalem's punishment was given by the Lord, and verse 20 ends the lament by saying it was the wrath and rebuke of God that caused the suffering.

21–23

However, the lament of those who are "drunk" with affliction is answered by the Lord God who identifies Himself as the one who pleads their cause. Remember the earlier trial scenes in D-I, where the Lord put the exiles and the pagan deities on trial; now the Lord is pleading for the people, stating that He has removed the cup of pain and wrath in order to give it to the Babylonians who had oppressed them.

52:1–3

[1]Awake, awake, put on your strength, O Zion; put on your beautiful garments, O Jerusalem, the holy city; for there shall no more come into you the uncircumcised and the unclean. [2]Shake yourself from the dust, arise, O captive Jerusalem; loose the bonds from your neck, O captive daughter of Zion. [3]For thus says the LORD: "You were sold for nothing, and you shall be redeemed without money.

Zion-Jerusalem is commanded to awake. The Lord will not only cause the oppressive Babylonians to suffer (51:22–23), but now Jerusalem will be free of her bonds, will be beautified by the removal of the unclean, and made a holy city. The removal of defilement and making holy are two sides of the coin that address the people's ability to restore true worship of the Lord to Jerusalem, an issue that will become a special theme of Trito-Isaiah.

Lesson 17

DEUTERO-ISAIAH 52:4–53:12

—— Isaiah 52:4–6 ——

4For thus says the LORD GOD: My people went down at the first into
Egypt to sojourn there, and the Assyrian oppressed them for nothing.
5Now therefore what have I here, says the LORD, seeing that my people
are taken away for nothing? Their rulers wail, says the LORD, and continually all the day my name is despised. 6Therefore my people shall
know my name; therefore in that day they shall know that it is I who speak; here am I."

A prose oracle looking back on Israel's historical relationships with two great empires—Egypt and Assyria—as a perspective on Babylon's situation. The Egyptians of the late Bronze Age and the Assyrian Empire of the eighth to seventh centuries did not gain anything by oppressing Israel, and neither has Babylon come out ahead by taking them into exile. Look back to the oracles against Egypt in Isaiah 19–20, against Assyria in 10:5–34, 14:24–27, and against Babylon in chapters 13 and 21, as well as the earlier oracles in D-I 46–47 (see lessons 6, 14, 15).

The evidence of Babylon's failure came when King Nabonidus went into hiding after the Persians defeated his armies at Opis in early October 539 BC. On October 20, the leaders inside the city of Babylon opened the gates to Cyrus's conquering army, and Nabonidus, though disguised, was captured and handed over to the Persians. Cyrus entered Babylon on October 29, welcomed by the people waving palm branches. This thorough defeat causes the Babylonians to wail while the people of Israel will recognize that the Lord had predicted this amazing turn of events and therefore have faith in Him. This overview is the Lord's definitive answer to His earlier calls to fear not (41:8–16; 43:1–7), the proclamations of salvation (43:16–21; 44:1–5; 49:7–12), and trial speeches (41:1–5; 43:8–15).

—— Isaiah 52:7–10 —— Hymn of Praise to God the King

This hymn is a response to the liturgical poem of 51:9–52:3, which moves from the community's lament through a promise of salvation and finally to a proclamation of salvation. The acceptance of this proclamation of salvation as true evokes this hymn of praise. Given the background of Cyrus's imminent takeover of Babylon, the people move from lament to praise. However, they do not praise the conquering Cyrus, whom the Lord had promised, but praise the Lord who made the promise in the first place. Hymns had concluded a number of D-I's sections—42:10–13; 44:23; 45:8; 49:13; 51:3; and here—perhaps seeking to replicate the Temple worship. However, the celebration is for the events that God is bringing about in history through the victories of Cyrus and the defeat of Babylon.

52:7–8

> **7How beautiful upon the mountains are the feet of him who brings good tidings, who publishes peace, who brings good tidings of good, who publishes salvation, who says to Zion, "Your God reigns." 8Hark, your watchmen lift up their voice, together they sing for joy; for eye to eye they see the return of the LORD to Zion.**

The announcement of salvation's good news is brought by someone whose feet are on the mountains. Babylon and Mesopotamia have no mountains whatsoever, while Jerusalem is on a hill and is surrounded by mountains. The messenger is bringing the good news of Babylon's defeat to Jerusalem, just as in 587 BC messengers had brought the news of the defeat of Jerusalem to Babylon. However, the content of this good news is not the defeat of Babylon but rather the eternal good news that "your God reigns" and that the people will see the return of the Lord to Zion.

52:9–10

[9]Break forth together into singing, you waste places of Jerusalem; for the LORD has comforted his people, he has redeemed Jerusalem. [10]The LORD has bared his holy arm before the eyes of all the nations; and all the ends of the earth shall see the salvation of our God.

This hymn implores the community to sing out to the Lord because He has already "comforted" His people (see the beginning of D-I in 40:1 where the plural imperative "comfort ye" was announced) and has redeemed Jerusalem. The redemption has taken place, so one may date this hymn after Cyrus's conquest of Babylon in October 539 BC and his decree to let Israel return home in November 538. Also, this hymn probably took place before the return to Jerusalem under Sheshbazzar in the spring of 537, since verse 7 only proclaims the tidings and publication of the good news of release.

—— Isaiah 52:11–12 ——

The final command to depart from Babylon begins with another repetition of the imperative, as in 40:1, 51:9, 17, and 52:1. This short section is the main point for all of Deutero-Isaiah: now is the time to depart from Babylon. This is probably not so much a description of what happened as it is a command to leave before it actually begins.

The History of the Departure from Babylon

On October 13, 539 BC, Gobryas, the governor of Gutium, led Cyrus's troops into Babylon without having to fight the inhabitants. Babylonian King Nabonidus was in the town of Uruk from October 14 to 20, not yet having heard about the capture of Babylon. He was captured on October 20 after returning to Babylon in disguise. On October 29, Cyrus himself entered Babylon, with the people placing branches and rejoicing at his arrival, since he planned to restore the full and proper worship of Marduk, which Nabonidus had neglected. Between December 539 and February 538, Cyrus ordered the return of the idols, which Nabonidus had taken from the various cities with much honor and ceremony and the rebuilding of new temples. In November 538, Cyrus returned to Ecbatana, the former capital of Media, where he issued his decree to let "the house of God which is in Jerusalem be built." It was to be paid for by the royal treasury and the sacred vessels which Nebuchadnezzar had removed from the Temple were to be returned (Ez 1:8; 6:3–5, 13–16). In the spring of 537 BC, Sheshbazzar and other Jewish exiles left Babylon and returned to Judah, arriving there in the month of Tishri (Sept./Oct.). They rebuilt the altar and offered sacrifice, "according to the Law of Moses, the man of God" (Ez 3:1–3). On the first day of Tishri, they offered the daily sacrifice at morning and evening. On 15 Tishri, they celebrated the Feast of Booths.

52:11

> **[11]Depart, depart, go out thence, touch no unclean thing; go out from the midst of her, purify yourselves, you who bear the vessels of the Lord.**

The command to "depart" includes orders to do so with ritual cleanness, bearing the vessels of the Lord's Temple which had been removed by Nebuchadnezzar.

52:12

> **[12]For you shall not go out in haste, and you shall not go in flight, for the Lord will go before you, and the God of Israel will be your rear guard.**

Therefore, the people need not fear to make the journey.

—— Isaiah 52:13–53:12 ——
Fourth Song of the Servant of the Lord

This final song of the "servant of the Lord" in D-I is connected with the others, emphasizing his call and future mission. However, this described the mission in terms of suffering for others. Isaiah 42:1–4 describes the Lord's call to bring "justice to the nations" (v. 1) and promise that he "will not fail or be discouraged till he has established justice in the earth" (v. 4). Here, the Lord begins with a promise to "prosper" and be exalted (52:13), along with a description of His coming suffering (vv. 14–15). The Lord's proclamation about the servant is followed by a report (53:1–11a) on the suffering of the servant by an unidentified group of people who simply speak as "we." Amazingly, they understand themselves as being at fault through their own sins while the servant is innocent. Furthermore, His suffering is for them, to justify them after their sins.

Finally, in 53:11b–12, the Lord again speaks promises that His servant will justify many, as the people's report states, and He will be vindicated in a great victory. With this general backdrop, we can examine each subsection in more detail.

52:13–15

> **13Behold, my servant shall prosper, he shall be exalted and lifted up,**
> **and shall be very high. 14As many were astonished at him—his ap-**
> **pearance was so marred, beyond human semblance, and his form be-**
> **yond that of the sons of men—15so shall he startle many nations; kings**
> **shall shut their mouths because of him; for that which has not been**
> **told them they shall see, and that which they have not heard they**
> **shall understand.**

The Lord makes a proclamation that describes his servant.

13

The Lord addresses an audience, presumably the people of Israel, with a promise that His servant shall prosper and be exalted.

14–15

In contrast to this promise, the Lord describes His servant as so marred in appearance that people will be astonished and nations and kings will be startled to silence.

53:1–11

> **1Who has believed what we have heard? And to whom has the arm**
> **of the Lord been revealed? 2For he grew up before him like a young**
> **plant, and like a root out of dry ground; he had no form or comeli-**
> **ness that we should look at him, and no beauty that we should desire**
> **him. 3He was despised and rejected by men; a man of sorrows, and**
> **acquainted with grief; and as one from whom men hide their faces**
> **he was despised, and we esteemed him not. 4Surely he has borne our**
> **griefs and carried our sorrows; yet we esteemed him stricken, smitten**

> **by God, and afflicted. 5But he was wounded for our transgressions, he was bruised for our iniquities; upon him was the chastisement that made us whole, and with his stripes we are healed. 6All we like sheep have gone astray; we have turned every one to his own way; and the LORD has laid on him the iniquity of us all. 7He was oppressed, and he was afflicted, yet he opened not his mouth; like a lamb that is led to the slaughter, and like a sheep that before its shearers is dumb, so he opened not his mouth. 8 By oppression and judgment he was taken away; and as for his generation, who considered that he was cut off out of the land of the living, stricken for the transgression of my people? 9And they made his grave with the wicked and with a rich man in his death, although he had done no violence, and there was no deceit in his mouth. 10Yet it was the will of the LORD to bruise him; he has put him to grief; when he makes himself an offering for sin, he shall see his offspring, he shall prolong his days; the will of the LORD shall prosper in his hand; 11ahe shall see the fruit of the travail of his soul and be satisfied.**

A chorus speaks of the servant.

1

A chorus of people ("we") begins with rhetorical questions about something amazing—namely, the Lord's suffering servant:

2–3

This section forms the chorus' initial report of the servant from his youth through his time of suffering during his manhood. The servant grew up before the Lord, coming from an unexpected place—the dry ground. When applied to Jesus Christ, this can be seen as a veiled reference to His birth of a Virgin.

Next, the chorus describes their own reaction to him—he had no physical beauty that attracted them to him.

In verse 3 comes the report that people despised him and therefore hid their faces from him. Even the chorus did not hold him in any esteem. Within himself, he was identified with his sorrows and the personal experience of grief.

4–5

The chorus states why the servant suffers: he is bearing "our" griefs, sorrows, transgressions, and iniquities. Normally, in Israel, the people would have brought animals to be sacrificed as sin offerings, but the Temple had been destroyed by the Babylonians in 587 BC. Consequently, no one was able to offer Temple sacrifice. Now we see a completely new idea in Israel: that a human being can take away sins by his suffering and death (53:8–9).

Verse 4 is directly cited by Saint Matthew in a summary statement on Jesus's healing ministry: "This was to fulfil what was spoken by the prophet Isaiah, 'He took our infirmities and bore our diseases'" (Mt 8:17). While verse 5c, "and with his stripes we are healed," is cited in 1 Peter 2:24: "He himself bore our sins in his body on the tree, that we might die to sin and live to righteousness. By his wounds you have been healed."

6

The chorus describes itself as straying sheep whose iniquity is laid upon the servant. The whole community acknowledges its guilt. However, the one responsible for laying everyone's guilt on the lamb-like servant is the Lord. The guilty people did not take that initiative, presumably because they do not have the power to lay their guilt on the suffering servant—only the Lord has that power and authority.

A reference to this verse and application to all Christians is found in 1 Peter 2:25: "For you were straying like sheep, but have now returned to the Shepherd and Guardian of your souls."

7–9

The servant resembling a lamb or sheep can be seen in two ways: he submits to his suffering and oppression quietly; he is without any guilt, having done no violence or spoken any deceit. Verse 8 states that his suffering is unjust, using a rhetorical question to show that he was stricken and died for the transgressions of the people, who do not comprehend what he is doing to justify them. One might consider here Luke 23:34: "Father, forgive them; for they know not what they do."

When the Holy Spirit directs the deacon, Philip, to come upon the Ethiopian eunuch on the Gaza road, the eunuch is reading Isaiah 53 and cites verses 7–8, 10, and 12, which perplex him in regard to the identity of the man about whom these things are said. Philip, jogging alongside the chariot, explains that Jesus Christ fulfills this passage, and the eunuch asks for baptism at a pool of water, which ancient Christians described as being only a few inches deep. This effective passage helps people recognize Jesus's messiahship; it was so important, that the rabbis of Jamnia forbade the inclusion of Isaiah 53 in the synagogue lectionary cycle from AD 85 to the present.

10–11a

At this conclusion of the people's report, three ideas are brought forth. First, the Lord willed that the servant suffer for the sake of everyone else (v. 10a). Second, the servant offers himself for sin, so his will is not at odds with the Lord's will (v. 10b). Third, he will be vindicated, even though he has died, with a prolonged life, prosperity from the Lord, and the satisfaction of seeing the fruit of his suffering (vv. 10c–11a). These ideas will be confirmed in the Lord's proclamation in the following verse (v. 12), thereby giving divine sanction and hope for the servant.

53:11b–12

> **11bBy his knowledge shall the righteous one, my servant, make many to be accounted righteous; and he shall bear their iniquities. 12aTherefore I will divide him a portion with the great, and he shall divide the spoil with the strong; 12bbecause he poured out his soul to death, and was numbered with the transgressors; 12cyet he bore the sin of many, and made intercession for the transgressors.**

The Lord concludes the song with a proclamation of promise. The servant will be vindicated after the purpose of his suffering is made known.

11b

Once again the Lord speaks, as indicated by identifying the "righteous one" as "my servant." While this proclamation assumes the suffering that is promised in 52:14–15 and described in the people's report of 53:1–11a, here, the servant's "knowledge" will cause others to be accounted as righteous. His knowledge will have this effect because the Lord's servant is himself "the righteous one," possessing a righteousness within himself that can make other people righteous. His "knowledge" of righteousness is interior and has a power to share righteousness with other people.

12a

This is God's promise of vindication that is directly related to the chorus' preceding description of the servant's sufferings in 53:1–11, as indicated by the "therefore" at the beginning of the verse. The promise of a "portion" and of "spoils" indicates that his vindication is similar to a war. The images of Cyrus and his conquering armies dividing up the spoils of the Babylonian Empire may well lie in the background.

12b

The promise of dividing the spoils is causally compared to his suffering "death" and being "numbered with the transgressors." His death will be his victory. Yet, if he has died through his sufferings and is still going to divide the spoils of victory, then it becomes logical to conclude that he will be raised up from the dead. Although not explicitly stated here, Ezekiel had received a vision of the dead's dry bones being raised up and the Lord promising to open the people's graves thirty-five or forty years earlier, in the 570s BC (see Ez 37:1–14). Sometime between Deutero- and Trito-Isaiah, the so-called "Isaiah Apocalypse" (Is 24–27) was composed, and it also promised a resurrection of the dead (Is 26:19; see lesson 20). Faith in the Resurrection was just beginning and would take greater shape in Daniel 12:3 and become far clearer in the New Testament.

Jesus cited this passage at the end of the Last Supper, showing that He understood Himself as the Servant of the Lord who fulfills the passage: "For I tell you that this scripture must be fulfilled in me, `And he was reckoned with transgressors'; for what is written about me has its fulfilment" (Lk 22:37).

Of course, Christians have regularly pointed out that Jesus Christ was "numbered among transgressors" when He was crucified between two thieves: "Two others also, who were criminals, were led away to be put to death with him. And when they came to the place which is called The Skull, there they crucified him, and the criminals, one on the right and one on the left" (Lk 23:32–33).

Verse 12b also states that "he poured out his soul to death." An echo of this occurs in Jesus's dying moment: "Then Jesus, crying with a loud voice, said, 'Father, into thy hands I commit my spirit! And having said this he breathed his last" (Lk 23:46). "And Jesus cried again with a loud voice and yielded up his spirit" (Mt 27:50; see also Mk 15:37; Jn 19:30).

12c

This suffering was not meant for the servant but for the "sin of many" and for transgressors, as is consistent with the message of the chorus in 53:5–6, 8. The difference is that the chorus understood his suffering for "our" sins and transgressions—that is, for the sins of Israel—while here the Lord confirms that the suffering is for the sins of the people.

Note how Jesus interceded for sinners even as He hung upon the cross: "Father, forgive them; for they know not what they do" (Lk 23:34).

This is particularly highlighted in the dialogue between Jesus and the two thieves: "One of the criminals who was hanged reviled him, saying, 'Are you not the Christ? Save yourself and us!' But the other rebuked him, saying, 'Do you not fear God, since you are under the same sentence of condemnation? And we indeed justly; for we are receiving the due reward of our deeds; but this man has done nothing wrong.' And he said, 'Jesus, remember me when you come into your kingdom.' And he said to him, 'Truly, I say to you, today you will be with me in Paradise'" (Lk 23:39–43).

Lesson 18

Deutero-Isaiah 54–55

—— Isaiah 54:1–10 ——

The basic form is an announcement of salvation to Zion, which understands itself as a barren widow since the destruction of Jerusalem. The Lord announces that she will have children in abundance, and therefore is not barren, and that He will betroth her as her true husband, even though she had committed “adultery” by worshiping other gods.

54:1–3

> **1“Sing, O barren one, who did not bear; break forth into singing and
> cry aloud, you who have not been in travail! For the children of the
> desolate one will be more than the children of her that is married, says
> the Lord. 2Enlarge the place of your tent, and let the curtains of your
> habitations be stretched out; hold not back, lengthen your cords and
> strengthen your stakes. 3For you will spread abroad to the right and to
> the left, and your descendants will possess the nations and will people
> the desolate cities.**

This hymn of praise states the reasons for such praise while announcing the end of Israel’s desolation.

1

As in hymns of praise, Israel, addressed as the “barren one,” is commanded to “sing,” “break forth,” and “cry aloud” in praise to God. Verse 1b explains the reason to praise God: Though Jerusalem was “desolate,” her children will exceed those of the “married” one, referring to Babylon. The promise that the small community of exiles would prosper with children in excess of the conquering Babylon would have seemed absurd. However, modern people can certainly observe the prosperity of Jerusalem and the fact that Babylon is a completely uninhabited ruin today.

2–3

Again, the imperatives ("enlarge," "be stretched out," "hold not back," "lengthen," and "strengthen") are addressed to the desolate Jerusalem. The Israelites had lived in houses in towns and cities since the twelfth century BC, but this reference to dwelling in tents calls to mind the nation's roots: Abraham, Isaac, and Jacob had dwelt in tents; after leaving Egypt, the people dwelt in tents again. Since D-I had frequently referred to the Exodus from Egypt as the model for the salvation from Babylonian exile, it is likely that he used the tent image from that period. Further, one of the three great festivals in Israel was Tabernacles, a feast when the Israelites dwelt in tents to remind them of their desert wandering. That feast was also associated with recognizing the Lord's kingship, as in the hymns of Psalms 97 and 99, and His superiority over the other deities and creation in Psalms 96 and 98.

The tent expansion follows the population growth. These new descendants will fill the desolate cities of Israel and will eventually possess other nations, as was the case in David's time.

54:4–6

> **4"Fear not, for you will not be ashamed; be not confounded, for you**
> **will not be put to shame; for you will forget the shame of your youth,**
> **and the reproach of your widowhood you will remember no more. 5For**
> **your Maker is your husband, the LORD of hosts is his name; and the**
> **Holy One of Israel is your Redeemer, the God of the whole earth he is**
> **called. 6For the LORD has called you like a wife forsaken and grieved in**
> **spirit, like a wife of youth when she is cast off, says your God.**

This third section also begins with imperatives to Israel: "fear not" and "be not confounded." D-I announced that shame would be the future of those who were angry with God (41:11), idolaters (42:17, 44:9, 11, 45:16), and for Babylon (47:3), but promised that those who trust the Lord would not be put to shame (49:23). Now, in the exultation of this hymn, God tells desolate Israel that shame and reproach are to be removed as they return home.

Furthermore, God seeks to restore the relationship between Israel as bride and the Lord as husband. This image of restoration of a marital relationship figures prominently in eighth-century Hosea 1–3 during the Assyrian crisis, as well as in Jeremiah 3:14–17 and Ezekiel 16 and 20 in the pre-exilic period. Israel had been an unfaithful wife, chasing after other gods like an adulteress chasing other men. Now she has repented, and D-I announces the reconciliation between the Lord and her.

54:7–10

> **7For a brief moment I forsook you, but with great compassion I will**
> **gather you. 8In overflowing wrath for a moment I hid my face from**
> **you, but with everlasting love I will have compassion on you, says**
> **the LORD, your Redeemer. 9For this is like the days of Noah to me:**
> **as I swore that the waters of Noah should no more go over the earth,**
> **so I have sworn that I will not be angry with you and will not re-**
> **buke you. 10For the mountains may depart and the hills be removed,**
> **but my steadfast love shall not depart from you, and my covenant**
> **of peace shall not be removed, says the LORD, who has compassion**
> **on you.**

The Lord speaks to Israel directly and tenderly as part of the reconciliation.

7–8

The time of the exile may have seemed long. The first exiles went to Babylon in 598 BC, the deportation after the destruction of Jerusalem was in 587 BC, and the liberation began in 538 BC. However, for the Lord, this is a "brief moment." His "great compassion," motivated by "everlasting love," is far more long lasting, since the Lord is the Redeemer. Again, recall that redeemer was a family role, requiring family members to "redeem" anyone who had been murdered by executing the murderer, or buying back family land that had been sold, or by bringing home anyone who had been enslaved. The Lord Redeemer now returns captured Israel and restores her to her land, as is key to the role of redeemer.

9–10

The Lord's words refer back to His promise to Noah, a rare reference within the Old Testament (elsewhere, only a mention is made of Noah in Ez 14:14, 20; Tb 4:12; Sir 44:17). Just as the Lord swore not to punish the earth with another flood, so does the Lord swear not to rebuke the exiles. In the time of Noah, this was part of a covenant (see Gn 9:11–16), so here does the Lord make a covenant of peace with the exiles out of His compassion and love for them. This promise is meant to allay fears of a repeated punishment, similar to the way the Lord had allayed Noah's fears of another flood.

His love and compassion will outlast the mountains and hills (v. 10). Such a line indicates that the Old Testament was by no means devoid of God's love, as some think. This is only one of many rich expressions of God's love, and as a culminating text in D-I, it points out the purpose of this whole prophetic work: God loves Israel, even after sin and punishment. He acts to redeem them because of His love.

—— Isaiah 54:11–17 ——

This passage has two sections, both promising salvation to the exiles.

54:11–12

> **11"O afflicted one, storm-tossed, and not comforted, behold, I will set your stones in antimony, and lay your foundations with sapphires. 12I will make your pinnacles of agate, your gates of carbuncles, and all your wall of precious stones.**

The New Jerusalem depiction is addressed to the afflicted, storm tossed, and discomfited people living in exile. While D-I just spoke of the return to Jerusalem in 54:1–10, the exiles can only imagine the ruined, burnt out city that they or their immediate forebears had left smoldering when Nebuchadnezzar forced them into exile. In contrast to their forsaken state, Nebuchadnezzar's palace included the "Hanging Gardens," one of the seven wonders of the ancient world. Now the Lord promises them a magnificent city, calling them to imagine His possibilities of beauty as a hope that can replace the ruined reality to which they would return.

In verse 11, the present participle "I am setting" rather than the RSV "I will set" your stones is better, indicating that since this action is already in God's mind, it is in process even as He speaks. This makes the promise of Jerusalem's future somewhat similar to the act of creation. "Antimony" means a dark powder used as eye make-up (Jer 4:30), and here is a dark cement used for setting stones in mosaic patterns. The sapphires may refer to lapis lazuli, such as was used to decorate walls and jewelry, while "agate" is an approximate translation for a term that refers to some kind of precious stone (mentioned only in Ez 27:16). The carbuncles seem to be a sparkling stone; the Septuagint Greek calls it crystal, and the Latin and other Greek translations speak of it as "sculpted stones." This description of the city may include words for precious or semi-precious stones whose meanings are unclear today; later descriptions of hope for a bejeweled Jerusalem appear in Tobit 13:16–18 and for the new and heavenly Jerusalem in Revelation 21:19–21.

54:13–17

> **13All your sons shall be taught by the LORD, and great shall be the prosperity of your sons. 14In righteousness you shall be established; you shall be far from oppression, for you shall not fear; and from terror, for it shall not come near you. 15If any one stirs up strife, it is not from me; whoever stirs up strife with you shall fall because of you.**
> **16Behold, I have created the smith who blows the fire of coals, and produces a weapon for its purpose. I have also created the ravager to destroy; 17no weapon that is fashioned against you shall prosper, and you shall confute every tongue that rises against you in judgment. This is the heritage of the servants of the LORD and their vindication from me, says the LORD."**

The form here is a promise of blessing of prosperity and protection from danger.

13

The Lord promises to teach the exiles' children, bestowing on them a wisdom that makes their prosperity possible. In Deuteronomy 4:6, Moses commands Israel to "keep and do" God's laws because they "will be your wisdom and your understanding in the sight of the peoples, who, when they hear all these statutes, will say, ‘Surely this great nation is a wise and understanding people.’” The restored exiles will be truly corrected along the ways of right and wrong, as the Lord teaches it. This is especially important since Israel’s disobedience had led to their destruction in the first place.

14–15

What flows from the Lord’s teaching is a “righteousness” that establishes them. Therefore, they will be protected from enemies. If they should dare to attack the people, the enemies shall fall. This promise is similar to the promise of blessing for those who bless Abram and a curse for those who curse him (Gn 12:3).

16–17

The promise of protection is confirmed by the promise to create a smith who produces a weapon of protection and a “ravager” to destroy Israel’s opponents. This double use of the verb “create” links the roles of God as Creator and Redeemer, as has been common in D-I. Since the Lord is doing this for Israel, no enemy will prosper either in battle or in legal judgment. Such confidence in the Lord is the “heritage” of His servants. This is more poignant in light of the vindication of the suffering servant of Isaiah 53, though here the promise of vindication is for all of His servants—that is, the whole nation.

—— Isaiah 55:1–5 ——

The Lord commands the exiles to prepare themselves to hear His proclamation of salvation, which will be a new covenant.

55:1–3a

> **1“Ho, every one who thirsts, come to the waters; and he who has no**
> **money, come, buy and eat! Come, buy wine and milk without money**
> **and without price. 2Why do you spend your money for that which is**
> **not bread, and your labor for that which does not satisfy? 2bListen dil-**
> **igently to me, and eat what is good, and delight yourselves in fatness.**
> **3aIncline your ear, and come to me; hear, that your soul may live;**

This is the introduction to the proclamation with repeated imperatives, as is typical of D-I's style (see 40:1–2; 51:9). The Lord commands Israel to "come . . . come, buy and eat," as the way to prepare themselves with the proper food and drink that He has prepared for them. One may look to Exodus 3:7–8, where the Lord has "heard" the cries and affliction of the Israelites in Egypt and now promises them freedom from slavery and to "bring them up out of that land to a good and broad land, a land flowing with milk and honey." This fits D-I's new exodus theme. Also, Lady Wisdom invites people to her feast so that the simple may gain wisdom (Prv 9:1–6), "Come, eat of my bread and drink of the wine I have mixed" (Prv 9:5), and see Sirach 24:19, "Come to me, you who desire me, and eat your fill of my produce."

1–2a

An ironic command for the people to come and buy food and drink without money. The backdrop to this invitation may lie in the Middle East marketplaces where men carry large containers of water, tea, or juice on their backs and cry out to the passers-by to buy a drink. However, such drinks do not ultimately satisfy a person and the Lord is offering food and drink that will provide a more ultimate satisfaction.

2b–3a

These verses are a summons to come and hear the proclamation about to be announced. The Lord's word is going to be the food that ultimately satisfies: "Man does not live by bread alone but by every word that comes from the mouth of God" (Dt 8:3).

55:3b–5

The actual proclamation.

> **3b and I will make with you an everlasting covenant, my steadfast, sure love for David. 4 Behold, I made him a witness to the peoples, a leader and commander for the peoples. 5 Behold, you shall call nations that you know not, and nations that knew you not shall run to you, because of the Lord your God, and of the Holy One of Israel, for he has glorified you.**

3b

The proclamation of salvation is that the Lord Himself will make an "everlasting covenant" with Israel. This covenant is linked to the Lord's steadfast love for David. Of course, Christians will link this promise of salvation with Christ's institution of the Eucharist when He says, "This is the cup of my blood, the blood of the new and everlasting covenant" (Mt 26:28; Mk 14:24; Lk 22:20; 1 Cor 11:25).

4–5

The promise is directed to David, who will no longer be the king of Israel only, but also a "witness," "leader," and "commander" for the peoples of the world (v. 4). Then the Lord addresses David and tells him, "you" will call nations who will come to you because the Lord has glorified him. The address in verse 5 is all in the second person singular, and therefore a direct promise to the Davidic leader rather than to the Israelites. The claim that the Lord has glorified him helps readers link the servant of the Lord who suffers and then is vindicated (Is 53) with this Davidic leader. For that reason, it is easy for Christians to see Jesus Christ, the Son of David, as the fulfillment of this promise. In its light, the mission to the Gentiles from Acts 10 forward makes sense as the fulfilment of this promise.

—— Isaiah 55:6–11 ——

This is the epilogue to Deutero-Isaiah that is linked with the prologue.

55:6–7

> **6"Seek the LORD while he may be found, call upon him while he is near; 7let the wicked forsake his way, and the unrighteous man his thoughts; let him return to the LORD, that he may have mercy on him, and to our God, for he will abundantly pardon.**

This is a series of four imperatives to seek the Lord and repent of evil in order to find God's mercy and pardon. The exiles need to live morally to receive the promise of salvation that the Lord has been making.

55:8–9

**[8]For my thoughts are not your thoughts, neither are your ways my ways,
says the LORD. [9]For as the heavens are higher than the earth, so are my
ways higher than your ways and my thoughts than your thoughts.**

The Lord substantiates these commands by declaring that not only are His thoughts and ways different from human thoughts but they are as far superior as the heavens are above the earth. This statement of wisdom is meant for the hearer to reflect and to draw the conclusion, "I want to follow the ways of the Lord rather than merely human wisdom."

55:10–11

**[10]"For as the rain and the snow come down from heaven, and return
not thither but water the earth, making it bring forth and sprout, giv-
ing seed to the sower and bread to the eater, [11]so shall my word be
that goes forth from my mouth; it shall not return to me empty, but
it shall accomplish that which I purpose, and prosper in the thing for
which I sent it.**

A second substantiation of the commands to seek the Lord and repent is the declaration that the Lord's word is inherently effective, as rain or snow on the arid soil. Once rain falls, the seed cannot help but grow. When God's word comes to people, it cannot help but effect the purpose for which the Lord sent it. This links back to 48:13–15, where God's Word caused creation to exist and His Word called Cyrus to be the instrument of salvation for Israel. Therefore, the words of D-I are also trustworthy.

—— Isaiah 55:12–13 ——

This concluding prophecy for the exiles proclaims that they shall indeed leave Babylon in joy and peace.

55:12a

[12a]"For you shall go out in joy, and be led forth in peace;

They will not sneak out but will return home in jubilation and peace will lead them. They will not be looking back in fear of pursuers but will look forward to God's salvation as the return home.

55:12b–13a

> **[12b]the mountains and the hills before you shall break forth into singing, and all the trees of the field shall clap their hands. [13a]Instead of the thorn shall come up the cypress; instead of the brier shall come up the myrtle;**

All of nature will rejoice with them, from mountains and hills to the trees. The nature, which God has created, shares in Israel's salvation by joining in the celebration. Of course, this will make the journey home easier for the exiles.

55:13b

> **[13b]and it shall be to the LORD for a memorial, for an everlasting sign which shall not be cut off."**

This great act of salvation will be a "memorial" (lit. Hebrew "a name") and an everlasting sign for the Lord since He had predicted it and it occurred. Recall the many trials in D-I where the proof of the Lord being the only God was that He had spoken predictions of the future and He made them take place, including the punishment of Israel for its sins. Here, too, God predicted the liberation from Babylon and He acts. Therefore, it is a sign of His divine power.

Lesson 19

Isaiah Apocalypse 24–25

—— Introduction to —— the Isaiah Apocalypse

Since 1892, Isaiah 24–27 has been designated the "Isaiah Apocalypse" by German scholars B. Duhm and Hermann Guthe because of its divine cataclysmic themes involving the destruction of the world, judgment of all nations, the redemption of Israel in the holy city of Jerusalem, and particularly, its teaching on the resurrection of the dead. Various battles and the resulting ruin of cities are portrayed. Scholars, however, have been unable to connect them with any specific historical events, except for the brief mention of Moab in 25:10b–12 and the obvious references to Zion and Jerusalem. This non-historical quality is best understood symbolically as the final destruction of all the earth, its cities, and kingdoms when God comes to judge at the end of time.

Studying these four chapters' poetic meter helps in dating them but requires knowledge of the Hebrew language. Such a study shows that chapters 24 through 26 use a quality of meter similar to Deutero-Isaiah, but in chapter 27, the quality of meter falls apart and moves to the poorer quality common throughout Trito-Isaiah. For that reason, these chapters are placed in a time between Deutero- and Trito-Isaiah—that is, between the return to Jerusalem in 538 BC and the end of the 500s. No specific historical events can be identified within these texts, perhaps supporting that time period when Israel was quietly, and in terms of world history, rebuilding itself. In 26:21, the Lord came from "his place" to "worship" on

His holy mountain (see 27:13), indicating that these texts came after the Temple was rebuilt. The Temple rebuild began when Sheshbazzar rebuilt the altar in September/October 537 BC (see Ez 3:1–3), and the foundation was laid in May/June of 536. Work on the Temple ceased temporarily, but at the instigation of the prophet Haggai, it was completed between 520 and 516 BC (Hg 1:1, 14–15). Perhaps these texts, filled with distress, refer to the Samaritans' repeated attempts to prevent the building of the Temple after 536 BC.

One possibility is that the tumult of the nations in these chapters refers to the Persian conquest of Egypt in 525 BC, when Cambyses II wiped out the Egyptian army at the Battle of Pelusium and captured Memphis the capital and Pharaoh Psammetichus. Also possible is the revolt in Persia, during which Cambyses II feared defeat and committed suicide in 522 BC, the year that Zerubbabel, the grandson of Judah's King Jehoiachin, and other exiles returned to Jerusalem. Cambyses's spear-bearer, Darius, left the territory of Israel to Persia to successfully take control of the empire by 520, the year Zerubbabel started working to finish the Temple. The ties between these political events and the rebuilding of the Temple may have inspired Isaiah 24–27 with its end of the world prophecies.

— Isaiah 24:1–13 —

This forms a prophecy of the destruction of the whole world in four stanzas.

24:1–3

> **1Behold, the Lord will lay waste the earth and make it desolate, and**
> **he will twist its surface and scatter its inhabitants. 2And it shall be, as**
> **with the people, so with the priest; as with the slave, so with his master; as with the maid, so with her mistress; as with the buyer, so with the seller; as with the lender, so with the borrower; as with the creditor,**
> **so with the debtor. 3The earth shall be utterly laid waste and utterly**
> **despoiled; for the Lord has spoken this word.**

The first stanza begins by stating that the Lord will lay waste the earth until it is desolate, and it concludes in verse 3 by stating that the utter destruction of the earth is sure because the Lord has spoken this prophetic word. In verse 2, between these verses, is a short list of various people on different spectrums. This indicates that all people on earth will be affected by the coming destruction.

24:4–6

[4]The earth mourns and withers, the world languishes and withers; the heavens languish together with the earth. [5]The earth lies polluted under its inhabitants; for they have transgressed the laws, violated the statutes, broken the everlasting covenant. [6]Therefore a curse devours the earth, and its inhabitants suffer for their guilt; therefore the inhabitants of the earth are scorched, and few men are left.

This stanza describes the mourning and withering experience of the earth and the heavens. Specifically, images of leaves wilting and drooping in a drought are employed (vv. 4–5a). Then comes the reason for the destruction: the people have "transgressed the laws, violated the statutes and broken the covenant" (v. 5b). This punishment is a "curse" because the people bear "guilt" for their sins. Receiving a "curse" for committing sin is stated in a liturgical way by the Levites in Deuteronomy 27:14–26, and a much longer list of curses for disobeying God's law is given in Deuteronomy 28:15–68. While those lists of curses were specifically meant for Israel in its life in the Promised Land, Isaiah 24:1–13 applies to the whole universe. Isaiah assumes that all the inhabitants of the earth are liable for keeping God's law, and, as will be restated in verse 13, only a few people will survive this total destruction that occurs because of sin.

24:7–9

[7]The wine mourns, the vine languishes, all the merry-hearted sigh. [8]The mirth of the timbrels is stilled, the noise of the jubilant has ceased, the mirth of the lyre is stilled. [9]No more do they drink wine with singing; strong drink is bitter to those who drink it.

This stanza assumes that people are immersed in drinking and merrymaking, with no thought for God's laws, judgment, or coming punishment. However, the worldwide destruction will affect the vines, wines, and strong drink, thereby bringing the merrymaking to an end.

24:10–12

[10]The city of chaos is broken down, every house is shut up so that none can enter. [11]There is an outcry in the streets for lack of wine; all joy has reached its eventide; the gladness of the earth is banished. [12]Desolation is left in the city, the gates are battered into ruins.

An unnamed city is described as "broken," referring to the protective walls and gates, while the individual houses are "shut up" as a last effort to protect the inhabitants. This is an absurd defense, since the larger, thicker walls could not protect them. Shutting up houses indicates desperate behavior by the panicked inhabitants. Again, the absence of wine and joy is described as having reached the city dwellers in their desolation. By leaving the city unnamed, the prophecy indicates the fate of all the earth's cities that the Lord will desolate.

24:13

[13]For thus it shall be in the midst of the earth among the nations, as when an olive tree is beaten, as at the gleaning when the vintage is done.

This verse sums up the whole situation by saying that only a few people will survive the worldwide destruction. This is symbolized by an olive tree. When the fruit is ripe, it is beaten with sticks, causing the olives to fall onto nets surrounding the tree. After the reapers are finished, others may come and glean the few olives remaining on the tree. Similarly, the majority of people among the nations will be "harvested" at the final destruction, and only a few just people will survive to be gathered afterward.

—— Isaiah 24:14–23 ——

This is a prophecy in two parts. The first part describes rejoicing from west to east over the Lord's coming destruction, presumably by those who are among the few that will be redeemed (vv. 14–16a). However, since one individual laments over ongoing treachery (v. 16b), a series of curses follows in verses 17–23.

24:14–16

**14They lift up their voices, they sing for joy; over the majesty of the
LORD they shout from the west. 15Therefore in the east give glory to
the LORD; in the coastlands of the sea, to the name of the LORD, the
God of Israel. 16aFrom the ends of the earth we hear songs of praise,
of glory to the Righteous One. 16bBut I say, "I pine away, I pine away.
Woe is me! For the treacherous deal treacherously, the treacherous deal
very treacherously."**

14–16a

The dark mood of the last scene is broken by the sound of excited cheers for Yahweh from far edges of the land.

16b

Though he recognizes that others are cheering, one individual laments that there are still people who act treacherously. The continued existence of these disloyal people causes the speaker internal grief. This is not simply due to any evil they have inflicted on him but because evil disrupts him.

24:17–23

**17Terror, and the pit, and the snare are upon you, O inhabitant of the
earth! 18He who flees at the sound of the terror shall fall into the pit;
and he who climbs out of the pit shall be caught in the snare. For the
windows of heaven are opened, and the foundations of the earth trem-
ble. 19The earth is utterly broken, the earth is rent asunder, the earth is
violently shaken. 20The earth staggers like a drunken man, it sways like
a hut; its transgression lies heavy upon it, and it falls, and will not rise
again. 21On that day the LORD will punish the host of heaven, in heav-
en, and the kings of the earth, on the earth. 22They will be gathered
together as prisoners in a pit; they will be shut up in a prison, and after
many days they will be punished. 23Then the moon will be confound-
ed, and the sun ashamed; for the LORD of hosts will reign on Mount
Zion and in Jerusalem and before his elders he will manifest his glory.**

The response to that lament is a series of four curses that threaten everyone and everything that opposes the Lord: the speaker can be assured that even at the end of the world, the wicked will not get away with their crimes.

17

A curse of terror on the inhabitant of the earth, presumably the one who acts treacherously in verse 16.

18

A second curse, similar to Amos 5:19, warns that escape from the Lord's punishment is impossible. The evil folk may attempt escape from God's punishment, but that is futile since the destruction is God's action, and it reaches from the heavens to the foundations of the earth. Therefore, everyone in between will be subject to the Lord's judgment.

19–20

The third curse on the earth will make it sway because it is "utterly broken," not merely by an earthquake, but ultimately by the heavy weight of human transgressions that lie upon it (v. 20).

21–22

The fourth curse is the punishment of the hosts of heaven and the kings on earth, who will be gathered into a prison for punishment. Those members of the "hosts of heaven"—that is, the angelic hosts—who rebelled against God will be as liable to punishment as the kings of earth who did evil. Similar judgment of the angels appears in Job: "Even in his servants he puts no trust, and his angels he charges with error; how much more those who dwell in houses of clay, whose foundation is in the dust, who are crushed before the moth" (Job 4:18–19).

Such is the picture of 2 Peter 2:4: "God did not spare the angels when they sinned, but cast them into hell and committed them to pits of nether gloom to be kept until the judgment." Also, in Revelation 12:4: "His tail swept down a third of the stars of heaven, and cast them to the earth." Later, these fallen spirits from heaven will be locked in the pit. In Revelation 20:2–3: "He seized the dragon, that ancient serpent, who is the Devil and Satan, and bound him for a thousand years, and threw him into the pit, and shut it and sealed it over him." In Revelation 20:10: "The devil who had deceived them was thrown into the lake of fire and sulphur where the beast and the false prophet were, and they will be tormented day and night for ever and ever."

23

In contrast to this destruction and punishment of all the "treacherous" (v. 16b), whether the heavenly hosts or earth's rulers, the concluding verse shows the Lord of hosts reigning in Jerusalem on Mount Zion. His brightness will shine so powerfully that the moon and the sun will seem pale in comparison, an idea that is picked up in Revelation 21:23–24: "The city has no need of sun or moon to shine upon it, for the glory of God is its light, and its lamp is the Lamb. By its light shall the nations walk; and the kings of the earth shall bring their glory into it."

The phrase, "the Lord of Hosts will reign" means that He is in full charge over nature and in Zion (see Ps 29:10; 93:2). That reign will mean the ultimate end of the rule of any and all evil forces, who have been securely imprisoned in pits.

—— Isaiah 25:1–5 —— A Song of Praise and Thanks Sung by Individuals

25:1a

1aO LORD, thou art my God; I will exalt thee, I will praise thy name;

The opening address to the Lord includes a covenantal statement of faith, "You are my God." The covenant had established a mutual relationship according to which the Lord says, "I will be your God and you shall be my people" (see also Lv 26:12; Dt 26:17–19; Hos 2:23; Jer 30:22; 31:1, 33; Ez 11:20; 36:28; 37:27; Zech 13:9; Heb 8:10; Rv 21:3). Notice how frequently this covenantal relationship was cited during the exilic times by Jeremiah and Ezekiel. Here the individual speaking this song personalizes the relationship.

His response to that relationship is to "exalt" and "praise" the Lord, not unlike Exodus 15:2, where Moses's song of praise at the sea personalizes his relationship with the Lord before expressing praise: "He is my God, and I will praise him, my father's God, and I will exalt him." A similar expression of personal relationship and praise also occurs in Psalms 118:28: "You are my God, and I will give you thanks; you art my God, I will extol you."

25:1b

> **[1b]for thou hast done wonderful things, plans formed of old, faithful and sure.**

The reason to offer praise is the wonderful things the Lord has already done in the past. "Wonder" is used to describe the Exodus in various hymns (the Song at the Red Sea, Ex 15:11; Ps 77:14; 78:11) and for the "wonders" God does in acts of redemption (Ps 88:10). Since the Lord has accomplished these wonders in Israel's history against the Egyptian Empire, He can do wonders at the consummation of the whole universe.

25:2–3

> **[2]For thou hast made the city a heap, the fortified city a ruin; the palace of aliens is a city no more, it will never be rebuilt. [3]Therefore strong peoples will glorify thee; cities of ruthless nations will fear thee.**

The destruction of a fortified city that will never be rebuilt (v. 2) gives the people of the present a reason to glorify the Lord and for the evil nations to fear Him (v. 3). The destroyed foreign city is not named and could apply to many ancient cities that were decimated by invading armies over the centuries. The key issue is not identifying the city but choosing to be among the strong peoples who praise the Lord rather than among the ruthless who fear Him.

25:4–5

> **[4]For thou hast been a stronghold to the poor, a stronghold to the needy in his distress, a shelter from the storm and a shade from the heat; for the blast of the ruthless is like a storm against a wall, [5]like heat in a dry place. Thou dost subdue the noise of the aliens; as heat by the shade of a cloud, so the song of the ruthless is stilled.**

The song now presents more reasons to praise the Lord, such as His protection for the poor and needy, especially from ruthless foreigners. The people composing or hearing this song would certainly identify themselves as the poor and needy in distress, such as the exiles who had been in Babylon. Since the Lord has protected these little people from larger alien enemies, He will continue to protect them in the present against forces much larger than they.

— Isaiah 25:6–8 —

The great banquet at the end of time will take place on "this mountain," a reference to Mount Zion in Jerusalem, the city to which Proto-Isaiah had said all nations will come (Is 2:1–4). In this apocalyptic section, the mountain of the Lord will be the site not so much of the Lord's instruction (as in Is 2:1–4) but of the victory banquet when the Lord is totally triumphant. This is similar to the "wedding feast of the Lamb" in Revelation 19:7, which comes after the destruction of Babylon (symbolizing the Roman Empire).

25:6

> **6On this mountain the LORD of hosts will make for all peoples a feast of fat things, a feast of wine on the lees, of fat things full of marrow, of wine on the lees well refined.**

This is the announcement of a banquet for all peoples, a feast of the richest foods. While modern people worry about high cholesterol in their food, the ancients (like poor people today), love the fatty meats and marrow in the bones.

25:7–8

> **7And he will destroy on this mountain the covering that is cast over**
> **all peoples, the veil that is spread over all nations. 8He will swallow up**
> **death for ever, and the LORD God will wipe away tears from all faces, and the reproach of his people he will take away from all the earth; for the LORD has spoken.**

At this banquet is announced the Lord's victory over death and its effects.

7

The "covering," or "veil," over the peoples is death and destruction, which the Lord will destroy.

8

Then, like a powerful lion, the Lord will "swallow up death forever." In general, Israelites speculated very little on life after death. Verse 8a identifies death as God's enemy, a notion that will develop elsewhere, such as in the book of Wisdom: "God did not make death, and he does not delight in the death of the living. For he created all things that they might exist . . . and the dominion of Hades is not on earth" (1:13–14).

In the New Testament, in the light of Christ's resurrection, death is an enemy in 1 Corinthians 15:26: "The last enemy to be destroyed is death." In 2 Timothy 1:10, Paul speaks of "our Savior Christ Jesus, who abolished death and brought life and immortality to light through the gospel." Also, in Hebrews 2:14–15, Christ shared in human nature "that through death he might destroy him who has the power of death, that is, the devil, and deliver all those who through fear of death were subject to lifelong bondage." In fact, Isaiah 25:8 will be cited in 1 Corinthians 15:54: "Death is swallowed up in victory," as is Hosea 13:14 in verse 55: "O death, where is thy victory? O death, where is thy sting?" God's enmity with death and victory over it becomes an important theme in the rest of the Bible.

Yet, the Lord, who is victorious over death, will act tenderly toward humans by "wiping away tears from all faces," a tenderness described also in Revelation 21:4: "He will wipe away every tear from their eyes, and death shall be no more, neither shall there be mourning nor crying nor pain any more, for the former things have passed away."

The basis for believing in this victory over death is "the Lord has spoken"; just as He had spoken the universe into existence in Genesis 1:3ff, and spoke redemptive actions through His prophets, so also does He declare that He will defeat death itself.

—— Isaiah 25:9–12 ——

This is hymn of thanksgiving by a community ("our God," "we," "us").

25:9–10a

> **9It will be said on that day, "Lo, this is our God; we have waited for him, that he might save us. This is the LORD; we have waited for him;**

let us be glad and rejoice in his salvation. [10a]For the hand of the LORD will rest on this mountain."

Before the hymn is the note that the proper time to sing this thanksgiving will be "on that day" of punishment for the wicked and a victory banquet for the redeemed. This hymn of thanksgiving is the proper response to the preceding celebration, which also takes place "on this mountain" (see 25:6 and 10a).

First, the community proclaims twice that they have "waited" for the Lord to save them, not unlike the prayer of the individual in Psalms 130, who cries to the Lord "out of the depths" (v. 1) to listen to him (v. 2), and who "waits . . . waits . . . waits for the Lord" (vv. 5–6) in full confidence in the Lord's love and redemption (v. 7) and forgiveness of iniquities (v. 8).

Second, they are celebrating that they "have waited" for God and the salvation was worth waiting for, so they announce, "Let us be glad and rejoice." Finally, in verse 10a, they state the reason for rejoicing: the hand of the Lord is upon "this mountain"—that is, Mount Zion in Jerusalem where the Temple of the Lord is.

25:10b–12

[10b]and Moab shall be trodden down in his place, as straw is trodden down in a dung-pit. [11]And he will spread out his hands in the midst of it as a swimmer spreads his hands out to swim; but the LORD will lay low his pride together with the skill of his hands. [12]And the high fortifications of his walls he will bring down, lay low, and cast to the ground, even to the dust.

This scene of the punishment of Moab is portrayed as the negative side of the coin of the Lord's salvation—at least negative for Moab, which had a longer oracle spoken against it in Isaiah 15:1–16:14 because of its arrogance against Israel (see also Zep 2:9 for the same accusation). Moab's thorough humiliation—swimming in deep dung pits and destroying its forts—is its proper punishment on a day when the Lord should have been praised for saving Israel.

Lesson 20

Isaiah Apocalypse 26–27

—— Isaiah 26:1–6 ——

The song of the redeemed who are streaming toward Jerusalem in triumph.

26:1a

> **[1a]In that day this song will be sung in the land of Judah:**

This section begins with an announcement of the song that will be sung when the people return to Judah.

26:1b–6

> **[1b]"We have a strong city; he sets up salvation as walls and bulwarks. [2]Open the gates, that the righteous nation which keeps faith may enter in. [3]Thou dost keep him in perfect peace, whose mind is stayed on you, because he trusts in you. [4]Trust in the Lord for ever, for the Lord God is an everlasting rock. [5]For he has brought low the inhabitants of the height, the lofty city. He lays it low, lays it low to the ground, casts it to the dust. [6]The foot tramples it, the feet of the poor, the steps of the needy."**

The actual song is about Jerusalem, the city that is the place of redemption.

1b

This is a statement of faith that the city is strong because the Lord makes His salvation its walls and bulwarks. When the exiles returned to Jerusalem, there were no city walls, and none would be built for about a hundred years after their return (see the books of Ezra and Nehemiah). This salvific act of faith reminds the people to trust in the Lord as their protective wall, not in themselves.

2

A command to those in the city to open its gates to permit a righteous nation that keeps faith to enter. Since God is the city's protector, those who enter must be characterized by faith in Him. This faith need have the effect of making a person righteous, because the unrighteous will be outside the city—see Revelation 21:27: "Nothing unclean shall enter it [the New Jerusalem], nor any one who practices abomination or falsehood, but only those who are written in the Lamb's book of life." The idea is captured well in 2 Peter 3:13–14: "According to his promise we wait for new heavens and a new earth in which righteousness dwells. Therefore, beloved, since you wait for these, be zealous to be found by him without spot or blemish, and at peace."

3

The preceding command is followed by an act of faith directed to the Lord, who gives peace to those who remain focused on Him and trust in Him steadfastly. This verse also shows the interrelation between the human act of keeping the mind on God in a trusting way and the grace of peace that the Lord bestows.

4–6

An exhortation to trust in the Lord for two reasons. By His divine nature, He is the "everlasting rock" upon which one can safely stand in faith. Second, the Lord has defeated and humbled the arrogant city and its inhabitants, permitting the people of Jerusalem to return to their own city made strong by the Lord. That proud city is not named, and it is impossible to identify it. Rather, the description and the humiliating fate of destruction awaits all arrogant human societies. This is a warning not only for ancient cities like Babylon but also "Babylon the great" in Revelation 18:2ff, which is declared "fallen, fallen."

— Isaiah 26:7–21 —

This section is a series of prayers addressed to the Lord, as indicated by the regular use of "you" in speaking directly to Him. The people express their present plight and tell the Lord some principles upon which they base their prayers. To these prayers, the Lord gives two responses, promising hope of resurrection of their bodies (v. 19) and instructions on the necessity of hiding during the coming period of wrath against the wicked (vv. 20–21).

26:7–18

> **7The way of the righteous is level; thou dost make smooth the path
> of the righteous. 8In the path of thy judgments, O LORD, we wait for
> thee; thy memorial name is the desire of our soul. 9My soul yearns for
> thee in the night, my spirit within me earnestly seeks thee. For when
> thy judgments are in the earth, the inhabitants of the world learn righ-
> teousness. 10If favor is shown to the wicked, he does not learn righ-
> teousness; in the land of uprightness he deals perversely and does not
> see the majesty of the LORD. 11O LORD, thy hand is lifted up, but they
> see it not. Let them see thy zeal for your people, and be ashamed. Let
> the fire for thy adversaries consume them. 12O LORD, thou wilt ordain
> peace for us, thou hast wrought for us all our works. 13O LORD our
> God, other lords besides thee have ruled over us, but thy name alone
> we acknowledge. 14They are dead, they will not live; they are shades,
> they will not arise; to that end thou hast visited them with destruction
> and wiped out all remembrance of them. 15But thou hast increased
> the nation, O LORD, thou hast increased the nation; thou art glorified;
> thou hast enlarged all the borders of the land. 16O LORD, in distress
> they sought thee, they poured out a prayer when thy chastening was
> upon them. 17Like a woman with child, who writhes and cries out in
> her pangs, when she is near her time, so were we because of thee, O
> LORD; 18we were with child, we writhed, we have as it were brought
> forth wind. We have wrought no deliverance in the earth, and the
> inhabitants of the world have not fallen.**

These prayers are expressed in very conversational ways, in which the people relate the difficulties they are enduring in the distress at the end of time.

7–9

As one would expect in a society formed by Israelite wisdom, living righteously leads to a "level . . . smooth" way of life, such as in some of the psalms: "Therefore the wicked will not stand in the judgment, nor sinners in the congregation of the righteous; 6 for the Lord knows the way of the righteous, but the way of the wicked will perish" (Ps 1:5). "All the paths of the Lord are steadfast love and faithfulness, for those who keep his covenant and his testimonies" (Ps 25:10). "Teach me thy way, O Lord; and lead me on a level path because of my enemies" (Ps 27:11; see also Ps 18:23–26; 26:12; Prv 1:1–6; 8:8–9; 15:19).

The people who speak this lament believe this doctrine and explain directly to God that they "wait" and "yearn" for Him. They still hope that when the Lord enacts His just judgments, the rest of the people on the earth will learn righteousness.

10–11

The converse principle is stated (v. 10) that favor to the wicked prevents them from learning righteousness, encourages them to act perversely, and they fail to understand the presence of God's majesty. Then the speaker informs the Lord in verse 11 that the wicked do not perceive His lifted, threatening hand. This is not right in his eyes, so he prays that the wicked can see the Lord's zeal for suffering faithful people by letting fire consume them. There is nothing like serious punishment to teach the wicked a lesson.

12–15

Having stated the principles about the safety that belongs to the way of the righteous (vv. 7–9) and the importance of punishing the wicked to teach them God's power (vv. 10–11), now the verses address a prayer of confidence that the Lord will deliver the people from the powerful enemy lords.

12

The Lord is addressed and a confident prayer that He will declare peace for the oppressed people, just as He had done throughout history.

13–14

The Lord is addressed with information about Israel's present situation. Even though the people have been faithful to Him and have acknowledged His name alone, other unnamed foreign leaders are ruling over them. In verse 14, these leaders are already dead. The term "shades" refers to the aspect of the person that continues in existence after death in Sheol—the Israelites did not refer to the souls of the dead but to their shades, since each person's shadow belongs only to that person, but it is dark and insubstantial and yet real. Of course, they are still among the living, but they are morally, spiritually dead. Therefore, at a later point, the Lord will visit them with complete destruction, finishing off the job that they started by making themselves morally dead.

15

A confident double statement that the Lord has "increased the nation" and enlarged its borders, even though the historical reality they can see is still the oppression by the foreign kings. This prayer expresses complete confidence that the Lord will reverse the fortunes of the foreigner oppressors and the oppressed Israel.

16–18

Notice the change from the Lord "our God" and other first person plural forms to third person plural "they." This change of perspective from "us" to speaking about "them" marks off this new section.

16

An individual here begins by informing the Lord about the people's distress, caused by the Lord's chastisement, and their prayer. This is lament, but it is not blaming the Lord for the problems. Rather, it speaks directly to the Lord, in the hope that He will cease the chastisement and distress.

17–18

Jesus uses the image of a woman in labor in a parable about His departure and return in John 16:21–22, where the disciples will have joy similar to a woman after her child is born. However, here the image fits the lament since they bring forth wind and not an actual child. Quite opposite of Jesus's parable, the people lament that they do not experience deliverance and the wicked inhabitants of the earth are still alive and in power.

26:19

19Thy dead shall live, their bodies shall rise. O dwellers in the dust, awake and sing for joy! For thy dew is a dew of light, and on the land of the shades thou wilt let it fall.

The Lord responds to these prayers with a promise that the dead will rise. Therefore, even if the good people die, their bodies shall rise and light will shine on the gloomy "land of the shades." The ancient Israelites spoke of a person's shade continuing after death in Sheol, the place of the dead. They understood Sheol neither as reward nor of torment, but definitely as inferior to life on earth. They did not want to go there, so prolonging life on earth was considered very good. However, this verse is revolutionary in telling people that their "shades" will rise from the gloom of Sheol and their bodies will live again. Ezekiel's vision of the valley of bones that come to life (see Ez 37:1–14) is the first clue of a resurrection of the dead; this passage promises hope for those who suffer and lament in 26:1–18.

26:20–21

20Come, my people, enter your chambers, and shut your doors behind you; hide yourselves for a little while until the wrath is past. 21For behold, the LORD is coming forth out of his place to punish the inhabitants of the earth for their iniquity, and the earth will disclose the blood shed upon her, and will no more cover her slain.

The Lord responds to these prayers and instructs the people at the time of His wrath against the wicked that they should hide until the wrath is over. While the just may be able to hide, the iniquitous, particularly those who killed the innocent, will be unable to hide. Earth itself will reveal their guilt by displaying the blood of the slain. This is reminiscent of the Lord's cross-examination of Cain after murdering Able: "The voice of your brother's blood is crying to me from the ground" (Gn 4:10). As in that murder, the Lord punishes the murderers at the end of time in His final wrath.

Note that in verse 21, the Lord comes from "his place," a reference to the Temple built on Mount Zion (see 27:13). Hence these texts are dated after the exiles have rebuilt the Temple, which was begun when Sheshbazzar rebuilt the altar in September of 537 BC (see Ez 3:1–3), and the foundation was laid in May/June of 536. Building was stopped for a while, but the Temple was completed between 520 and 516 BC (see Hg 1:1, 14–15).

—— Isaiah 27:1 ——

1In that day the LORD with his hard and great and strong sword will punish Leviathan the fleeing serpent, Leviathan the twisting serpent, and he will slay the dragon that is in the sea.

The day of the Lord will see Him punish the dragon Leviathan. The ancient city of Ugarit was discovered in Syria in 1927, and clay tablets tell the story of Baal, his sister and wife, Anath, and the defeat of the sea and its dragons, including their defeat of "the dragon" (*tnn*) by muzzling him and destroying the "crooked serpent" (*btn*) Shalyat (meaning the "accursed") having "seven heads" (Baal and Anath, 37–39). Shalyat is identified on another tablet as "Lotan," the Ugaritic form of Leviathan. The Lord's battle against Leviathan is in Psalms 74:14: "You crushed the heads of Leviathan, you gave him as food for the creatures of the wilderness." Whereas he is the Lord's pet living in the sea in Psalms 104:26: "There go the ships, and Leviathan which you formed to sport in it." The Lord speaks to Job about His power to control and play with Leviathan: "Can you draw out Leviathan with a fishhook, or press down his tongue with a cord? Can you put a rope in his nose, or pierce his jaw with a hook? Will he make many supplications to you? Will he speak to you soft words? Will he make a covenant with you to take him for your servant for ever? Will you play with him as with a bird, or will you put him on leash for your maidens?" (Job 41:1–5).

Isaiah 27:1 promises that at the end of the world ("in that day"), the Lord will thoroughly defeat the seven-headed Leviathan. This may refer not only to the ancient sea monster but also to the great political powers and empires He will destroy "on that day." In Revelation 12:3, "the great red dragon, with seven heads" plans to destroy the boy child of "the Woman clothed in the sun" but fails (12:4–6). Saint Michael and his angels then defeat the dragon and his angels (12:7–9), where the dragon is identified as "that ancient serpent, who is called the Devil and Satan, the deceiver of the whole world." Though it is a short unit, this verse has an important influence on Revelation.

—— Isaiah 27:2–6 ——

27:2–5

> **[2]In that day: "A pleasant vineyard, sing of it! [3]I, the LORD, am its keeper; every moment I water it. Lest any one harm it, I guard it night and day; [4]I have no wrath. Would that I had thorns and briers to battle! I would set out against them, I would burn them up together. [5]Or let them lay hold of my protection, let them make peace with me, let them make peace with me."**

This song of the vineyard at the end of time ("in that day" is a key designation for the end of time beginning in Ex 32:34, 1 Sm 8:18, and Amos 5:18, where it is called "the day of the Lord"). However, it clearly hearkens back to the Song of the Vineyard in Isaiah 5:1–7, condemning Israel for being an unfruitful vine that bears smelly grapes, even though the Lord had done everything possible to make it a good vineyard. That song is followed by a series of woes, indicating the coming destruction of the vineyard. Here, the Lord again sings this song about His vineyard to pronounce all that He has done to protect it. However, He sings, "I have no wrath." He would be happy to fight against encroaching thorns and briars, but there are none. Therefore, in verse 5, He invites the people to be at peace with Him.

27:6

> **[6]In days to come Jacob shall take root, Israel shall blossom and put forth shoots, and fill the whole world with fruit.**

At this song's conclusion is a promise for the end of time ("in those days") that Jacob/Israel, the Lord's vine, will go through the whole process of growth and development, from taking root to blossom to bearing fruit. However, Israel's fruit will benefit the whole world. This takes the reader back to Genesis 12:1–3, when the Lord calls Abram to become a blessing for all the world's nations. At the end of time will come the fulfillment of that vocation. This idea may have influenced Revelation 7:4: "I heard the number of the sealed, a hundred and forty-four thousand sealed, out of every tribe of the sons of Israel," which is followed by a listing of twelve thousand virgin men (see Rv 14:4) from each of the twelve tribes of Israel. This indicates that Israel plays a key role at the end of time according to Revelation and Isaiah 27:1–6.

—— Isaiah 27:7–9 ——

A question and answer about the Lord's reasons for the punishment of Israel in the exile.

27:7

> **7 Has he smitten them as he smote those who smote them? Or have they been slain as their slayers were slain?**

An unnamed person raises two parallel questions as to whether the Lord ("he") has punished "them" (Israel) as severely as He punished the foreigners ("those who smote," "their slayers"). Such questions are concerned with the fairness of the degree of punishment meted out to various people.

27:8–9

> **8 Measure by measure, by exile thou didst contended with them; he removed them with his fierce blast in the day of the east wind. 9 Therefore by this the guilt of Jacob will be expiated, and this will be the full fruit of the removal of his sin: when he makes all the stones of the altars like chalkstones crushed to pieces, no Asherim or incense altars will remain standing.**

The answer is that the Lord punished Israel with exile, a suffering similar to the very hot east winds that come off the desert. Verse 9 explains this punishment as the Lord's means to remove Israel's sin, which included the building of altars to other deities, such as the Asherim. The exile led to the destruction of the altars, and Israel's exile gave them distance from the scene of this crime of polluting the land with idolatry. Therefore, the reader should conclude that the Lord was fair to Israel.

—— Isaiah 27:10–11 ——

10For the fortified city is solitary, a habitation deserted and forsaken, like the wilderness; there the calf grazes, there he lies down, and strips its branches. 11When its boughs are dry, they are broken; women come and make a fire of them. For this is a people without discernment; therefore he who made them will not have compassion on them, he that formed them will show them no favor.

A description of the sad, tragic fate of a fortified city. It will become solitary, no longer having allies or subject cities. It will de deserted by people and inhabited by cattle. Its trees will wither and become firewood. However, the identity of the city is unknowable. Part of this last chapter's ambiguity is that the writer leaves the readers with too little information. Perhaps the best one can do is apply the fate of desolation to any society that lacks "discernment." Such people will find neither compassion nor favor from the Lord, who judges them and decrees their destruction.

—— Isaiah 27:12–13 ——

12In that day from the river Euphrates to the Brook of Egypt the LORD will thresh out the grain, and you will be gathered one by one, O people of Israel. 13And in that day a great trumpet will be blown, and those who were lost in the land of Assyria and those who were driven out to the land of Egypt will come and worship the LORD on the holy mountain at Jerusalem.

The visions conclude with a summons of Israel from the northeast (River Euphrates) and southwest (Brook of Egypt) into one people at the end of time. The great trumpet that assembles them from Assyria (in modern Iraq) and Egypt is clearly the Lord's trumpet that sounds beyond human borders. Proper worship is the purpose of their return to the Lord's holy mountain in Jerusalem. Worship is the proper way for creatures to relate to their creating God, and Israel has learned how to worship the one true God from the Lord's own instructions in Exodus and Leviticus. Their return will fulfill their ultimate purpose of knowing, loving, and serving the Lord.

Lesson 21

Isaiah 34–35

—— Isaiah 34:1–17 ——

These verses foretell the end of the world and the destruction of Edom.

This chapter has been associated with Deutero-Isaiah, but it is more likely a later addition to Isaiah because of its apocalyptic themes, and yet focuses on Edom's destruction, without mentioning Babylon.

Many post-exilic texts bring up Edom's condemnation because the Edomites had encouraged the Babylonians to destroy Jerusalem completely: "Remember, O Lord, against the Edomites the day of Jerusalem, how they said, 'Raze it, raze it! Down to its foundations!'" (Ps 137:7; see also Jer 49:7–22; Ez 25:12–14; Ob 10–14, 18–21; Lam 4:21–22).

Therefore, the Jews who returned to Jerusalem after the exile wanted to see Edom punished. In addition, the Edomites had used the Babylonian exile to expand their own territory into Judah, even taking Hebron, the site of Abraham's tomb. Such encroachment was seen as a good reason for singling Edom out during the destruction of all the nations.

34:1–4

**1Draw near, O nations, to hear, and hearken, O peoples! Let the earth
listen, and all that fills it; the world, and all that comes from it. 2For
the Lord is enraged against all the nations, and furious against all
their host, he has doomed them, has given them over for slaughter.
3Their slain shall be cast out, and the stench of their corpses shall rise;
the mountains shall flow with their blood. 4All the host of heaven shall**

rot away, and the skies roll up like a scroll. All their host shall fall, as leaves fall from the vine, like leaves falling from the fig tree.

The Lord calls the whole earth and the heavens to His ultimate judgment.

1

The Lord summons the nations of the whole world to learn of the impending doom of all.

2–4

The coming judgment and destruction of all the nations and the hosts of heaven.

2–3

The Lord states the reason for the assembly of everyone in the world: He is enraged and furious against all nations and has doomed them all to slaughter and death.

4

Even the skies will be destroyed and their hosts fall. This may refer to both the stars and to the evil spirits. A similar scene is depicted in Revelation 12:4 when the great red dragon's "tail swept down a third of the stars of heaven, and cast them to the earth," referring to the stars and to his evil angels.

34:5–8

[5]For my sword has drunk its fill in the heavens; behold, it descends for judgment upon Edom, upon the people I have doomed. [6]The LORD has a sword; it is sated with blood, it is gorged with fat, with the blood of lambs and goats, with the fat of the kidneys of rams. For the LORD has a sacrifice in Bozrah, a great slaughter in the land of Edom. [7]Wild oxen shall fall with them, and young steers with the mighty bulls. Their land shall be soaked with blood, and their soil made rich with fat. [8]For the LORD has a day of vengeance, a year of recompense for the cause of Zion.

The slaughter that begins in the heavens will then focus on Edom.

5

This punishment begins at the top in the heavens, as the Lord's sword drinks its fill in punishing the hosts of heaven that had rebelled against

Him. When He finishes there, the sword comes down upon Edom for His judgment, since He has doomed them.

6–8

The Lord's sword continues its work on the lambs, goats, and sheep of Edom, effecting a great slaughter here described as a sacrificial feast on a "day of vengeance, a year of recompense" against Edom and its capital city Bozrah. The purpose of this slaughter is to gain recompense for the wrongs Edom had committed against Zion, the chosen place for authentically worshiping the Lord. A similar scene of slaughter appears in the final judgment in Revelation 19:11–15, 17–21 before the Lord brings down the new and heavenly Jerusalem in Revelation 21–22.

34:9–15

These verses are a description of the devastation of Edom.

> **9And the streams of Edom shall be turned into pitch, and her soil into**
> **brimstone; her land shall become burning pitch. 10Night and day it**
> **shall not be quenched; its smoke shall go up for ever. From generation**
> **to generation it shall lie waste; none shall pass through it for ever and**
> **ever. 11But the hawk and the porcupine shall possess it, the owl and**
> **the raven shall dwell in it. He shall stretch the line of confusion over**
> **it, and the plummet of chaos over its nobles. 12They shall name it No**
> **Kingdom There, and all its princes shall be nothing. 13Thorns shall**
> **grow over its strongholds, nettles and thistles in its fortresses. It shall**
> **be the haunt of jackals, an abode for ostriches. 14And wild beasts shall**
> **meet with hyenas, the satyr shall cry to his fellow; yes, there shall the**
> **night hag alight, and find for herself a resting place. 15There shall the**
> **owl nest and lay and hatch and gather her young in her shadow; yes,**
> **there shall the kites be gathered, each one with her mate.**

9–10

Edom will be destroyed by fire as its streams turn into burning tar and its soil into burning brimstone. Such a fire will stink of sulphur, in addition to burning through many generations. The fire and smell will make Edom uninhabitable.

11–15

Verses 11, 13–15 mention that scavenger animals will inhabit the land, consuming the dead. Not being buried but eaten by scavengers was considered a horrible fate in the ancient world, since only the shades of those who have been buried in the ground were permitted any kind of rest in Sheol. The shades of the unburied were required to wander aimlessly.

The result of this destruction is that Edom would no longer be considered a kingdom and its rulers will become nothing (v. 12).

34:16–17

> **16Seek and read from the book of the LORD: Not one of these shall be missing; none shall be without her mate. For the mouth of the LORD has commanded, and his Spirit has gathered them. 17He has cast the lot for them, his hand has portioned it out to them with the line; they shall possess it for ever, from generation to generation they shall dwell in it.**

As a postscript, the reader is to know that Scripture will testify to this destruction because the word of the Lord has "commanded" it, and His Spirit gathers the peoples for His judgment. Therefore, the judgment is inevitable. This is one of the earliest claims within Scripture for its own authority (see also Is 30:8; Mal 3:16; Jn 5:39; 10:35; 2 Tm 3:16).

—— Isaiah 35:1–10 ——

The preceding scene of judgment and destruction in Isaiah 34 is here contrasted with the Israelites' happy journey back to Zion where great joy awaits.

35:1–2

> **1The wilderness and the dry land shall be glad, the desert shall rejoice and blossom; like the crocus 2it shall blossom abundantly, and rejoice with joy and singing. The glory of Lebanon shall be given to it, the majesty of Carmel and Sharon. They shall see the glory of the LORD, the majesty of our God.**

This verse describes the Lord transforming the desert to prepare a way to Zion. Lebanon is famous for its tall cedars growing in the mountains; such is its glory. Carmel is covered with pines and many olive trees, while Sharon is a coastal plain just south of Carmel and is full of flowers. These regions are windward to the Mediterranean and have enough water to bring about growth; now the Lord promises the same beauty and abundant flora for the leeward deserts. They, too, will see God's glory, and that glory will effect the growth and beauty.

35:3–10

> **[3]Strengthen the weak hands, and make firm the feeble knees. [4]Say to**
> **those who are of a fearful heart, "Be strong, fear not! [4b]Behold, your**
> **God will come with vengeance, with the recompense of God. He will**
> **come and save you." [5]Then the eyes of the blind shall be opened, and**
> **the ears of the deaf unstopped; [6a]then shall the lame man leap like**
> **a deer, and the tongue of the mute sing for joy. [6b]For waters shall**
> **break forth in the wilderness, and streams in the desert; [7]the burning**
> **sand shall become a pool, and the thirsty ground springs of water; the**
> **haunt of jackals shall become a swamp, the grass shall become reeds**
> **and rushes. [8]And a highway shall be there, and it shall be called the**
> **Holy Way; the unclean shall not pass over it, and fools shall not err**
> **therein. [9]No lion shall be there, nor shall any ravenous beast come up**
> **on it; they shall not be found there, but the redeemed shall walk there.**
> **[10]And the ransomed of the LORD shall return, and come to Zion with**
> **singing; everlasting joy shall be upon their heads; they shall obtain joy**
> **and gladness, and sorrow and sighing shall flee away.**

3–6a

3–4a

First, a series of imperative plural verbs addresses a group, commanding them to strengthen the weak and feeble, and to encourage the fearful.

4b

Next comes an announcement that God's recompense will work vengeance, as promised in 34:8, and He will save the people.

5–6

The result of their obedience to God's commands and of His saving deeds will be the gift of sight to the blind, hearing to the deaf, leaping for the lame, and speaking for the mute. The Church includes this reading in Advent to show that Jesus Christ fulfills the hopes prophesied here by means of His various healing miracles.

6b–9

This description of the highway through the desert to Zion is similar to the description of those highways for the exiles leaving Babylon in Deutero-Isaiah (see Is 40:3–4; 42:16; 49:11–12) and Trito-Isaiah (see Is 57:14; 62:10). Because Jews remained scattered throughout the world, the hope for a highway through the desert that has plenty of water available (vv. 6b–7) and freedom from dangerous predators (v. 9) was very welcome.

More important is verse 8, where the highway is designated "the Holy Way," and the kind of people who do and do not walk the highway is laid out: the unclean and the fools are as unwelcome as the lions and jackals. The reader is meant to draw the conclusion: do not be unclean or a fool.

10

The arrival in Zion is meant for the ransomed who have come out of exile or diaspora living. The highlighted characteristic is their joy and gladness, attitudes that belong to liturgical celebrations. Zion is the proper place for worshiping the Lord, so the ransomed will dispel any sorrow and grief because they worship the Lord in His sanctuary on Mount Zion.

Lesson 22

Trito-Isaiah 56–57

Isaiah 56–66 is identified by modern scholars as "Trito-Isaiah," or "third Isaiah." The Hebrew style is quite distinct from Proto- or Deutero-Isaiah, or the Isaiah Apocalypse. In general, the meter of the Hebrew is poorly done, and the writing is of a lesser quality from D-I. I place the Isaiah Apocalypse in between D-I and Trito-Isaiah (T-I) because the Hebrew changes from a style more like D-I in the first three chapters to a decline reminiscent of T-I.

The text makes no reference to historical events, but Isaiah does assume certain historical circumstances that may help in dating these chapters. First, the Temple ("my house" 56:5, 7; 60:7, which mentions the altar and "my glorious house") is in operation, indicating that the writing is after the dedication of the new Temple in 516 BC. Second, Isaiah 62:2 mentions "the year of the Lord's favor," a reference to a Jubilee year, which was held every fifty years. The touchstone for dating the Jubilees is Ezekiel 40:1: "In the twenty-fifth year of our exile, at the beginning of the year, on the tenth day of the month." Mention of the "beginning of the year, on the tenth day" marks this as a Jubilee, since only the Jubilee year began on the tenth day of the month (which happens to be Yom Kippur, the Day of Atonement) instead of beginning on the first day of the month, as in the other forty-nine years (see Lv 23:27). The twenty-fifth year after his exile, which began in 598 BC, was 573 BC. From this can be determined that the Jubilee was every seventy-third and twenty-third year of the century. Since the Temple was not nearly completed in the 523 BC Jubilee, it is more likely that Isaiah 61:2 is referring to 473 BC, a time of difficulties within the Jerusalem community, as reflected in the prophet Malachi and described in Ezra and Nehemiah. Nothing else makes for any specific dating.

Trito-Isaiah presents a number of great ideals for the Jerusalem community, but he also prophesies against a number of problems and disillusionment by the returnees from exile. He describes the triumph of the ideals over the problems by the end of the book with a hope for a glorious, eschatological Jerusalem at the end of time. This was crucial for the community to have a hope that could take them beyond disappointments with life as it is in the restored Jerusalem to a far greater hope for what God can still do for the people of faith.

— Isaiah 56:1–2 —

This is an oracle, which is indicated by the messenger formula, "Thus says the Lord."

56:1

> **1Thus says the Lord: "Keep justice, and do righteousness, for soon my salvation will come, and my deliverance be revealed.**

The oracle begins with a double exhortation in the plural form to "keep" or "guard" justice and "do righteousness." This opening to Trito-Isaiah is a challenge to the community now settled in Jerusalem. The return to their homeland and the rebuilding of the Temple is not a satisfactory accomplishment if the people do not live with justice governing their interrelationships and moral righteousness guiding each one's personal lives.

The second part of the verse motivates the exhortation: the Lord's salvation and deliverance is still to come. Again, the return home is not the fullness of salvation: the quality of moral life and, perhaps, hope of complete independence from the Persian Empire, of which Jerusalem was a tiny part. In the first years after the return, the nation included no more than twenty square miles of territory. The returnees may well have been somewhat disappointed.

56:2

> **[2]Blessed is the man who does this, and the son of man who holds it fast, who keeps the Sabbath, not profaning it, and keeps his hand from doing any evil."**

This is a beatitude for the person who "does this"—that is, righteousness—and "holds it fast"—that is, judgment. In addition to the personal and social mores, the blessed will keep the Sabbath by not doing any evil, a reference to manual labor. This beatitude integrates morality with religious observance, both goals for possessing the Promised Land since the days Moses presented the covenant on Sinai. There the moral laws and the liturgical laws were presented together from Exodus 19, where the people are called to become a kingdom of priests, through the end of Leviticus. Israel was meant for worship, but with moral integrity as its guiding principle. So, too, here in this beatitude.

— Isaiah 56:3–8 —

This section begins with an exhortation to stop foreigner's and eunuchs from lamenting (v. 3), to which the Lord responds with two oracles that promise an everlasting name and the opportunity to worship (vv. 4–7) and a promise to include still more outcasts (v. 8).

56:3

> **[3]Let not the foreigner who has joined himself to the LORD say, "The LORD will surely separate me from his people"; and let not the eunuch say, "Behold, I am a dry tree."**

Lying in the background is a lament that foreigners who converted to the Lord fear that they will be separated out from the community, since Deuteronomy 23:3–6 excluded certain foreigners from Israel's assembly. Therefore, their new faith will leave them separated from their own people as well as from Israel. Similar concerns about the conversion of Gentiles to Christianity also caused problems for many Jewish Christians in the early Church. The eunuchs who have joined the returnees also feel abandoned, "like a dry tree" that has no fruit. Men who worked in the royal palaces in Babylon or Persia were able to have a good living and considerable influence. However, kings would trust them, especially around the harem, only if they were castrated, whether willingly or by force. Some of these men came back to Jerusalem but were excluded from worship because of Deuteronomy 23:1, which precluded eunuchs from "entering the assembly."

56:4–7

> **[4]For thus says the LORD: "To the eunuchs who keep my Sabbaths, who choose the things that please me and hold fast my covenant, [5]I will give in my house and within my walls a monument and a name better than sons and daughters; I will give them an everlasting name which shall not be cut off. [6]"And the foreigners who join themselves to the LORD, to minister to him, to love the name of the LORD, and to be his servants, every one who keeps the Sabbath, and does not profane it, and holds fast my covenant – [7]these I will bring to my holy mountain, and make them joyful in my house of prayer; their burnt offerings and their sacrifices will be accepted on my altar; for my house shall be called a house of prayer for all peoples.**

The first oracle ("thus says the Lord") addresses the concerns of the eunuchs and foreigners.

4–5

First, the Lord addresses the eunuchs who keep His Sabbaths and His covenant. He promises them an everlasting name that will be better than having children, which of course would be physically impossible for eunuchs. Jesus later taught a still more positive attitude that became the basis for freely chosen celibacy: "Not all men can receive this saying, but only those to whom it is given. For there are eunuchs who have been so from birth, and there are eunuchs who have been made eunuchs by men, and there are eunuchs who have made themselves eunuchs for the sake of the kingdom of heaven. He who is able to receive this, let him receive it" (Mt 19:11–12).

Here, T-I presents an oracle that supersedes the prohibition of Deuteronomy 23:1 and offers an everlasting promise to the eunuchs.

6–7

Then he informs the foreigners who converted to the Lord, minister to Him, love Him, and keep Sabbath and the covenant that they are welcome to find joy in worshiping God in the Temple and in offering sacrifices. Like all of Israel, maintaining the covenant's moral requirements enables a person to worship, even if born in a foreign nation.

56:8

> **8Thus says the LORD God, who gathers the outcasts of Israel, I will gather yet others to him besides those already gathered."**

The second oracle is addressed by the Lord God, who identifies Himself as the one who gathers Israel's outcasts. He promises to remain true to His character and gather still more outcasts. The implication is that just as the community of returnees needs to incorporate the outcasts already living among them, so must they do for the outcasts that the Lord intends to keep bringing into the community. When the Temple was rebuilt in 516 BC, the prophet Zechariah also prophesied that "many peoples and strong nations shall come to seek the Lord of hosts in Jerusalem, and to entreat the favor of the Lord" (Zech 8:22).

— Isaiah 56:9–12 —
A Proclamation of Judgment

56:9

> **9All you beasts of the field, come to devour – all you beasts in the forest.**

A command, presumably from God, for the predator animals of the wild to come devour those who are supposed to be the watchmen of Israel. This opening verse of the prophecy starts with the declaration of punishment before the sinners or their misdeeds are identified.

56:10–11a

> **10His watchmen are blind, they are all without knowledge; they are all dumb dogs, they cannot bark; dreaming, lying down, loving to slumber. 11aThe dogs have a mighty appetite; they never have enough.**

The watchmen are the various leaders in Jerusalem who are blind and therefore without knowledge or the ability to speak out against what is wrong in society. They use their position for personal gain, but that can never be satisfied (v. 11a). Calling them "dogs" was particularly insulting since Jews considered dogs unclean animals rather than pets, as in the modern world.

56:11b–12

> [11b]**The shepherds also have no understanding; they have all turned to their own way, each to his own gain, one and all. [12]"Come," they say, "let us get wine, let us fill ourselves with strong drink; and tomorrow will be like this day, great beyond measure."**

Here the "watchmen" are called shepherds because they do not understand their role as guardians of the flock. Instead, they seek their own gain so they can get drunk. Their saying that "tomorrow will be like this day" implies their denial of a day of judgment or a day of salvation by God. Therefore, drink and be merry from day to day in this life, since such pleasure is all that one can hope for. Tragically for them, they seem unaware of the punishment the Lord is effecting through the wild beasts.

— Isaiah 57:1–2 —

> [1]**The righteous man perishes, and no one lays it to heart; devout men are taken away, while no one understands. For the righteous man is taken away from calamity, [2]he enters into peace; they rest in their beds who walk in their uprightness.**

This shorter section describes a situation that contradicts the standard teaching of wisdom, according to which the righteous prosper and the wicked perish. Here in 57:1, the righteous and devout (literally, "people of covenant love") perish and are taken away. A further connection with wisdom ideas is that "no one understands" this disordered society, while in Proverbs 1:23, the readers are expected to understand insight and righteousness. The last part of verse 1 may be better translated, "While no one understands that from the presence of calamity the righteous is taken." This means that the righteous are not supposed to experience calamity in a just world, and yet they do. What kind of salvation have the returnees experienced? In verse 2, the righteous are supposed to enter peace, but that is far from their present situation in Jerusalem at this point in history.

—— Isaiah 57:3–6 ——

This section is a trial of the evildoers that concludes in their judgment.

57:3

> **3But you, draw near hither, sons of the sorceress, offspring of the adulterer and the harlot.**

The judge summons the accused to draw near for trial. Already the accused are identified as the children of a sorceress and an adulterer. The father would neglect his illegitimate children and the mother would teach them wrong religion.

57:4–5

> **4Of whom are you making sport? Against whom do you open your mouth wide and put out your tongue? Are you not children of transgression, the offspring of deceit,**
> **5you who burn with lust among the oaks, under every green tree; who slay your children in the valleys, under the clefts of the rocks?**

The trial's interrogation begins with rhetorical questions, making it clear that the transgressors on trial are "playing around" with God Himself, and not merely with the weak, vulnerable righteous people. Verses 4b–5 pose a leading question, that as children of transgression and deceit, they are in fact worshiping other gods with orgies and child sacrifices (Baal worship).

57:6

> **6Among the smooth stones of the valley is your portion; they, they, are your lot; to them you have poured out a drink offering, you have brought a cereal offering. Shall I be appeased for these things?**

Their guilty verdict results in them living among the "smooth stones" in a dried-up riverbed. The punishment fits the crime since they made offerings to the gods in that location. The final rhetorical question implies that they claimed to offer worship in the Temple, but the Lord will not be appeased if their sacrifices to Him are made in conjunction with pagan worship.

— Isaiah 57:7–13 —

An accusation of apostasy among the returnees and a condemnation for the guilty but safety for those who authentically take refuge in the Lord.

57:7–10

> **7Upon a high and lofty mountain you have set your bed, and thither
> you went up to offer sacrifice. 8Behind the door and the doorpost you
> have set up your symbol; for, deserting me, you have uncovered your
> bed, you have gone up to it, you have made it wide; and you have
> made a bargain for yourself with them, you have loved their bed, you
> have looked on nakedness. 9You journeyed to Molech with oil and
> multiplied your perfumes; you sent your envoys far off, and sent down
> even to Sheol. 10You were wearied with the length of your way, but you
> did not say, "It is hopeless"; you found new life for your strength, and
> so you were not faint.**

In this section, the Lord speaks directly to the Jerusalem community members who reverted back to pagan practices, which are described in detail here.

7

Setting a bed on a high mountain was done for the orgiastic worship of fertility gods, who observed humans in sexual relations so as to induce the father storm god to mate with mother earth goddess. Adding sacrifices to the orgies was meant to ensure fecund animal husbandry and fields.

8

In addition to orgies outside the city, they also set up idols in the hidden places of their homes and engaged in sexual practices to honor the gods. They forsake God for pagan gods.

9–10

The Hebrew says they journeyed to "melek," which means "king" and was the name of a Canaanite deity. They anointed his idol with oil and perfumed ointments, similar to the way Jacob anointed the stone at Bethel in honor of the Lord (see Gn 27:18). Their "envoys" refer to various practitioners of magic and mediums who conjure spirits from Sheol, the place of the dead, practices which are called "abominations" in Deuteronomy 18:9–11.

Even when they were "wearied" with this journey for inappropriate spiritual knowledge, due to the usual failures of charmers, mediums, and occultists, they were blind to its futility and "were not faint."

57:11

> **[11]Whom did you dread and fear, so that you lied, and did not remember me, did not give me a thought? Have I not held my peace, even for a long time, and so you do not fear me?**

The Lord interrogates these idolaters about whom they dread and fear. Their actions showed apparently that they feared the fertility gods more than the Lord. However, they will soon realize that they feared the wrong deities, and now they will experience dread of the true Lord God.

57:12–13

> **[12]I will tell of your righteousness and your doings, but they will not help you. [13]When you cry out, let your collection of idols deliver you! The wind will carry them off, a breath will take them away. But he who takes refuge in me shall possess the land, and shall inherit my holy mountain.**

First, the pronouncement of sentence states that their righteous deeds will not help them because their sins of apostasy are greater than any good works they are able to do (v. 12). Second, since they want the Canaanite gods' help, who are flimsy enough to be blown away in a wind, let the gods deliver them from the Lord. Of course, that will be impossible (v. 13a). Finally, in verse 13b, taking refuge in the Lord is the only way of salvation. It is the prerequisite for possessing the land and the Lord's holy mountain, where He is worshiped in holiness and truth, not in sexual orgies or false necromancy.

— Isaiah 57:14–21 —

After these descriptions of troubles in the community (57:1–2) and condemnations of the unrighteous and the idolaters (57:3–6, 7–13), the Lord issues a proclamation of salvation for the contrite and humble.

57:14

> **[14]And it shall be said, "Build up, build up, prepare the way, remove every obstruction from my people's way."**

The call to prepare the way. While D-I made this call as a literal summons to prepare a highway for Israel's departure from exile in Babylon, here it is a figure for a way of life.

57:15–21

> **[15]For thus says the high and lofty One who inhabits eternity, whose name is Holy: "I dwell in the high and holy place, and also with him who is of a contrite and humble spirit, to revive the spirit of the humble, and to revive the heart of the contrite. [16]For I will not contend for ever, nor will I always be angry; for from me proceeds the spirit, and I have made the breath of life. [17]Because of the iniquity of his covetousness I was angry, I smote him, I hid my face and was angry; but he went on backsliding in the way of his own heart. [18]I have seen his ways, but I will heal him; I will lead him and requite him with comfort, creating for his mourners the fruit of the lips. [19]Peace, peace, to the far and to the near, says the LORD; and I will heal him. [20]But the wicked are like the tossing sea; for it cannot rest, and its waters toss up mire and dirt. [21]There is no peace, says my God, for the wicked."**

An oracle ("thus says") substantiates the prophet's summons to prepare the way by proclaiming salvation.

15

The Lord describes Himself as high, lofty, eternal, and holy, but His word is addressed to humans who are contrite and humble: they will be revived.

16–17

These verses look back on a period when the Lord was angry at the "iniquity of his covetousness" and "backsliding" and punished him. The Lord's reason not to contend forever is that the spirit and breath of life proceed from Him, and He will not hold His anger against His creature forever.

18–19

This is a promise of salvation which is experienced as healing, comfort to mourners, and peace.

20–21

However, Isaiah concludes with God's warning that peace is not for the wicked, since the uproar of wickedness makes their peace impossible.

Lesson 23

TRITO-ISAIAH 58–59

—— Isaiah 58:1–12 ——

An admonition about proper fasting attitudes during communal fasting, such as the Day of Atonement or some other fast day.

58:1–3a

> **1"Cry aloud, spare not, lift up your voice like a trumpet; declare to my**
> **people their transgression, to the house of Jacob their sins. 2Yet they**
> **seek me daily, and delight to know my ways, as if they were a nation**
> **that did righteousness and did not forsake the ordinance of their God;**
> **they ask of me righteous judgments, they delight to draw near to God.**
> **3a'Why have we fasted, and thou seest it not? Why have we humbled**
> **ourselves, and thou takest no knowledge of it?'**

The Lord introduces the prophet to his mission of admonishing the people who are acting sinfully when they fast.

1

The Lord commands the prophet to shout aloud the people's transgressions and sins to them.

2

The people think they are pleasing God by seeking Him and acting as if they were righteous in obeying His laws and ordinances, but in fact they are not. Hence, the need for the loud cry.

3a

The Lord quotes the people's question about God's lack of response to their fasting. They declare their innocence.

58:3b–4

> [3b]**Behold, in the day of your fast you seek your own pleasure, and oppress all your workers.** [4]**Behold, you fast only to quarrel and to fight and to hit with wicked fist. Fasting like yours this day will not make your voice to be heard on high.**

Here the prophet speaks directly to the people and accuses them of fasting in a way that is divorced from their moral behavior. Fasting is meant to be a time of abnegation, but the people seek their "own pleasure." Fasting usually makes people weaker and subdues their emotions, but here they quarrel, fight, oppress, and hit others. God refuses to accept a fast connected with behavior that contradicts the very nature of fasting.

58:5–7

> [5]**Is such the fast that I choose, a day for a man to humble himself? Is it to bow down his head like a rush, and to spread sackcloth and ashes under him? Will you call this a fast, and a day acceptable to the LORD?** [6]**"Is not this the fast that I choose: to loose the bonds of wickedness, to undo the thongs of the yoke, to let the oppressed go free, and to break every yoke?** [7]**Is it not to share your bread with the hungry, and bring the homeless poor into your house; when you see the naked, to cover him, and not to hide yourself from your own flesh?**

In the name of the Lord, the prophet admonishes the people with a series of rhetorical questions. Such questions evoke the correct answers from the people, who already know deep within themselves what kind of fasting the Lord truly desires from them.

5

The questions here are meant to show what is wrong with their fasting.

6–7

The questions here point to proper fasting, one that accomplishes a number of good deeds: loosing bonds and ending oppression; feeding the hungry, housing the homeless, and covering the naked, especially when these people are fellow Jews ("your own flesh"). While some modern people emphasize good works instead of fasting, these verses show that proper fasting leads to the accomplishment of good deeds and that fasting and righteous action are not mutually exclusive.

58:8–9a

> **[8]Then shall your light break forth like the dawn, and your healing shall spring up speedily; your righteousness shall go before you, the glory of the LORD shall be your rear guard. [9a]Then you shall call, and the LORD will answer; you shall cry, and he will say, Here I am.**

The Lord promises salvation to each individual (throughout the promise is addressed to "you" singular) who repents from doing evil during the fast but chooses to act righteously for the needy during the fast. Each person will receive light and healing. Using an image from a military campaign, and perhaps making a reference to the Exodus from Egypt, righteousness will go in front of the person, like a forward guard, while the glory of the Lord will be a guard of protection from the rear. Then (v. 9a), in answer to the complaint of verse 3a, the Lord promises to answer prayers and be personally present.

58:9b–12

> **[9b]"If you take away from the midst of you the yoke, the pointing of the finger, and speaking wickedness, [10a]if you pour yourself out for the hungry and satisfy the desire of the afflicted, [10b]then shall your light rise in the darkness and your gloom be as the noonday. [11]And the LORD will guide you continually, and satisfy your desire with good things, and make your bones strong; and you shall be like a watered garden, like a spring of water, whose waters fail not. [12]And your ancient ruins shall be rebuilt; you shall raise up the foundations of many generations; you shall be called the repairer of the breach, the restorer of streets to dwell in.**

Here, the Lord sets out the conditions for receiving His salvation.

9b–10a

The Lord sets conditions revolving around acts of justice and charity. Both the removal of the yoke of oppression plus generosity to the poor and afflicted are requirements for receiving salvation. Doing what is good makes a person liable to receiving good from the Lord.

10b–12

These verses clearly state that the Lord's salvation flows from the individuals choosing to do good. First, they will see light, as promised in verse 8. Then comes the Lord's guidance, since they can see more clearly. Satisfying them with good things that make them strong refers to receiving food in abundance after having fasted properly. Finally (v. 12), the ruins shall be rebuilt. This indicates that Jerusalem was not yet fully rebuilt and the walls were still a ruin. That would not be accomplished until the second half of the fifth century, when Nehemiah comes from Persia to oversee the construction of the city walls, despite the Samaritans' opposition and harassment.

—— Isaiah 58:13–14 ——

> **13If you turn back your foot from the Sabbath, from doing your pleasure on my holy day, and call the Sabbath a delight and the holy day of the LORD honorable; if you honor it, not going your own ways, or seeking your own pleasure, or talking idly; 14then you shall take delight in the LORD, and I will make you ride upon the heights of the earth; I will feed you with the heritage of Jacob your father, for the mouth of the LORD has spoken.**

An oracle ("the mouth of the Lord has spoken") exhorts the people to keep holy the Sabbath and promises reward if they do so. Earlier, 56:1–2 had opened T-I with a beatitude for the one who keeps the Sabbath, and the conclusion of chapter 59 with a Sabbath exhortation may provide bookends for the whole of 56 to 59 as a major section of T-I. This verse shows how important the prophet considered the Sabbath, as well as indicate that the people did not take it so seriously, despite the commandment (see Ex 20:8–11, where keeping the Sabbath holy by resting is done in imitation of the Lord's rest during the creation—see Gn 2:1–4a). This commandment was repeated in Exodus 31:13–14, where keeping the Sabbath "is a sign between me and you" to know that the Lord "sanctifies" Israel (31:13); plus, anyone who works on the Sabbath profanes it and must be put to death (31:14). Here the condition of a good Sabbath is avoiding doing whatever a person wants, seeking pleasure of idle talk while taking delight in the Sabbath as a holy day. No longer is it a threat of the death penalty (see Ex 31:14) but the promise that the observant will "take delight in the Lord." Sabbath will not be a burden but a deep delight. Further, they will find success (riding upon the heights), and the Lord will bless the land with produce, even though the people take a day off from work.

—— Isaiah 59:1–21 ——

A prophetic word against false fasting while favoring true fasting during a community fast. This long section may have been incorporated into a liturgical celebration; the prophet addresses the people's complaint that the Lord does not care about their fasting by accusing them of improper fasting and by calling them to repent.

59:1–3

> **[1]Behold, the LORD's hand is not shortened, that it cannot save, or his ear dull, that it cannot hear; [2]but your iniquities have made a separation between you and your God, and your sins have hid his face from you so that he does not hear. [3]For your hands are defiled with blood and your fingers with iniquity; your lips have spoken lies, your tongue mutters wickedness.**

The Lord accuses the people of iniquity in response to their accusation of His weakness.

1

Lying behind this verse is some unnamed person's accusation that the Lord has "shortened" His hand—that is, He was too weak to save or hear the people.

2–3

However, the Lord turns the accusation around by claiming that the people have committed a variety of iniquities—defiling themselves with blood, which may refer to murder (see v. 7), lying, and speaking wicked things.

Such serious sins can separate them from God, causing Him to hide His face from listening to their prayers for help.

59:4–8

> **[4]No one enters suit justly, no one goes to law honestly; they rely on**
> **empty pleas, they speak lies, they conceive mischief and bring forth**
> **iniquity. [5]They hatch adders' eggs, they weave the spider's web; he who**
> **eats their eggs dies, and from one which is crushed a viper is hatched.**
> **[6]Their webs will not serve as clothing; men will not cover themselves**
> **with what they make. Their works are works of iniquity, and deeds of**
> **violence are in their hands. [7]Their feet run to evil, and they make haste**
> **to shed innocent blood; their thoughts are thoughts of iniquity, des-**
> **olation and destruction are in their highways. [8]The way of peace they**
> **know not, and there is no justice in their paths; they have made their**
> **roads crooked, no one who goes in them knows peace.**

The Lord goes beyond answering the people's accusation of His weakness by laying out more accusations against them.

4

First, He accuses the people of abusing the law courts by false pleas, lying, and mischief. In this way, they break the eighth commandment against bearing false witness, which specifically is directed to protecting justice in the legal system (Ex 20:16; see other laws on this topic in Ex 23:6–7; Lv 19:11, 16; Dt 19:1521, all of which show how important the issue was in Israel).

5–6

The people's long-term plots and plans are described as "hatching adders' eggs" and a "spider's web." These are both vile realities that kill (adders are a very poisonous snake) and entrap people like insects in a spider's web. That the webs cannot be spun as clothing refers to the impossibility of having something good come out of these plots and plans of iniquity and wickedness.

7–8

These people are so wicked that they hurry to do evil; they cannot wait to "shed innocent blood." These verses portray two roads: desolation and destruction versus peace and justice. This image returns to the choice Moses laid before Israel in Deuteronomy 30:15–20: to choose life and good or death and evil. Similarly, Jesus described this choice as the narrow and hard road that leads to heaven or the wide and easy road that leads to hell (see Mt 7:13–14).

59:9–11

> **9Therefore justice is far from us, and righteousness does not overtake us; we look for light, and behold, darkness, and for brightness, but we walk in gloom. 10We grope for the wall like the blind, we grope like those who have no eyes; we stumble at noon as in the twilight, among those in full vigor we are like dead men. 11We all growl like bears, we moan and moan like doves; we look for justice, but there is none; for salvation, but it is far from us.**

Upon hearing the Lord's accusations, the people ("we," "us") lament their sins, admitting that justice, righteousness, and light are far from them. They accept their moral blindness that makes them "like dead men."

59:12–15a

> **12For our transgressions are multiplied before thee, and our sins testify against us; for our transgressions are with us, and we know our iniquities: 13transgressing, and denying the LORD, and turning away from following our God, speaking oppression and revolt, conceiving and uttering from the heart lying words. 14Justice is turned back, and righteousness stands afar off; for truth has fallen in the public squares, and uprightness cannot enter. 15aTruth is lacking, and he who departs from evil makes himself a prey.**

The community's lament continues here, humbly confessing their sin and moral failings. Since they turned away from God and speak oppression, they accept that their own justice, righteousness, and truth is turned away from them. In order to find these virtues as God's gift, they must first seek them in their own lives.

59:15b–20

> **15bThe LORD saw it, and it displeased him that there was no justice. 16He saw that there was no man, and wondered that there was no**

one to intervene; then his own arm brought him victory, and his righteousness upheld him. [17]He put on righteousness as a breastplate, and a helmet of salvation upon his head; he put on garments of vengeance for clothing, and wrapped himself in fury as a mantle. [18]According to their deeds, so will he repay, wrath to his adversaries, requital to his enemies; to the coastlands he will render requital. [19]So they shall fear the name of the LORD from the west, and his glory from the rising of the sun; for he will come like a rushing stream, which the wind of the LORD drives. [20]And he will come to Zion as Redeemer, to those in Jacob who turn from transgression, says the LORD.

The Lord responds to their confession of sin by saving the people from their enemies.

15b–16

The Lord sees that the people are without anyone to save them and to bring them justice and righteousness. The Lord is not about to intervene simply out of favoritism; rather, He seeks to bring victory in order to effect justice and righteousness because these virtues are good in themselves.

17

The Lord readies Himself to fight against the enemies by putting on armor. However, the Lord does not need physical protection. Rather, His "breastplate" is the virtue of righteousness and His "helmet" is His act of salvation. Such imagery has precedents in Isaiah 11:5, where the future messiah will clothe Himself in righteousness and faithfulness, or Job 29:14, where Job says of himself, "I put on righteousness, and it clothed me; my justice was like a robe and a turban." Saint Paul uses such imagery on several occassions: "Put on the breastplate of faith and love, and for a helmet the hope of salvation" (1 Thes 5:8); "Put on the armor of light" (Rom 13:12); and the most developed of all: "Stand therefore, having girded your loins with truth, and having put on the breastplate of righteousness, and having shod your feet with the equipment of the gospel of peace; besides all these, taking the shield of faith, with which you can quench all the flaming darts of the evil one. And take the helmet of salvation, and the sword of the Spirit, which is the word of God" (Eph 6:14–17).

18–19

The Lord promises to repay the enemies according to their own evil deeds, since the Lord is acting out of justice. As a result, the enemies will fear the Lord across the world and they will see His glory.

20

This oracle ("says the Lord") indicates that He will come to Zion, the mount where the Temple is located and be present among His recently repentant people. His presence will be as a Redeemer for those who turn away from their sins and transgressions. However, in the context of verses 1–15a, He will not be a Redeemer for those who persist in their sin.

59:21

> **21"And as for me, this is my covenant with them, says the LORD: my spirit which is upon you, and my words which I have put in your mouth, shall not depart out of your mouth, or out of the mouth of your children, or out of the mouth of your children's children, says the LORD, from this time forth and for evermore."**

In this oracle ("says the Lord"), the Lord makes a covenant with the people according to which His Spirit and His words will remain with them. Nothing specific is required of the people in this covenant, but the reader can assume that the Lord's abiding Spirit and word will transform them, just as the Spirit hovering over the waters and God's word began creation (Gn 1:2–3). Later, Christians could read this promise through the lens of John's Gospel, where the Word, who is God (Jn 1:1–3) and became flesh (1:14), would later promise the gift of the Paraclete, the Holy Spirit of truth (Jn 14–16) and then breathe Him upon the apostles on Easter Sunday (Jn 20:22).

Lesson 24

TRITO-ISAIAH 60–61

With good sense, a number of scholars consider Isaiah 60–62 the core of Trito-Isaiah. The prophet says that the Lord sent him to proclaim salvation to Zion (62:1), and these chapters all form a proclamation of salvation to the returnees from Babylon to Jerusalem. Except for 60:12, this section contains no condemnations of the nations nor criticisms of Israelites acting unjustly. The Lord proclaims salvation and a promise of yet greater things than the return home.

—— Isaiah 60:1–22 ——

A proclamation of salvation that the Lord's presence in Jerusalem will be the sole light in the world's darkness that draws all people there.

60:1–3

> **1Arise, shine; for your light has come, and the glory of the LORD has risen upon you. 2For behold, darkness shall cover the earth, and thick darkness the peoples; but the LORD will arise upon you, and his glory will be seen upon you. 3And nations shall come to your light, and kings to the brightness of your rising.**

The thick darkness that covers the peoples and the earth stands in contrast to the Lord's light. Given the general attitude toward pagan religion, this contrast concerns the knowledge of God and His presence. While the text clearly sees the nations' lack of the true God as darkness, verse 3 clearly recognizes that the nations ultimately want to come to the light. Therefore, when they see that the one source of light shines upon Jerusalem, they will be attracted to it.

60:4–7

> **4Lift up your eyes round about, and see; they all gather together, they come to you; your sons shall come from far, and your daughters shall be carried in the arms. 5Then you shall see and be radiant, your heart shall thrill and rejoice; because the abundance of the sea shall be turned to you, the wealth of the nations shall come to you. 6A multitude of camels shall cover you, the young camels of Midian and Ephah; all those from Sheba shall come. They shall bring gold and frankincense, and shall proclaim the praise of the LORD. 7All the flocks of Kedar shall be gathered to you, the rams of Nebaioth shall minister to you; they shall come up with acceptance on my altar, and I will glorify my glorious house.**

The effects of the Lord's light will cause Israel to be radiant and rejoice.

4

The command to "look up and see" assumes a somewhat downcast attitude among the returnees to Jerusalem. However, once the people see the nations streaming towards the light of the Lord, they will notice their sons and daughters—that is, the other Israelites living in diaspora—being brought home by these Gentiles streaming toward the light.

5–7

The return of Israel's children will cause joy and radiant hearts among the people. In addition, the nations will bring wealth from Arabia (Midian and Ephah, which was a clan of Midian) and Sheba, which may have been on the Horn of Africa, and Kedar and Nebaioth, regions of modern Jordan famous for livestock. Ezra 7 describes exiles who return from Persia with treasures, such as silver and gold, with which they will provide for offerings in the Temple at the expense of the king of Persia. Persia is not mentioned in Isaiah 60, but Ezra's description fits the actions of bringing gold and flocks for offering sacrifices in Isaiah 60: 6b–7.

60:8–9

> **8Who are these that fly like a cloud, and like doves to their windows? 9For the coastlands shall wait for me, the ships of Tarshish first, to bring your sons from far, their silver and gold with them, for the name**

of the LORD your God, and for the Holy One of Israel, because he has glorified you.

The Lord asks the people about the identity of these nations streaming to Jerusalem (v. 8), and He answers the question Himself: even ships of Tarshish (a Phoenician colony in Spain) and the coastlands of Asia Minor (now western Turkey) will bring Israel's scattered children, plus silver and gold. The reason is not found within the foreigners' human weakness or in Israel's strength but in the Lord's name—He has glorified Israel. God Himself and His actions for Israel is the attraction for these peoples.

60:10–16

10Foreigners shall build up your walls, and their kings shall minister to
you; for in my wrath I smote you, but in my favor I have had mercy
on you. 11Your gates shall be open continually; day and night they
shall not be shut; that men may bring to you the wealth of the nations,
with their kings led in procession. 12For the nation and kingdom that
will not serve you shall perish; those nations shall be utterly laid waste.
13The glory of Lebanon shall come to you, the cypress, the plane, and
the pine, to beautify the place of my sanctuary; and I will make the
place of my feet glorious. 14The sons of those who oppressed you shall
come bending low to you; and all who despised you shall bow down
at your feet; they shall call you the City of the LORD, the Zion of the
Holy One of Israel. 15Whereas you have been forsaken and hated, with
no one passing through, I will make you majestic for ever, a joy from
age to age. 16You shall suck the milk of nations, you shall suck the
breast of kings; 16band you shall know that I, the LORD, am your Savior
and your Redeemer, the Mighty One of Jacob.

The description of salvation here focuses on the rebuilding and the beautifying of Jerusalem.

10

When the Babylonians destroyed Jerusalem in 587 BC, they made sure the walls were dismantled to prevent any further revolts. When the people returned, the Persians did not give them permission to rebuild the walls, making them vulnerable to attack. Since the walls were not built, according to Trito-Isaiah, this chapter is placed before the arrival of Nehemiah in 444 BC, who received permission from Persian King Artaxerxes I to build the walls (Neh 2:7–9).

11

In fact, after the walls and gates were built, notice of closing them to keep out people was made in Nehemiah 13:19. However, in this proclamation of salvation, the gates will not be shut, because the Lord will be the city's protection. That same idea appears in the new and heavenly Jerusalem, whose "gates shall never be shut by day and there shall be no night there" (Rv 21:25), since God protects the city.

12

This is the sole threatening verse in Isaiah 60–62, threatening any nation who does not cooperate with the salvation the Lord is effecting in Jerusalem.

13

The excellent wood that comes from the Lebanon forests will be used to beautify the Temple, which was rebuilt between 520 and 516 BC, though in a smaller and less glorious way than the previous one. Those who were old enough to remember the old Temple wept in disappointment when they saw the new one (Ezra 3:12). Here is a promise that it will be made excellent. That would not take place until 19 BC, when Herod the Great constructs a completely magnificent Temple in place of the post-exilic building.

14–16a

This salvation will reverse Israel's place among the nations. Former oppressors will bow before Jerusalem and recognize it as the City of the Lord, the Holy One of Israel (v. 14). On the other hand, Jerusalem, which had been abandoned, will become majestic and an everlasting joy (v. 15). Suckling milk from foreign nations means they will provide sustenance for the city.

16b

This whole transformation will be the proof that the Lord is Savior, Redeemer, and the Mighty One capable of effecting such a marvel.

60:17–22

17Instead of bronze I will bring gold, and instead of iron I will bring
silver; instead of wood, bronze, instead of stones, iron. I will make
your overseers peace and your taskmasters righteousness. 18Violence
shall no more be heard in your land, devastation or destruction with-
in your borders; you shall call your walls Salvation, and your gates
Praise. 19The sun shall be no more your light by day, nor for brightness
shall the moon give light to you by night; but the LORD will be your
everlasting light, and your God will be your glory. 20Your sun shall
no more go down, nor your moon withdraw itself; for the LORD will
be your everlasting light, and your days of mourning shall be ended.
21Your people shall all be righteous; they shall possess the land for ever,
the shoot of my planting, the work of my hands, that I might be glori-
fied. 22The least one shall become a clan, and the smallest one a mighty
nation; I am the LORD; in its time I will hasten it.

Salvation will mean a complete transformation of the present circumstances into a new and far more wonderful ideal.

17–18

Common materials will all be upgraded to more precious ones: bronze to gold, iron to silver, wood to bronze, stone to iron. Such work may require taskmasters and overseers, but they will have the virtues of peace and righteousness rather than oppressive human beings (v. 17). Such new taskmasters will bring violence, devastation, and destruction to an end, and salvation and praise will become the protective walls (v. 18). This last idea can be illustrated by the Christian martyrs throughout the centuries. These brave men and women trusted powerfully in Christ's salvation as their ultimate protection. Many went into the arenas with praise on their lips, knowing that God was bringing them to the New Jerusalem through their terrible sufferings.

19–20

Not only will the building materials of the city be transformed into precious materials, but even the sun and moon will be replaced by the presence of the Lord God, who is the light promised in 60:1–3. This understanding of the Lord God as the light of the new and heavenly Jerusalem is also stated in Revelation 21:23; 22:5.

21–22

After detailing salvation's impact on Jerusalem, the last two verses describe the changes effected in the inhabitants. They "shall all be righteous," which can certainly refer to a moral change within them. However, the word "righteousness" can refer to victories in war, so being righteous may here refer to the state of being among those the Lord has saved. This need not be too strong a distinction, since morally righteous people are the ones God wants to count among the redeemed.

The other descriptions—possessing the land, increasing from a small population to a large one—are standard features of redemption. They, too, will occur among the righteous, proclaiming again that the Lord is glorified throughout the whole process of salvation.

—— Isaiah 61:1–3 ——

This short section is a proclamation by an individual chosen by the Lord for a mission to the rest of the people, in their weaknesses, to proclaim the year of the Lord's favor. This proclamation will transform the mourning in Zion into gladness, and to make the faint into "oaks of righteousness."

61:1

> [1]**The Spirit of the Lord God is upon me, because the Lord has anointed me to bring good tidings to the afflicted; he has sent me to bind up the brokenhearted, to proclaim liberty to the captives, and the opening of the prison to those who are bound;**

Whereas in Isaiah 42:1 the Lord says, "I have put my Spirit upon him," here the prophet speaks by saying "the Spirit of the Lord is upon me." He recognizes that his power to speak "good news," to bind up the broken hearted, and to proclaim liberty is truly beyond his personal ability, but the Spirit of the Lord "anointed" him, enabling him to do such things.

61:2

> **[2]to proclaim the year of the LORD's favor, and the day of vengeance of our God; to comfort all who mourn;**

This verse identifies "the year of the Lord's favor" with the "day of vengeance of our God." This seems to be a reference to the Jubilee Year, which occurs every fifty years (see Lv 25:19) on the seventy-third or twenty-third year of each century. This verse may be a way to date Trito-Isiah to around 473 BC, the first Jubilee after the construction of the Temple.

The whole year was a Jubilee with various national obligations to restore a just society, including the proclamation of liberty (see Lv 25:10), letting the land lie fallow for a rest (see Lv 25:11), the return of land to those who had to sell it (see Lv 25:13–17, 23–34), the remission of debts (see Lv 25:35–38), and freeing of slaves (see Lv 25:39–43, 47–55). Yet it began with the Day of Atonement, on the tenth day of the seventh month, instead of the first day, which is Jewish New Year normally. These activities fit the ministry of the prophet in 61:1.

Isaiah 61:1–2 is read by Jesus in the synagogue at Nazareth (see Lk 4:18–19). He stated that the passage was fulfilled in Him (see Lk 4:21). Father Bargil Pixner, OSB, argues from John 2:20 that Jesus's ministry began in AD 27, which was a Jubilee year, which makes Jesus's use of Isaiah 61:1–2 all the more poignant.

61:3

> **[3]to grant to those who mourn in Zion—to give them a garland instead of ashes, the oil of gladness instead of mourning, the mantle of praise instead of a faint spirit; that they may be called oaks of righteousness, the planting of the LORD, that he may be glorified.**

In addition to external transformations in society, the ministry empowered by the Holy Spirit will also grant interior changes of gladness and praise to "faint" spirits. Their transformation into strong oaks of righteousness will enable the people to glorify the Lord.

— Isaiah 61:4–11 —

This proclamation of salvation is a follow-up to the messenger's self-proclamation of having the ministry of the Spirit of the Lord. Verses 4–11 describe societal changes and how they will be accomplished.

61:4

> **[4]They shall build up the ancient ruins, they shall raise up the former devastations; they shall repair the ruined cities, the devastations of many generations.**

The first step, so obvious to the returnees from Babylon, is that Jerusalem's "ancient ruins" will be rebuilt, along with the other cities.

61:5–6

> **[5]Aliens shall stand and feed your flocks, foreigners shall be your plowmen and vinedressers; [6]but you shall be called the priests of the LORD, men shall speak of you as the ministers of our God; you shall eat the wealth of the nations, and in their riches you shall glory.**

A direct address by the messenger to the inhabitants of Jerusalem ("you") that sets them apart for a priestly ministry to "our God." This would fulfill their vocation from the beginning of God's call to them at Mount Sinai (Ex 19:6: "you shall be to me a kingdom of priests and a holy nation"). As a priestly people, they are to offer sacrifices for all the nations. Hence, they will become a source of blessing for the whole world, as the Lord told Abram when He first called him (Gn 12:2–3 "you will be a blessing . . . by you all the families of the earth shall bless themselves"). For Israel to be a priestly people, the foreign nations will tend their animals, farms, and vineyards and bring them riches to pay for the sacrifices they offer for all the nations.

The New Testament also understands the whole Christian people as a priestly people in 1 Peter 2:4–5 and Revelation 1:6; 5:10; 20:6, which is a type of fulfillment of 61:6.

61:7–9

> **[7]Instead of your shame you shall have a double portion, instead of dishonor you shall rejoice in your lot; therefore in your land you shall**

possess a double portion; yours shall be everlasting joy. [8]For I the LORD love justice, I hate robbery and wrong; I will faithfully give them their recompense, and I will make an everlasting covenant with them. [9]Their descendants shall be known among the nations, and their offspring in the midst of the peoples; all who see them shall acknowledge them, that they are a people whom the LORD has blessed.

Israel's transformation includes exchanging a double portion of food instead of shame and rejoicing instead of dishonor (v. 7). The Lord's love of justice is the catalyst for Israel's change. The Lord pays back what Israel deserves and seeks to make an everlasting covenant with them (v. 8). Finally, in verse 9, the shame of verse 7 is also transformed by the fame of their descendants among all nations as a people whom the Lord has blessed. This will stand in contrast to the prophets' earlier threats that Israel would become a byword of cursing and a hissing because of the destruction of Jerusalem by the Babylonians (Dt 28:37: "You shall become a horror, a proverb, and a byword, among all the peoples where the Lord will lead you away." See also Jer 19:8; 24:9; 25:18; 26:6; 42:18; 44:22; Ez 23:10; 25:23; 36:2).

61:10

[10]I will greatly rejoice in the LORD, my soul shall exult in my God; for he has clothed me with the garments of salvation, he has covered me with the robe of righteousness, as a bridegroom decks himself with a garland, and as a bride adorns herself with her jewels.

A song of praise in which an individual greatly rejoices and exults because the Lord effects a transformation that clothes the person in salvation and righteousness. This type of song might be sung by a groom or bride at their wedding feast. A similar parallelism of rejoicing and exulting appears in the Magnificat: "My soul magnifies the Lord, and my spirit rejoices in God my Savior" (Lk 1:46–47), which Mary proclaims after conceiving Jesus, who personifies salvation.

61:11

[11]For as the earth brings forth its shoots, and as a garden causes what is sown in it to spring up, so the LORD God will cause righteousness and praise to spring forth before all the nations.

A statement of faith that the Lord will cause righteousness as a quality of the people and praise as their activity to grow as surely as the plants from the earth or in a planted garden. Since the garden is planted by humans who have a definite plan for what they want to grow, it is a good image for the Lord's plans for righteousness and praise to grow in Israel.

Lesson 25

TRITO-ISAIAH 62–64

—— Isaiah 62:1–12 ——

This chapter assumes that the people have been lamenting that the Lord has been silent because He has forsaken Zion. As a result, this chapter is a proclamation of salvation that counters those complaints.

62:1–5

> **1For Zion's sake I will not keep silent, and for Jerusalem's sake I will**
> **not rest, until her vindication goes forth as brightness, and her salva-**
> **tion as a burning torch. 2The nations shall see your vindication, and**
> **all the kings your glory; and you shall be called by a new name which**
> **the mouth of the LORD will give. 3You shall be a crown of beauty in**
> **the hand of the LORD, and a royal diadem in the hand of your God.**
> **4You shall no more be termed Forsaken, and your land shall no more**
> **be termed Desolate; but you shall be called My delight is in her, and**
> **your land Married; for the LORD delights in you, and your land shall**
> **be married. 5For as a young man marries a virgin, so shall your sons**
> **marry you, and as the bridegroom rejoices over the bride, so shall your**
> **God rejoice over you.**

The Lord answers the lament by a promise of working constantly for Jerusalem until she sees God's vindication in her transformation into a beautiful city.

1–2

In a number of the psalms of lament, the Lord is asked "how long" the present suffering or desolation will last (see Ps 4:2; 6:3; 13:1, 2; 35:17; 74:10;

89:46; 94:3). These proclamations are answered with: "until" Jerusalem's vindication arrives. The people assumed that the Lord was silent and now He speaks until the nations see Jerusalem's vindication, glory, and a new name given by the Lord (v. 2).

3–5

The transformation is portrayed with images from marriage scenes. The idea of the Lord loving Israel like a husband loving his wife goes back to Hosea 1–3, where He divorces Israel for Her infidelity by worshiping other gods but then restores her to an everlasting marriage covenant. Here Jerusalem will become a "crown" and "diadem" after having been forsaken to the Babylonian destroyers that left only charred ruins. From being forsaken and desolate, the city will be called by the Lord "My Delight" and "Married" (Hebrew "Beulah"). God will rejoice over her like a bridegroom because she will be rebuilt in magnificence.

62:6–7

> **6Upon your walls, O Jerusalem, I have set watchmen; all the day and all the night they shall never be silent. You who put the LORD in remembrance, take no rest, 7and give him no rest until he establishes Jerusalem and makes it a praise in the earth.**

Once again, the use of "until" implies that the people's lament of "How long?" will be answered. Here the image is that the Lord has set watchmen until He establishes Jerusalem as a place that is praised by the whole world.

62:8–9

> **8The LORD has sworn by his right hand and by his mighty arm: "I will not again give your grain to be food for your enemies, and foreigners shall not drink your wine for which you have labored; 9but those who garner it shall eat it and praise the LORD, and those who gather it shall drink it in the courts of my sanctuary."**

Cyrus the Persian had given the Jewish exiles permission to return to Jerusalem. But they remained part of the empire and were forced to pay taxes in forms of grain and wine. These verses respond to a complaint about paying Persian taxes with a promise of independence that allows them to eat the produce of their fields in the Temple as part of their joyful celebration of the Lord's glory.

62:10–12

> **[10]Go through, go through the gates, prepare the way for the people; build up, build up the highway, clear it of stones, lift up an ensign over the peoples. [11]Behold, the Lord has proclaimed to the end of the earth: Say to the daughter of Zion, "Behold, your salvation comes; behold, his reward is with him, and his recompense before him." [12]And they shall be called the holy people, the redeemed of the Lord; and you shall be called Sought out, a city not forsaken.**

The proclamation of salvation to the returnees living in Jerusalem uses some ideas from Deutero-Isaiah: verse 10 refers back to Isaiah 40:3 and 52:11, and verse 11 refers to Isaiah 40:9–11. However, the words are no longer addressed to the exiles but to the inhabitants of Jerusalem. The Lord is telling them to go through the city gates and build up a highway for those people still living abroad so that they can return to Jerusalem (v. 10). Meanwhile, in verse 11, the Lord will go out to the "end of the earth" to tell all the scattered Israelites that their salvation is coming with a reward. The people will be identified as "holy people"—that is, people set apart for the Lord and the redeemed. As a result of this transformation from exiled to redeemed, the rest of the world's inhabitants will seek them out.

—— Isaiah 63:1–6 ——

The city watchman poses questions to someone unknown to him, and the Lord answers that it is He coming to save the city.

63:1

> **[1]Who is this that comes from Edom, in crimsoned garments from Bozrah, he that is glorious in his apparel, marching in the greatness of his strength? "It is I, announcing vindication, mighty to save."**

The first question seeks the identity of the approaching stranger coming from Bozrah, the capital of Edom, in crimsoned garments. The Lord answers without stating His name but by identifying Himself as the one who "speaks with righteousness, great to save." The translator interpreted the term "righteousness" as "vindication", but it is better to translate it consistently with the other uses of this word in T-I (Is 60:17, 21; 61:3, 10, 11) in order to link the various proclamations of the Lord's salvation with each other. The watchman learns that the Lord has approached in order to save Jerusalem in a mighty way.

63:2–3

> **[2]Why is your apparel red, and your garments like his that treads in the wine press? [3]"I have trodden the wine press alone, and from the peoples no one was with me; I trod them in my anger and trampled them in my wrath; their lifeblood is sprinkled upon my garments, and I have stained all my raiment.**

The watchman's second question concerns the reason for the Lord's red garments. He answers that He has exercised judgment in wrath and anger against the wicked, and their blood has stained His garments. The same image of a winepress as the way to condemn sinners appears in Lamentations 1:15, written after the destruction of Jerusalem, and Revelation 14:19–20; 19:13–15, at the final judgment.

63:4–6

> **[4]For the day of vengeance was in my heart, and my year of redemption has come. [5]I looked, but there was no one to help; I was appalled, but there was no one to uphold; so my own arm brought me victory, and my wrath upheld me. [6]I trod down the peoples in my anger, I made them drunk in my wrath, and I poured out their lifeblood on the earth."**

Having answered the questions posed by the watchman, the Lord connects His presence with the day of vengeance and year of favor in Isaiah 61:2. In 63:5, the Lord seems surprised that no one was available to effect the judgment on sinners. In the absence of people who will punish the wicked, the Lord takes on this responsibility, reiterating in verse 6 that He trod the wicked in His winepress of judgment.

— Isaiah 63:7–64:12 —

This long section employs a community lament, a liturgical prayer for the peoples to present its needs in a difficult situation, presumably in the Temple. This form appears in Psalms 44 and 89, where a close examination will show several of the same elements as are also found in this section of T-I. The great promises of the preceding proclamations of salvation contrasted with the actual situation of problems in the small community of returned exiles living in Jerusalem. The territory under their control was no more than twenty square miles, hardly the glorious city to which the nations would one day stream. Instead of the light shining upon them (Is 60), they see present difficulties. In such a situation, the faithful do not deny either God's promise or their present plight. Rather, they turn toward God and let both realities come together in prayer, here, in a form like the psalms.

63:7–14

[7]I will recount the steadfast love of the LORD, the praises of the LORD, according to all that the LORD has granted us, and the great goodness to the house of Israel which he has granted them according to his mercy, according to the abundance of his steadfast love. [8]For he said, Surely they are my people, sons who will not deal falsely; and he became their Savior. [9]In all their affliction he was afflicted, and the angel of his presence saved them; in his love and in his pity he redeemed them; he lifted them up and carried them all the days of old. [10]But they rebelled and grieved his holy Spirit; therefore he turned to be their enemy, and himself fought against them. [11]Then he remembered the days of old, of Moses his servant. Where is he who brought up out of the sea the shepherds of his flock? Where is he who put in the midst of them his holy Spirit, [12]who caused his glorious arm to go at the right hand of Moses, who divided the waters before them to make for himself an everlasting name, [13]who led them through the depths? Like a horse in the desert, they did not stumble. [14]Like cattle that go down into the valley, the Spirit of the LORD gave them rest. So thou didst lead your people, to make for thyself a glorious name.

These verses recount the Lord's historical dealings with Israel. As in Psalms 44 and 89, this serves to reawaken faith in the Lord's loving action since He seems absent during their current predicament.

7

The introductory verse remembers the Lord's love and the times when the people had praised Him for all of His goodness, mercy, and love.

8–10

The first part of recounting the past focuses on the history of the Lord's relationship with Israel: the Lord assumes He can trust them, but they rebelled.

8–9

This part draws the reader into the pathos of the Lord's love. The Lord thinks the people will not be false to Him, and therefore, He became their Savior. Their afflictions became His own, so He pitied them in their misery, particularly referring to their servitude in Egypt (see Ex 3:7–9, where the Lord "saw the people's affliction" and "heard their cry"). The "angel of his presence" refers to the role of angels in the Exodus (see Ex 14:19; 23:20–21; 33:14).

10

However, the Lord's trust was met with rebellion rather than obedience. The theme of rebellion and "murmuring" appears from the beginning of their wilderness journey and escalates when the people make a golden calf to lead them (see Ex 32). Later, they refuse to begin the conquest of Canaan after the spies' report of the strength of the Canaanite cities and people (see Nm 13–14). The Lord became their enemy, punishing them after the golden calf episode and forcing them to wander in the desert for forty years after the spy episode.

11–14

A lament that the Lord remembered "Moses his servant" and saved Israel. However, the lament raises the questions, "Where is he" now? The Lord brought the people out of the Red Sea (vv. 12–13) and His Spirit gave them rest, but where is the Lord in our present needs?

63:15–16

> **[15]Look down from heaven and see, from thy holy and glorious habitation. Where are thy zeal and thy might? The yearning of thy heart and thy compassion are withheld from me. [16]For thou art our Father, though Abraham does not know us and Israel does not acknowledge us; thou, O LORD, art our Father, our Redeemer from of old is thy name.**

A petitionary prayer is offered for the Lord to look down upon Jerusalem of the post-exilic time and see its difficulties as He had seen the afflictions of Israel in Egypt.

15

The prayer contains the question that implies lament, "Where are thy zeal and might?" The Lord had shown that in the past, but where is that now as compassion and empathetic yearning for Israel are absent?

16

The writer implores the Lord to answer for two reasons. First, the Lord is a Father and therefore a Redeemer, whose compassion to Israel was described in verses 8–9. Therefore, revive that paternal love and redeem Jerusalem. Second, their ancestors, Abraham and his grandson Israel, do not acknowledge them; therefore, they have only the Lord to care for them.

63:17–19

> **[17]O LORD, why dost thou make us err from thy ways and harden our heart, so that we fear thee not? Return for the sake of thy servants, the tribes of thy heritage. [18]Thy holy people possessed thy sanctuary a little while; our adversaries have trodden it down. [19]We have become like those over whom thou hast never ruled, like those who are not called by thy name.**

As is typical of community lament psalms, the writer returns to the theme of lament, with a question directed to the Lord and then a description of the problems.

17

The lament opens with an odd question from people who need to repent: they ask the Lord why He makes them "err," using a Hebrew word meaning to "wander," and "harden"—that is, make stubborn—their hearts. They imply that their circumstances are the reason they sin and harden their hearts, and God caused the circumstances; therefore, it is His fault. The solution appears in the petition, "return" to us and be a protection.

18–19

They complain that unnamed enemies have trampled and therefore defiled the Temple sanctuary that they had only recently rebuilt. This may refer to some event unknown involving the Samaritans, who are mentioned as harassing Jerusalem before Nehemiah came with permission to build the city walls (see Neh 4). Because of this attack, the people seek the Lord's help even more. They have become like people without a ruler.

64:1–5a

> **1O that thou would rend the heavens and come down, that the mountains might quake at thy presence – 2as when fire kindles brushwood and the fire causes water to boil—to make thy name known to thy adversaries, and that the nations might tremble at thy presence! 3When thou didst terrible things which we looked not for, thou camest down, the mountains quaked at thy presence. 4From of old no one has heard or perceived by the ear, no eye has seen a God besides thee who works for those who wait for him. 5aYou meet him that joyfully works righteousness, those that remember thee in thy ways.**

These verses contain the petition for the Lord to appear in great power and give them protection.

1–3

As in very old hymns, they want the Lord to "rend the heavens and come down, making the mountains "quake," with fire and "terrible" (i.e., "fearful") things as signs of His presence (see similar images in Jgs 5:4–5; Ps 18:7–15).

4–5

The petition is accompanied by a confession of faith: there is no "God besides you" who does such wonders for the people who wait for Him in faith and who joyfully do works of righteousness. This profession of faith is also a prayer directed to the Lord.

64:5b–7

**5bBehold, thou wast angry, and we sinned; in our sins we have been a
long time, and shall we be saved? 6We have all become like one who
is unclean, and all our righteous deeds are like a polluted garment.
We all fade like a leaf, and our iniquities, like the wind, take us away.
7There is no one that calls upon thy name, that bestirs himself to take
hold of thee; for thou hast hid thy face from us, and have delivered us
into the hand of our iniquities.**

The prayer recognizes the Lord's anger and the people confess their sin. They accept that all of them are "unclean" and that makes their righteous deeds "polluted," like a rag that a woman uses after her menstrual cycle.

In verse 6b, the image of being a faded leaf that blows away because of their iniquities is drawn from Psalms 1:4–6, where the wicked are like dried chaff blown away in the wind.

A final plea is made to the Lord. Since the Lord "hid" His face from their sins and delivered the people into their iniquities, no one calls upon Him. Implied in this plea is that if the Lord wants someone to pray to Him, then He ought to forgive the people.

64:8

**8Yet, O LORD, thou art our Father; we are the clay, and thou art our
potter; we are all the work of thy hand.**

Profession of confidence in the Lord as a Father who has shaped the people like clay. This is yet another, though positive, inducement for the Lord to answer them and forgive their sins.

64:9–11

**9Be not exceedingly angry, O LORD, and remember not iniquity for
ever. Behold, consider, we are all thy people. 10Thy holy cities have
become a wilderness, Zion has become a wilderness, Jerusalem a deso-
lation. 11Our holy and beautiful house, where our fathers praised thee,
has been burned by fire, and all our pleasant places have become ruins.**

From the preceding confession of sin and profession of faith comes the following prayer that the Lord be not angry with Zion nor remember their sin. Then the prayer lists the things they want the Lord to consider in His answer. First, they are His people, as in verse 8, where they are the work of His hands (v. 9b). Then recall the mess they are in: cities are ruined, Jerusalem is desolate, the Temple has been burned, and their houses are ruined.

64:12

> **[12]Wilt thou restrain thyself at these things, O LORD? Wilt thou keep silent, and afflict us sorely?**

The petition concludes with a rhetorical question in light of these problems: Lord, will You restrain yourself, be silent, and afflict us? They lay this question before Him in the hope that He who has "formed" them like a potter will answer positively and help them.

Lesson 26

Trito-Isaiah 65–66

—— Isaiah 65:1–16 ——

An announcement of the Lord's doom (vv. 1–7) follows an announcement of His salvation (vv. 8–16a). This passage introduces a new concept in the Old Testament. Whereas the prophets present messages of judgment and doom and of salvation elsewhere, each message is generally applied to the whole nation because they all bore a corporate responsibility for their sins or repentance. Here the passage announces doom to those who sin and salvation to the righteous, distinguishing between the groups in the community and assigning their fate before God's judgment on the merits of the people within the groups. This is a major step in recognizing that the Lord judges each person for their deeds and conscience.

At the same time, this passage gives us a window into the tensions that existed among the returnees to Jerusalem. Not all returnees were pious and faith-filled. Some reverted back to old sins, such as idolatry.

65:1–7

Here, the announcement of doom is pronounced on the sinners.

> **[1]I was ready to be sought by those who did not ask for me; I was ready**
> **to be found by those who did not seek me. I said, "Here am I, here am I,"**
> **to a nation that did not call on my name. [2]I spread out my hands all the**
> **day to a rebellious people, who walk in a way that is not good, following**
> **their own devices; [3]a people who provoke me to my face continually, sac-**
> **rificing in gardens and burning incense upon bricks; [4]who sit in tombs,**
> **and spend the night in secret places; who eat swine's flesh, and broth of**

abominable things is in their vessels; [5]who say, "Keep to yourself, do not come near me, for I am set apart from you." These are a smoke in my nostrils, a fire that burns all the day. [6]Behold, it is written before me: "I will not keep silent, but I will repay, yea, I will repay into their bosom [7]their iniquities and their fathers' iniquities together, says the LORD; because they burned incense upon the mountains and reviled me upon the hills, I will measure into their bosom payment for their former doings."

1–2

In a direct address to the people, the Lord lays out His case for sinners by pointing out that He had offered His gracious salvation to even those who were not asking, seeking, or calling on Him because of their rebellion. This harkens back to the prophetic ministries of D-I during the exile and T-I after the return to Jerusalem. The image of the Lord spreading out His hands is one of opening His arms to embrace the rebellious people in love, similar to the father of the prodigal son (see Lk 15:20).

3–5

These verses describe the rebels' sins who "provoke" the Lord by sacrificing in their own gardens instead of worshiping in the Temple, which was the only place to offer sacrifices and incense. These people sat in tombs in order to consult the dead and speak with ghosts in secret. Eating pork and other forbidden "unclean" animals further separated them. It is no wonder that they tell the Lord to keep to Himself, and that He says they are a "smoke in my nostrils" and a fire, an image of the doom they are already living out.

6–7

The Lord announces that He will not remain silent but will punish their iniquities, both recent and past. The present sins of idolatry and necromancy are in continuity with the sins committed before the exile, so the Lord will add the new sins to their account of past sins.

65:8–16

[8]Thus says the LORD: "As the wine is found in the cluster, and they say, 'Do not destroy it, for there is a blessing in it,' so I will do for my

> **servants' sake, and not destroy them all. [9]I will bring forth descen-
> dants from Jacob, and from Judah inheritors of my mountains; my
> chosen shall inherit it, and my servants shall dwell there. [10]Sharon
> shall become a pasture for flocks, and the Valley of Achor a place for
> herds to lie down, for my people who have sought me. [11]But you who
> forsake the LORD, who forget my holy mountain, who set a table for
> Fortune and fill cups of mixed wine for Destiny; [12]I will destine you
> to the sword, and all of you shall bow down to the slaughter; because,
> when I called, you did not answer, when I spoke, you did not listen,
> but you did what was evil in my eyes, and chose what I did not delight
> in." [13]Therefore thus says the LORD God: "Behold, my servants shall
> eat, but you shall be hungry; behold, my servants shall drink, but you
> shall be thirsty; behold, my servants shall rejoice, but you shall be put
> to shame; [14]behold, my servants shall sing for gladness of heart, but
> you shall cry out for pain of heart, and shall wail for anguish of spirit.
> [15]You shall leave your name to my chosen for a curse, and the LORD
> God will slay you; but his servants he will call by a different name. [16]So
> that he who blesses himself in the land shall bless himself by the God
> of truth, and he who takes an oath in the land shall swear by the God
> of truth; because the former troubles are forgotten and are hid from
> my eyes.**

This announcement of salvation for the Lord's chosen promises to distinguish the rebels from the chosen, with punishment for the former and salvation for the latter.

8

The section begins with an oracle ("Thus says the Lord") about a cluster of grapes—some look rotten but some are still good and possess "a blessing." This is the image for the community which includes idolaters, who will be destroyed like rotten grapes, and the Lord's own servants, who will be saved.

9–10

The oracle continues with a promise that the Lord's "chosen" will have descendants who inherit His mountains in the center of the country and plains. (Sharon is a coastal plain in the west; Achor is a section of the Jordan valley in the east.)

11–12

On the other hand, the Lord speaks directly to those who "forsake the Lord" and "forget his holy mountain" where the Temple rests and who set themselves up for the feast of the judgment. They will be slaughtered because they did not listen to the Lord and did evil things that the Lord rejects.

13–16

The oracle formula is repeated as the Lord God lays out the separation of sinners from the Lord's servants and decrees the future of each in pairs of opposites: servants eat, sinners hunger; servants drink, sinners thirst; servants rejoice, sinners are shamed; and ultimately the names of sinners will become a curse used by the servants (vv. 13–15). Verse 16 concludes the whole with a promise of blessing and taking oaths in the name of the God of truth "because" the former troubles are forgotten. These "former troubles" refer in this context to the judgments of the whole nation as a unity, while in the present, the Lord will judge each person's own actions, with reward to those who serve the Lord and punishment to the sinners.

—— Isaiah 65:17–25 ——

Having made the judgment between the wicked and the authentic servants of the Lord, the Lord now promises a new creation that brings ultimate joy to His people.

65:17–18

> **17"For behold, I create new heavens and a new earth; and the former things shall not be remembered or come into mind. 18But be glad and rejoice for ever in that which I create; for behold, I create Jerusalem a rejoicing, and her people a joy.**

These opening verses use the Hebrew word "create" (*bara'*), which always has God as the subject: no one else can create. While D-I referred to the Lord's creation of the original heaven and earth as a proof that He is the only God (Is 45:18), here T-I speaks of the Lord creating "new heavens," "new earth," and Jerusalem in order to forget past suffering and offer future joy.

65:19–24

**19 I will rejoice in Jerusalem, and be glad in my people; no more shall
be heard in it the sound of weeping and the cry of distress. 20 No more
shall there be in it an infant that lives but a few days, or an old man
who does not fill out his days, for the child shall die a hundred years
old, and the sinner a hundred years old shall be accursed. 21 They shall
build houses and inhabit them; they shall plant vineyards and eat their
fruit. 22 They shall not build and another inhabit; they shall not plant
and another eat; for like the days of a tree shall the days of my people
be, and my chosen shall long enjoy the work of their hands. 23 They
shall not labor in vain, or bear children for calamity; for they shall be
the offspring of the blessed of the LORD, and their children with them.
24 Before they call I will answer, while they are yet speaking I will hear.**

Here the Lord focuses on the description of the New Jerusalem.

19

The Lord sets the tone for the Israelites in His description of the new Jerusalem. He declares that He Himself will rejoice in the city and His people. They will not weep anymore and He will delight in them. This points out the fellowship that the Lord and the people will share.

20

This new Jerusalem will be characterized by a much longer life expectancy. At this time, life expectancy was about forty years, and that remained the average life expectancy for most peoples until the nineteenth century AD. The main reason for short life expectancy was high infant mortality, so the promise that babies will survive was itself a tremendous idea. Considering one hundred years a short life would have been considered fantastic. This is a hint, but no more, to eternal life, as revealed by Jesus Christ in the New Testament and emphasized in the book of Revelation.

21–22

The new Jerusalem is not a paradise already built, as Jesus promises in John 14:1–4 or Revelation portrays. Rather, people will work to construct the houses and vineyards. However, the promise involves the people enjoying the fruit of their labor, without fear of thieves, invaders, or the empire's taxation that could take their property away from them.

23–24

The new Jerusalem will permit people to labor fruitfully and bear children for longevity. This renewal is due to the Lord's blessings, not because of the people's own power. And the Lord will answer their needs even before they ask for His help. This indicates again the communion of the redeemed with their Lord in His new creation.

65:25

> [25]**The wolf and the lamb shall feed together, the lion shall eat straw like the ox; and dust shall be the serpent's food. They shall not hurt or destroy in all my holy mountain, says the Lord."**

The creation of the new earth is portrayed as a paradise in which dangerous animals dwell with the gentle domestic animals without any suffering among the animals or, of course, the humans, as portrayed in Isaiah 11, especially verses 6–9.

—— Isaiah 66:1–4 ——

These loosely connected oracles criticize some of the people's false attitudes toward worship after returning to Jerusalem.

66:1–2

> [1]**Thus says the Lord: "Heaven is my throne and the earth is my footstool; what is the house which you would build for me, and what is the place of my rest? [2]All these things my hand has made, and so all these things are mine, says the Lord. But this is the man to whom I will look, he that is humble and contrite in spirit, and trembles at my word.**

The first two verses are an oracle ("Thus says the Lord") that put the rebuilt Temple into perspective and assert what the Lord wants. The Bible frequently mentions that the Lord's throne is heaven (see Ps 2:4; 11:4; 103:19; 115:3). When Solomon dedicated his magnificent Temple, he admitted readily that not even heaven could contain the Lord, let alone a building (see 1 Kgs 8:27). The point here is that even though the Lord instructed Haggai to promote rebuilding the Temple, He still looks to the humble and contrite of heart who tremble at His word (v. 2). The real issue is the kind of person who worships rather than the place of worship.

66:3

> **3"He who slaughters an ox is like him who kills a man; he who sacrifices a lamb, like him who breaks a dog's neck; he who presents a cereal offering, like him who offers swine's blood; he who makes a memorial offering of frankincense, like him who blesses an idol. These have chosen their own ways, and their soul delights in their abominations;**

This verse criticizes those who bring sacrifices to the Temple while still following their own ways and perform abominations. Such an arrogant person's sacrifices are worse than useless: they are abominations as bad as killing a man, offering unclean animals, such as dogs or pigs, or blessing an idol. Just as anyone who commits those abominable acts deserves punishment, so also does the arrogant person who does his or her own will rather than obey God's word.

66:4

> **4I also will choose affliction for them, and bring their fears upon them; because, when I called, no one answered, when I spoke they did not listen; but they did what was evil in my eyes, and chose that in which I did not delight."**

The arrogant who do not listen to the Lord and do evil will receive affliction. The Lord will cause the things they fear to come upon them, thereby making their punishment tailor suited to them.

—— Isaiah 66:5 ——

> **5Hear the word of the LORD, you who tremble at his word: "Your brethren who hate you and cast you out for my name's sake have said, 'Let the LORD be glorified, that we may see your joy'; but it is they who shall be put to shame.**

This oracle is addressed to those who "tremble at his word"—that is, the humble people He delights in (v. 2). Their brothers—that is, their fellow Jews living in Jerusalem—mock their humble obedience and cast them out of the elite parts of society because they honor the Lord's name. The arrogant mock authentic worship and demand to see the Israelites' joy. However, the Lord here assures the humble that the arrogant will be put to shame, a dire fate in a society that treasures honor as highly as people of the Middle East do.

—— Isaiah 66:6–16 ——

This unit forms an apocalyptic description of the Lord's coming, who will judge the nations and bring salvation to Israel.

66:6

> **6"Listen, an uproar from the city! A voice from the temple! The voice of the LORD, rendering recompense to his enemies!**

The judgment is introduced by a witness announcing that the Lord is making His voice resound in an uproar from the Temple to pay back His enemies. This is not unlike the opening of Amos, "The Lord roars from Zion, and utters his voice from Jerusalem" (1:2), which opens the judgment on the nations and Israel in Amos 1–2.

66:7–9

> **7"Before she was in labor she gave birth; before her pain came upon**
> **her she was delivered of a son. 8Who has heard such a thing? Who has**
> **seen such things? Shall a land be born in one day? Shall a nation be**
> **brought forth in one moment? For as soon as Zion was in labor she**
> **brought forth her sons. 9Shall I bring to the birth and not cause to**
> **bring forth? says the LORD; shall I, who cause to bring forth, shut the**
> **womb? says your God.**

These verses are an announcement of salvation, using the image of childbirth for the beginning of the new era.

7–8

The image of birth pangs is used a number of times to describe the travail at the end of the world (see Is 26:16–18; Mt 24:7–8; Mk 13:8; Jn 16:20–21; 1 Thes 5:3). Here T-I proclaims that Israel's salvation will arrive without the pain. The wonder of such a promise is expressed in the rhetorical questions of verse 8.

9

The Lord asks a different question here, one that assumes many people had doubts about His promise of a new era and the new birth. The answer each question expects is "No." In fact, the Lord will bring the new era to birth, and their doubts are unfounded.

66:10–11

> **10"Rejoice with Jerusalem, and be glad for her, all you who love her; rejoice with her in joy, all you who mourn over her; 11that you may suck and be satisfied with her consoling breasts; that you may drink deeply with delight from the abundance of her glory."**

In these verses, the prophet summons those who "love" Jerusalem and the "people who mourn" over her distress to rejoice with her now so that they might partake of her abundance, like a baby at its mother's breasts. T-I had also summoned the people to rejoice like a groom or bride (61:10) and to rejoice over Jerusalem (65:18). However, notice that this summons is directed to the ones who love Jerusalem and mourn over her, implying that it will not be for those who act wickedly.

66:12–14

> **12For thus says the LORD: "Behold, I will extend prosperity to her like a river, and the wealth of the nations like an overflowing stream; and you shall suck, you shall be carried upon her hip, and dandled upon her knees. 13As one whom his mother comforts, so I will comfort you; you shall be comforted in Jerusalem. 14You shall see, and your heart shall rejoice; your bones shall flourish like the grass; and it shall be known that the hand of the LORD is with his servants, and his indignation is against his enemies.**

This is a description of the salvation the Lord extends to Jerusalem—prosperity will be like an overflowing river, or like a child suckling and receiving his mother's comfort, or a flourishing like the grass. Very importantly, the Lord directs this description as a promise to the people directly, using the "you" plural form for the verbs and pronouns. The listening community will take part in this salvation themselves.

66:15–16

> **[15]"For behold, the LORD will come in fire, and his chariots like the stormwind, to render his anger in fury, and his rebuke with flames of fire. [16]For by fire will the LORD execute judgment, and by his sword, upon all flesh; and those slain by the LORD shall be many.**

The other side of the preceding promises of salvation will be the destruction of the wicked who will participate in the terrifying approach of the Lord in fire, storm, and sword to slay many people. Their punishment will be painful and will mean their exclusion from the prosperous, comforting salvation of Jerusalem. This description is stated as a fact; each hearer must decide whether to love Jerusalem or to be destroyed by the Lord who comes forth from Jerusalem.

—— Isaiah 66:17 ——

> **[17]"Those who sanctify and purify themselves to go into the gardens, following one in the midst, eating swine's flesh and the abomination and mice, shall come to an end together, says the LORD.**

This verse is a warning against a false type of worship that may have been similar to the pagan practices described in Ezekiel 8. These people eat mice, reptiles, and pork in some secret practices in a garden as they "follow one in the midst," a feminine noun that may refer to some priestess or cult prostitute. False worship will lead to punishment and extermination.

—— Isaiah 66:18–24 ——

These verses tell of the last judgment and assignment of eternal reward or eternal punishment.

66:18

> **[18]"For I know their works and their thoughts, and I am coming to gather all nations and tongues; and they shall come and shall see my glory,**

The Lord God begins with His assertion that He knows the works everyone does as well as their thoughts. The latter idea is an important background for the various occasions when Jesus Christ knows the unspoken thoughts of various people throughout the Gospels (see Mt 9:4; 12:25; Lk 5:22; Jn 5:42; Rv 2:2 for the context of Christ's judgment of a church). Though knowledge of thoughts is not a clear indicator of Jesus's divinity, this verse and others like it raises the question for Jews who knew this text.

With that knowledge of all people, the Lord announces that He is coming to gather all the nations and languages so that they can see His glory. Jesus makes the same claim about Himself in Matthew 25:31–32: "When the Son of man comes in his glory, and all the angels with him, then he will sit on his glorious throne. Before him will be gathered all the nations." (See also Mt 16:27–28; 19:28; 26:64; Mk 8:38; 14:62; Lk 9:26; 22:69–70; Jn 5:27–29; Acts 1:11; 2 Thes 1:7–9.)

66:19

> **19and I will set a sign among them. And from them I will send survivors to the nations, to Tarshish, Put, and Lud, who draw the bow, to Tubal and Javan, to the coastlands afar off, that have not heard my fame or seen my glory; and they shall declare my glory among the nations.**

The Lord promises a sign to the nations, though the text does not clarify what the sign will be. The clearer point is that the "survivors," either those who survived the Lord's gathering of the nations or the Israelites who survived the exile, will be sent throughout the world to declare the Lord's glory to those who do not know it. Such a missionary approach to the nations was not typical in Israelite religion, particularly since they form both a religion and an ethnic identity as the descendants of Abraham, Isaac, and Jacob/Israel. However, the mission to proclaim God's glory is here a sign before the final judgment. Tarshish was a Phoenician colony in southern Spain, Put was on the Horn of Africa, and Lud was in Africa (see Jer 46:9; Ez 30:5), though it was also used for a people in Asia Minor, probably the Lydians, whom Cyrus conquered. Tubal was south of the Black Sea, while Javan is Greece and the Greek islands. This list indicates the geographical diversity of people to whom the missionaries were sent by the Lord.

66:20

> **[20]And they shall bring all your brethren from all the nations as an offering to the LORD, upon horses, and in chariots, and in litters, and upon mules, and upon dromedaries, to my holy mountain Jerusalem, says the LORD, just as the Israelites bring their cereal offering in a clean vessel to the house of the LORD.**

A further task for the missionaries was to bring "your brethren"—that is, all the Israelites scattered among these nations—to the Lord's holy mountain, which is Jerusalem. They will not be required to walk but will be carried on animals and in vehicles, which indicates their great importance and a change from the state of the exiles who had to walk from Babylon. The most interesting part of this verse is that they are to be "an offering to the Lord," like a cereal offering in a clean vessel. They were not going to be sacrificed, since human sacrifice was strictly forbidden in Israel. Rather, the very act of returning these Israelites with so much dignity is treated as an act of worship by the nations, and the Lord will accept this gift of His people being brought back to Him.

In the New Testament we see the idea of self-sacrifice develop in Romans 12:1 when Saint Paul writes, "Present your bodies as a living sacrifice, holy and acceptable to God, which is your spiritual worship" (see also Phil 2:17: "Even if I am to be poured as a libation upon the sacrificial offering of your faith;" Heb 13:15–16). Ultimately, self-sacrifice is related to and finds its fulfilment in Christ being a sacrifice offered on the cross: "Christ, our paschal lamb, has been sacrificed" (1 Cor 5:7; see also Heb 6–10). This is understood in terms of offering oneself, in union with Jesus Christ, in service to God and as a martyr, in the extreme.

66:21

> **[21]And some of them also I will take for priests and for Levites, says the LORD.**

The promise to take "some of them" as priests and Levites is amazing, given that the Israelite priesthood was hereditary, as was, of course, membership in the Levite tribe that assisted at the Temple. The term "them" is not defined, and some scholars consider the possibility that priests might even be taken from the Gentiles who come to Jerusalem.

66:22–24

22"For as the new heavens and the new earth which I will make shall
remain before me, says the LORD; so shall your descendants and your
name remain. 23From new moon to new moon, and from Sabbath
to Sabbath, all flesh shall come to worship before me, says the LORD.
24"And they shall go forth and look on the dead bodies of the men that
have rebelled against me; for their worm shall not die, their fire shall
not be quenched, and they shall be an abhorrence to all flesh."

The Lord announces the final and eternal state of reality after his judgment of all the nations.

22–23

First, the Lord uses His eternal "new heavens and new earth" as the norm for the eternal life of Jerusalem's inhabitants, including not only Israel ("your name" referring to Israel's name) but also "all flesh," the various nations who come to worship the Lord.

24

The Old Testament presented the punishment of the wicked in terms of their annihilation—that is, until this passage. For the first time, the wicked will experience eternal punishment, where the "worm shall not die" and "their fire shall not be quenched." Their corpses will undergo this torment forever, within sight of the city and its inhabitants. This prepares the way for later Jewish imagery of hell as "Gehenna" ("Gei" meaning "Valley" of Hinnom), a valley that goes around the western and southern sides of the city. Jesus will take up this imagery frequently, since only He, and the book of Revelation, explicitly threaten eternal damnation in Gehenna or hell (see Mt 3:12; 5:28–29; 10: Mk 9:44–49; Rv 14:10–11).